Poor Relations

Poor Relations

The Children of the State in Illinois, 1818–1990

Joan Gittens

University of Illinois Press
Urbana and Chicago

This book is printed on acid-free paper.

Library of Congress Cataloging-in-Publication Data

Gittens, Joan.
    Poor relations : the children of the state in Illinois, 1818–1990
/ Joan Gittens.
        p.   cm.
    Includes bibliographical references and index.
    ISBN 0-252-02064-2 (alk. paper).—ISBN 0-252-06411-9 (pbk.: alk. paper)
    1. Child welfare—Illinois—History. 2. Juvenile delinquency—
Government policy—Illinois—History. 3. Juvenile delinquents—
Government policy—Illinois—History. 4. Handicapped children—
Government policy—Illinois—History. I. Title.
HV742.I3G57   1994
362.7'09773—dc20   93-10945
                                                                CIP

This book is dedicated in loving memory
to my brother Jimmy, who taught me
to care about the children of the state.

Contents

Acknowledgments

Writing this book has been a long and sometimes daunting enterprise, and it is a pleasure to reach the point at last where I can thank the people who have helped me to take it from its most tentative stages to its finished form. I owe a special debt of gratitude to Father Paul Prucha, who first taught me to write history and who read this book in all its incarnations. His astute and astringent criticism has sustained it and me from the start. In moments of discouragement, I persisted because he saw something worthwhile in the project and gave unstintingly of his time and wise advice. Few writers can have been blessed with a critic so generous and so unequivocal.

I am indebted to Professor Joseph Hawes of Memphis State University whose thoughtful and extensive critique helped me immeasurably in revising the manuscript. Lela B. Costin, University of Illinois Professor Emerita, offered clear and incisive suggestions that helped me to articulate the major themes of the manuscript more confidently.

Richard Wentworth, director of the University of Illinois Press, has patiently encouraged this book through a long revision, while Lisa Warne-Magro, the assistant to the director, has cheerfully helped me through numerous details and complexities to bring it to a conclusion. With tact and an unerring eye, Rita D. Disroe, manuscript editor, helped me to sharpen and clarify the manuscript.

The Social Policy Research Center, an affiliate of the National Opinion Research Center at the University of Chicago, supported a first phase of the dependency and delinquency sections of this book, which were issued as working papers by NORC and Chapin Hall Center for Children. I am grateful to former NORC director Robert Michael for his support and encouragement at a crucial stage of this work.

Maggie Williams and Eileen Libby of the School of Social Service Administration Library at the University of Chicago were unfailingly helpful to me, as were Pat Bova and Michael Worley of NORC's library and the librarians of the Regenstein Library, the John Crerar Library and the University of Chicago Law Library.

Galen Wilson shared with me the photographic treasures of the Chicago Public Library Special Collections, along with other material helpful for the work. Thanks also to Mary Ann Bamburger of the University of Illinois Special Collections and JoAnn Weems of the Cook County Detention Center for assistance with photographs.

Interviews were an important resource for the later decades covered in *Poor Relations*. My thanks to the many individuals and organizations cited in the chapter notes for their time and expertise. I was especially fortunate to know Marilyn Clarke, who so generously put the accumulated wisdom of more than twenty years of child welfare experience at my disposal. Malcolm Bush, president of the Woodstock Institute, was a critical resource, helping to bring the often baffling questions of child welfare into sharper focus for me. Marlene Stern and the staff of the Citizens Committee for the Juvenile Court were helpful in countless ways from the earliest stages of this book to its conclusion. Mary Lopata and Debbie Greenebaum were my guides in writing the section on disabled children. Eileen Subak of the League of Women Voters supplied important resources at the first stages of the work.

Student assistants Elizabeth Leaver, James Leaver, Lisa Meyer, John Carpenter, and Jenny Austin helped with the often tedious tasks connected with the research, writing, and word processing of the manuscript. I am grateful to all of them for their good nature and their fastidious work. Especially because computers have largely remained a mystery to me, I appreciate all the help I received in rendering an apparently malevolent machine benign. Cassandra Britton and her staff did much of the original word processing of the manuscript. Michael Glass and Cindy Sims not only read (or had read to them) most of this work in bits and pieces but also gave their own valuable time to produce the first finished draft at a point where I could no more work a computer than I could fly an airplane. My friend and colleague John Hittinger, an undisputed WordPerfect Master, worked his magic to convert the manuscript from one program to another and put it into a proper form. Shawn Hedman of Southwest State University's Computer Services patiently worked with me at the final stages of the manuscript. A grant from the Charles P. and Lavinia Schwartz Foundation helped to support the technical aspects of the book.

My Illinois decade had a Dickensian quality to it, and I am more grateful than I can say to the many people, family and friends, who supported this book through all the vicissitudes and helped me keep my sense of humor and my sense of proportion. A special thanks to the stalwarts of the yellow ribbon brigade for their help in the long winter of 1992.

Throughout the time that I have been writing this book, my students have been a constant source of energy. They have shared information and ideas, have helped to explore difficult issues, and have been unflaggingly enthusiastic about the prospect that the manuscript would one day be a book. They were my mind's eye audience as I wrote, and if I have found a voice at all, it is because they were always so willing to listen.

Much of this book was written without institutional support, an exhausting process that I do not recommend. Happily, in the manuscript's final stages I have had the felicity to work in a department that has given me support in every sense. My thanks to my colleagues at Southwest State University whose good will and encouragement have made the last phase of this project so civilized that I can contemplate with equanimity the prospect of writing another book.

Introduction

In the spring of 1991, in the midst of a prolonged child welfare crisis, a *Chicago Tribune* editorial calling for more adequate funding for children's services began with the uncompromising headline "Illinois: The Cheapskate State."[1] The editorial, condemning the disparity between the state's wealth and its funding for children in need, concentrated on contemporary issues. But to anyone familiar with Illinois' checkered past in relation to its children, the bald indictment "cheapskate" could serve as a short and unequivocal summary of the almost 175 years of state child welfare activities. Illinois, bustling and prosperous in economic terms, has always behaved less like its Progressive neighbors Wisconsin and Minnesota than a poor southern state in the care of its vulnerable people. Not only recently, but consistently throughout its history, the state has underfunded, underbuilt, and undertaxed in regard to children's needs, with the result that its programs are often so inadequate as to constitute downright neglect.

Even in education, the endeavor for children that might be expected to tap the greatest spirit of consensus and provoke the most ungrudging response, Illinois' history has been marred from the beginning by cynicism and penury. The clearest example of this is the use to which early legislators put the income from the state's school lands, a legacy from the Northwest Ordinances that had organized Illinois and contiguous territory into states. The school lands, set aside for sale or rent that would raise revenue for free public schools in Illinois, were in reality the first federal aid to education, a recognition of the necessity for education in a republic. That this notion—Thomas Jefferson's, in fact—was too advanced for Illinois lawmakers was demonstrated in the first two decades of the state's existence. The state passed a free school act in 1826, but by the 1830s, the legislators (without congressional approval) had sold all the reserved lands, not to expand education but simply to spare unwilling citizens the burden of general taxes.[2]

The same mentality that put low taxes above children's right to education pervaded the state's relationship with dependent, delinquent, and disabled children over time. These children, far more dependent on the state's bounty than the average school child, found the state to be an erratic and, on the whole, reluctant parent. Dependent children—those who were orphaned or abused or simply impoverished—were one of the most obvious groups needing state care. Yet the state has resisted thoroughgoing acceptance of responsibility for this group from the earliest poor law provisions to the elaborate bureaucracy of the modern Department of Children and Family Services.

On the other hand, deaf and blind children received early attention from the state, even though neither group was particularly large or in a crisis situation. Deaf children especially received strong continuing support because they had a skillful lobbyist in their school's superintendent. At the same time, children with orthopedic handicaps, tuberculosis, and heart disease were long neglected altogether, while mentally handicapped children for many years experienced the worst of both zeal and neglect, deemed unfit to live outside institutions that were chronically underfunded. Delinquent children, like the mentally handicapped, received state attention because of fear. If they proved threatening enough, the legislature might consider innovations as varying as the establishment of the juvenile court or the passage of laws that automatically sent juveniles to adult courts to be tried. But passing legislation was an entirely different matter from supporting programs, institutions, and staff. The legislature was never loath to make an honorific statement. It was the ensuing appropriations bills that so often illustrated the gap between the lawmakers' pious wishes and their willingness to support such sentiments with actual funding.

Politicization as well as a lack of adequate funding characterized the state's relationship with its children. The practical care of the state's children was politicized from the beginning, since a large number of caretakers were patronage appointments. From the politically appointed superintendent of the Soldiers' Orphans' Home to the merest probation officer or worker at the Lincoln Home for the Feebleminded, partisan politics rather than commitment and training were the basis for selecting the staff who held children's lives in their hands. During his 1907 testimony to a legislative committee investigating an accident at the Lincoln institution, one caretaker gave a chilling demonstration of just how hazardous this mode of hiring could be for children. An epileptic boy in the man's care had been terribly burned due to his neglect; yet he showed not a jot of contrition in his responses to the committee, referring to the boy, throughout his surly and unregenerate testimony, as "it."[3]

The tensions between private and public agencies caring for children, especially religious agencies, added another layer of political complexity to an already intensely political situation. As a state with a vast immigrant population, Illinois experienced many of the tensions that resulted from the settling of immigrant and religious groups and the resistance of those who regarded themselves as "natives." In the schools of the state and the nation, the issues of religion and ethnicity were a battleground for many years. The concerns of an immigrant, largely Catholic, population about America's intent to convert their children took on an even greater urgency when the children in question were institutionalized and thus peculiarly subject to proselytizing. Particularly in the care of dependent children, private agencies stepped in early to insure that homeless and orphaned children be trained in the religion and culture of their ancestors. The Catholic and immigrant lobby, an embattled minority in the nineteenth century, was a force to be reckoned with by the turn of the century. So, too, was the network of private, Protestant-based child welfare organizations. Through the years, they resisted state interference and state control, materially affecting both the writing of laws and the functions of agencies for children, particularly the two major agencies, the juvenile court and the Department of Children and Family Services.

Against the backdrop of parsimony and politics, reformers struggled to act in behalf of children, contending simultaneously with the state's indifference and the jealous regard of ethnic and religious groups. Illinois has been on one level anomalous, a rich, industrial state with a powerful bias toward minimal intervention and taxation. But the story of its reformers in children's issues, "childsavers" in the convenient shorthand of the late nineteenth century, fits a much broader national pattern than its fiscal minimalism. The nineteenth century reformers who established orphanages, the Chicago Reform School, and the special schools for handicapped children reflected the national reforming mood before the Civil War. The national connection was even more apparent during the Progressive Era, when Illinois reformers established the first juvenile court and the first state mothers' pension

program, both notable innovations of the time. And, in the reforming 1960s and 1970s, a new breed of Illinois reformers, in concert
with like-thinking comrades across the nation, challenged the institutions and assumptions of the Progressive Era, charging that
they were interventionist at the expense of basic justice and civil
liberties.

The history of the state's *parens patriae* role toward children is
strikingly circular. Regarding delinquent children, a nineteenth century court limited the intervention of reformers into "predelinquents'" lives in the name of civil liberties. A century later, in the
1967 Gault case, the United States Supreme Court did much the
same thing. In dealing with dependent children, the oldest solution
was to settle them promptly into families, with little or no further
intervention from the state. In the Adoption Act of 1980, reformers again espoused a limitation on state intervention in favor of simple familial care. And in the education of handicapped children, the
pre–Civil War special schools' goal of returning mentally and physically handicapped children to their communities as soon as possible finds an echo in the modern day commitment to deinstitutionalization and mainstreaming of handicapped children.

Although it would be simplistic to argue that modern solutions
exactly imitated the nineteenth-century philosophy of minimal
state action, it is certainly clear that by the second half of the
twentieth century, reformers had lost faith in the Progressive commitment to intervention and had come to see the state not as a
benevolent parent but as a juggernaut, as likely to destroy as to
help children in need. The story of point/counterpoint, Progressive intervention and later reformers' rejection of such intervention, is the major focus of this book.

The 1899 Illinois Conference of Charities and Corrections posed
the question "Who are the children of the state?" dedicating the
entire conference to the exploration of that issue. The answer that
the conference gave to the question was that all children, rich and
poor, of whatever nationality, were the proper concern of the state,
both for humanitarian reasons and because the adequate nurture
of its children was the only real means of the state's preservation.
Nineteenth-century American culture had devoted great attention
to the celebration of childhood as a unique and important stage
of the human experience. At an earlier point in American history, the ancient and revered sentiment "Foolishness is bound in the
heart of the child"[4] summarized the general view of childhood as
a condition that people must be trained out of with as much dis-

patch as possible. But by the end of the nineteenth century, childhood was lauded as a precious time, a time of innocence and a critical stage of development—a stage to be circumvented at society's
peril. A carefully nurtured childhood was crucial to the creation
of a responsible and competent adult, according to the experts, and
competent adulthood was the very essence of the great republican experiment that seemed so much at risk as the American nation moved into its second century.

Reformers contrasted the special needs of children to the reality that they saw in their changing and beleaguered society. Urban
squalor, industrial strife, ever-increasing immigration, a growing
separation of the rich and poor—this was what the forces of modernism had wrought. And evidence that children fared poorly in
this complicated new world was everywhere. Children worked ten
and twelve hours a day at brain-numbing tasks that ruined their
health, taught them nothing, and robbed them of the opportunity
to attend school and prepare themselves to cope in the complicated and constantly changing modern world. There seemed to be
hoards of ill-cared-for children either on the street or housed in a
variety of institutions from orphanages to the poorhouse, because
their parents were dead or missing or could not afford to keep
them. Most dismaying of all, children were locked in adult jails
for a host of petty reasons, exposed to the worst that a strained
and unraveling society could inflict upon them.

And despite the generally held conviction that the city was the
source of all ills, the problems for children in rural regions were
no less grave. Though their numbers were smaller than the hoards
of city children in need, their situation was in some ways even
more vulnerable, since the services of many private organizations
that aided Chicago children were not available to them. In rural
Illinois, dependent and handicapped children, when they could not
be ignored, could at best expect placement with a family, with little or no review by public officials of their subsequent care. At
the worst, they would be placed in the local poorhouse, the inadequacies of which formed the subject of a forty-year lament by the
state's monitoring agency, the State Board of Charities. It was institutionalized children in southern Illinois who made up a good-
ly portion of the workers in the hellish glass factories of the state.
Children with adult protectors were not often subjected to such a
fate.[5]

Progressive reformers, critical of a society that acted so fitfully
in children's interests, argued that the time for mere localism and

volunteering was over. They felt that the country's welfare needed consistent, coherent attention that could best be provided by
central policies. They argued first for control on a state level and
later for intervention by the federal government. Compulsory education, an ongoing crusade of the era, was an example of their
argument for state intervention. The state's interest in a child's
education was so critical, they contended, that it overrode the ancient common law right of the father to control the education of
his children. The circumstances of modern society had changed
enough to necessitate this profound intervention into family life,
since an uneducated child was both robbed of childhood and
shaped for life by the inability to cope in a world that demanded
literary skills and training.[6]

The pervading sense among Progressives was that times had
changed and that in order to deal with modern problems, modern solutions must be used.[7] They put their faith not in immu-
table laws but in flexibility. The juvenile court, one of the most
famous of all Progressive reforms, had flexibility as a key com-
ponent. Unlike the adversarial stance of adult proceedings, the
court sought first to respond to the sense that the needs of children were different from adults and second to individualize the
response so that each child might get the care that he or she needed. The fact that, in achieving flexibility, civil liberties protections were lost seemed mere quibbling to most reformers, since
they saw civil liberties as doing so little to protect dependent and
delinquent children from the hazards of turn-of-the-century life.
What would help children was not rigid adherence to legal procedures but rather vigorous early intervention by benignly involved citizens and professionals.

The Progressive persuasion in social welfare certainly met with
resistance: from those who feared its invasion into family life (and
here the immigrant church was especially active); from private
agencies objecting to state attempts to dominate the child welfare
field; and from those who objected to the money that Progressive
programs cost the taxpayer.

None of the programs or institutions established under Progressive auspices were ever funded at anything approaching an adequate level in Illinois. In the Great Depression of the 1930s some
of the programs, notably mothers' pensions, were federalized, and
by the 1960s and 1970s, there was some federal funding for virtually every group of the state's children. But the funding, even in
the palmy days of the 1960s, was not sustained long enough to
prove adequate to the needs of children's programs and institu-

tions, particularly when the baby boom, also a phenomenon of the era, strained existing services so badly. A review of Progressive interventions for children in the first half of the twentieth century in Illinois reveals a record that at best might be called indifferent, certainly not successful. Yet the general faith in the Progressive commitment to active intervention was preserved intact for at least fifty years.

Some of the earliest groups to challenge the Progressive consensus were the advocates for mentally handicapped children. No group had suffered more from intervention than the retarded and their families. The "modern" approach, legitimized in the Progressive Era, was to institutionalize mentally handicapped children at birth, ostensibly to put them in a setting where they might have expert care, but in reality to isolate them, since they were viewed as potential contaminators of the race. The 1915 Illinois involuntary commitment law directed at mentally retarded people showed Progressivism at its interventionist worst. And the total failure to build and staff adequate institutions illustrated the inevitable gap between reformers' plans and the legislature's actions. By the 1940s, this group of vulnerable citizens was the most isolated of all people in need, and their families—sternly told that they owed it to their other children and the community—faced the prospect of sending loved children to dismally inadequate institutions—and then only if they could get past the long waiting lists. Organizations like the National Association for Retarded Children began to challenge the conventional wisdom that retarded children must be segregated from society and to challenge as well the dominance of doctors, social workers, and other professionals in their relationships with their children.

The challenge to what reformers only a few years earlier had called a "pro-state philosophy"[8] became stronger in the 1960s. In a sense the challenge in social welfare was part of a broader intellectual realignment, in which a new generation of liberals rejected foreign policy assumptions begun in the Progressive Era and developed more fully in the presidency of Franklin Roosevelt and beyond. At home as well as abroad, these critics argued, the old liberalism was far less humane and democratic than it purported to be, less the vehicle of improvement and reform than of repression. The Progressive commitment to expertise especially came in for criticism, as the second half of the twentieth century began to feel the side effects of some of the medical and pharmaceutical marvels that had promised so much a few decades earlier.[9]

In social policy, these new critics challenged the liberal consensus that class was not important in the United States, arguing that class and race were critical determinants in American life, aspects that could not be discounted. This group, composed of social theorists, social activists, and historians, began to scrutinize the social welfare of their day and to see in its Progressive origins not evidence of good will and creativity that might have fallen short in actual practice. Rather, they argued, from the beginning those mechanisms were instruments not of benevolence but of social control, an attempt by worried "native" Americans to restrain the poor and immigrant newcomers who were flooding their society. Schools, the juvenile court, welfare programs, volunteer efforts were examined for intention as well as results and found wanting in both respects. They were not benign efforts of well-meaning, civic people but instruments of repression and ineptitude.

One of the earliest and best known critiques of the Illinois juvenile court sounded this theme unequivocally. Anthony Platt's book *The Child Savers: The Invention of Delinquency* presented a social control theme, characterizing the juvenile court reformers as frightened members of the upper class whose intention was to Americanize children and neutralize the threat from immigrants who were invading their shores. He had especially harsh words for Louise Bowen and Jane Addams of Hull-House, women he saw as misplaced elites who sought status at the expense of hapless adolescents whose more vigorous and earthy lifestyle offended the reformers' middle-class sensibilities.

Platt was making a case for a more adversarial system of justice for juveniles. Thus he presented the court from its foundation as an aggressor against youth rather than regarding it, as more moderate critics did, as a good invention gone badly out of tune over the years. Platt argued that children had done better in the adult system that preceded the juvenile court than reformers had been willing to acknowledge. He insisted that children were frequently absolved by reason of noncompetence and pointed out that one English youth convicted of breaking and entering had not been executed as the court prescribed. With a breezy disregard for the horrors of life aboard an eighteenth-century convict ship, Platt assured his readers that the boy was merely "transported to New South Wales for the rest of his life."[10]

Platt's history, selective and disingenuous in its attack on reformers, was nevertheless widely read, and in time the theme of social control became a new orthodoxy in the writing of reform history.

The range of this argument was broad. Platt's work was an uncompromising attack on the motives of reformers. David Rothman's *Conscience and Convenience,* on the other hand, was a
more judicious assessment. Rothman argued that Progressive reformers' intentions were good but their innovations granting broad
interventionist powers in the name of effectiveness and flexibility actually played into the hands of the invested bureaucracies of
prisons, reformatories, and asylums to create a nightmare of intrusion. Michael Katz's history of welfare, *In the Shadow of the
Poorhouse,* insisted that not just poor funding but "inherent contradictions" in Progressive policies toward children "crippled every innovation from the start," while Rothman went so far as to
argue that underfunding by state legislatures was in retrospect a
good thing, since it constrained invasive behavior that might otherwise have infringed on even more lives in a combination of zeal
and bureaucratic ruthlessness.[11]

The conviction that social control motivation had shaped Progressive reforms and still impelled social welfare found acceptance
among practitioners and those shaping policy, as well as historians. Starting in the 1960s, the thrust of much legislation and many
legal challenges of the time was to limit state intervention and
protect the civil liberties of those subject to treatment or judgment
by the state. Much of what went on was a lawyers' revolution, and
as such, put great emphasis on procedure, reducing the very flexibility that Progressives had seen as the key to effective social and
legal responses.

It was appropriate, as the country celebrated the bicentennial
of its founding, that the emphasis of reformers should return to
civil liberties, to the freedoms that had originally impelled the
American colonists to confront England and to reject her invasive
rule. With their consciousness of race and class, reformers of the
new breed showed far more sensitivity to the rights of children
and their parents than had previously been practiced in American
social welfare. Even in the early republic, when interventionist
social welfare measures were a thing of the future, the rights of
the poor had been routinely trampled in both law and custom.

But the new libertarian emphasis had its limits in dealing with
children. Few reformers were prepared to make the argument that
the only problems that families had were caused by state intervention. In fact, the notion of a more benign and efficient state
support was implicit in many arguments against current practice.
For example, in urging adoption of older, hard to place children,

there was an assumption that the state would provide subsidies to willing families in order to make such actions by private citizens feasible. The aim was not so much to eliminate state support altogether as to limit it primarily to financial aid and reduce the erratic and destructive bureaucracy that seemed an inevitable concomitant of foster care.

Late twentieth-century critics of Progressive reformers pointed to flaws in Progressive innovations that made them vulnerable to cynical manipulation by legislators and bureaucrats. But their own programs were in fact also prey to cynical manipulation. Deinstitutionalization of the mentally handicapped and mentally ill was originally expected to be a program that would require more, not less, funding from government.[12] The intent was to redirect funds to community resources, but what happened in reality as funds dried up and the temper of the times became more conservative was that only the first half of the program, deinstitutionalization, was accomplished. Rather than responsive community services, the country saw a policy of "dumping" and the growth of the homeless population as institutions closed.

Similarly, in the 1960s critics of excessive state intervention into the lives of juveniles drew firm lines between predelinquents or status offenders and youths convicted of crimes. Formerly, misuse of the elastic categories of "delinquent" and "dependent" had resulted in flagrant injustices to children. But drawing a sharp distinction between the guilty and innocent child had its own hazards, playing to the "get tough" attitude toward youthful offenders that was part of the growing conservatism of the age and leading to policies like Illinois' ever increasing "automatic transfers" to the adult courts.

Even the emphasis on procedure had discouraging aspects, causing delays in the system and demonstrating the age-old maxim that too much emphasis on the letter of the law stifled the spirit of many reforms.

As the century drew to a close, American society seemed prepared once more to turn reformers' best intentions to cynical ends. The aim of modern reformers had been to restrain government in order to preserve the privacy, dignity, and civil liberties of families. Many disenchanted Americans, rejecting the complicated responses of reform, opted simply to stop thinking of children altogether. The rhetoric of the right, in ascendancy especially in the 1980s, essentially agreed that government had not solved the problems of poverty, adding that the state had in fact caused most of these problems by creating dependency and eroding initiative.[13] As good as their word, politicians pledged to get government off the backs of the American people slashed programs for children. The loss of these supports, combined with a growing rate of single parent households, put children in the unenviable class of America's poorest people—pauperized, malnourished, unvaccinated, uneducated.[14] The wariness about government intervention had been translated into actions that went far beyond what most critics of state intervention had anticipated.

And yet the ideology of left and right were confusing when it came to state intervention. In areas of child abuse and child welfare, critics from the political right sometimes proposed extraordinary intervention into family life, while in other respects the same critics might argue for a far more restricted state role. Similarly, social theorists on the left of the political spectrum had a mixed response to the role of government, clearly viewing the state and bureaucracy with wariness, especially in regard to civil liberties, yet looking to the government to support more effective programs in education, child welfare, and delinquency prevention. The notion of "early intervention," a concept older than the Progressives, began to have currency again.[15]

The many contradictions in the issue of state intervention in children's lives reflected the reality that, though the Progressive consensus had been plucked to pieces by relentless criticism from both the left and right, no new consensus had appeared in regard to social welfare generally and children's issues in particular. As new problems like homeless families, cocaine addicted babies, and staggering violence toward and among children assaulted the anxious public, Americans were coming to realize that they lived in a society where the gap between the rich and poor had grown dramatically, creating a sense of crisis very similar to that experienced by their Progressive forbears. Whether or not the crisis would foster a new urgency, whether Americans were capable of a new consensus on how best to act for children in need, was the key question, a fitting one as the century neared its conclusion. Would the new century and the new millennium bring effective action for the nation's ills or merely witness a growing chasm between the children of the privileged and the children of the state?

Part 1

Dependent Children

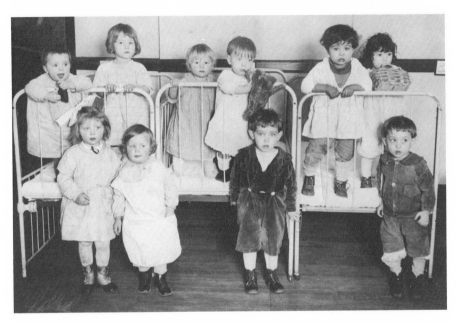

Children in the Olivet Institute Day Care Center, Chicago, 1928. Papers of Norman Burton Barr, Special Collections of the Chicago Public Library.

1

Minimal Offerings, 1818–99

There is perhaps no greater catastrophe for children than when their families, for whatever reason, no longer function for them. Not only must they contend with emotional upheaval; they are left without caretakers and must look to the broader society for sustenance and protection. If they are fortunate, relatives or friends will step in and fill the gap—if not emotionally, at least on a practical level. The children unlucky enough to have no surrogate parents must look to the society at large to take an interest in their well-being. That this is at best a tenuous situation for a child is demonstrated by the prevalence of the pathetic and mistreated orphan in folk and popular culture.

Yet folklore could scarcely exaggerate life's hazards for children dependent on public bounty in Illinois. Despite the citizenry's occasional intense regard—usually when a particularly brutal story hit the newspapers—dependent children have been generally isolated, remote from public consciousness, and without natural allies. "Their very innocence and inoffensiveness leads to their disregard," wrote one observer bitterly. "They make no loud outcry and menace no one. Since there are so few voices raised in their behalf, it is not surprising that the persons charged with their care should be ignorant of any problems they present, and blind to their real interests."[1]

Besides being easy to ignore, dependent children have historically been costly to the state, requiring years of expense before they could become self-sufficient. How much the issue of their poverty has shaped their prospects the State Board of Charities noted late in the nineteenth century, citing the telling fact that as early as 1795 the territory of Illinois had created an orphans' court to deal with the estates of children who had lost their parents. The children most desperately in need, children without means or property, had no court to watch over their interests. They had instead the overseer of the poor, who could apprentice children from destitute families even over their parents' objections.

Another territorial law underscored the inferior protection accorded to dependent children. The law provided that apprentices and masters could take grievances to a justice of the peace to rule on, thus enforcing on the one hand the master's right to obedience and hard work and on the other the apprentice's right to decent treatment and competent education. The law specifically excluded from protection children apprenticed by the local poor law officials.[2]

The conscious separation of "the state's children" from those with parents continued in the Poor Law of 1819, the social welfare law passed the year after Illinois attained statehood. But revisions of apprenticeship and poor laws in the next fifteen years reflected a growing sense that the state owed a more even-handed treatment to the vulnerable children who looked to them for support. The Apprenticeship Law of 1826 and the Poor Law of 1833 made it the concern of the state that dependent children's apprenticeships be monitored to some extent by the probate judge, who was charged to keep the bonds of indenture in his office and to investigate indentured children's situations from time to time. The laws also articulated some of the expectations that the children might have: the right to decent treatment, adequate education, a new Bible, and two suits of clothes (suitable to their station in life) at the end of apprenticeship. Masters still had great discretion to decide what was fit and proper treatment, but there was at least some sense that children dependent on the state had a right to proper care.[3]

The Apprenticeship Law of 1826, in addition to voicing some concerns about the protection of dependent children, gave a further indication of an increasing sense of state responsibility by expanding the definition of children requiring state attention. This law gave wide latitude to the overseer of the poor in indenturing children whom he deemed to be inadequately cared for, like the children of beggars, habitual drunkards, and widows of "bad character." This was the first recognition that the state might need to intercede even in families who had not turned to the overseers of the poor for help. And it was the first articulation that the state had an interest in doing more than warding off imminent starvation, that it also had an interest in the proper rearing of children and an obligation on some level to step in if such proper rearing was not going forward.[4]

This concern about proper child rearing was a nineteenth-century phenomenon all across Western culture, but in the United States it was especially tied to the republican experiment that must have been very much on citizens' minds in 1826, that fiftieth-anniversary year of the Declaration of Independence. The adequate raising of children was a humanitarian concern, but it was also a practical matter for the survival of the noble but risky political enterprise that was the focus of so much anxiety and so much international attention. In the 1840s the Illinois Supreme Court gave this rationale for the state's presumption to interfere in family life:

> The power of chancery to interfere with and control, not only the estates but the persons and custody of all minors within the limits of its jurisdiction, is of very ancient origin, and can not now be questioned. This is a power which must necessarily exist somewhere in every well regulated society, and more especially in a republican government, where each man should be reared and educated under such influences that he may be qualified to exercise the rights of a freeman and take part in the government of the country. It is a duty, then, which the country owes as well to itself, as to the infant, to see that he is not abused, defrauded or neglected, and the infant has a right to this protection.[5]

To some extent the laws dealing with the adult poor reflected increased humanitarian concern as well—Illinois outlawed the practice of auctioning off the destitute to the lowest bidder in 1827, for example—but it is striking that in its increased concern about neglected children, the state paid little or no heed to the rights of poor parents. Earlier poor laws had given the overseer of the poor the right to indenture children without parental consent if the family had become a charge upon the state, even if their poverty was only a temporary catastrophe. The 1826 law expanded the overseer's discretionary powers to decide on the fitness of parents, and while on the one hand that showed an increased concern for the well-being of children, it also reflected a callousness toward the civil rights of poor parents that had always pervaded American poor laws.[6]

This cavalier approach toward destitute families remained characteristic of those engaged in child welfare right through the nineteenth century, a striking anomaly in a society where the sanctity of family ties was a paramount value. It was not until the end of the nineteenth century that some child welfare theorists would begin to argue for the rights of poor parents and to insist that the best care society could offer children was to support them in their homes rather than removing them.

Urbanization and the Growth of the Child Welfare Problem

The growing awareness of children in need was a key characteristic of nineteenth-century social welfare endeavors. In Illinois, as in other areas of the country, this concern had its roots in a mix of philosophical, social, and practical considerations. The years before the Civil War saw an outpouring of reform efforts on all levels, and because of their vulnerability and dependence on adults, children were prime subjects of this heightened humanitarian sense. They appealed further because during the course of the nineteenth century the concept of childhood as a special stage of development grew apace, drawing the attention of everyone from popular novelists to learned theologians. Nineteenth-century culture celebrated childhood's intuitive goodness and innocence, in contrast to the gloomy assessment of earlier centuries, which had seen children at best as profoundly ignorant and at worst as little bundles of depravity. Another reason for the attention to children's needs was the abiding concern that they be trained to be independent, responsible citizens, not merely for their own sake but for the health of the republic. Finally, attention turned to dependent children because their numbers swelled so markedly with the rapid growth of urban centers during the nineteenth century.[7]

Chicago, a frontier outpost at its incorporation in 1833, grew in the next sixty-seven years to be the second largest city in the United States, an industrial center that attracted immigrants from all over the world. According to the national census, the population of Chicago was 4,470 people in 1840; 298,977 in 1870; and 1,698,575 in 1900. The rapid growth of the city brought great wealth to some, but it brought in its wake much suffering as well. Immigrants who came to the city seeking a better life sometimes found Chicago to be a place of opportunity, but many found themselves enmeshed in a web of poverty, desperation and squalor, and the devastating effects of urban life were particularly visible in children. In 1851 the city charter noted a group that greatly concerned officials: "children who are destitute of proper parental care, wandering about the streets, committing mischief, and growing up in mendicancy, ignorance, idleness, and vice." These children, popularly called "street arabs," were viewed as potential trouble makers and therefore received official attention early.[8]

In addition to these children there were others affected by the disruption of city life. The legislature had made minimal legal provisions for illegitimate children, for example, in the early years of statehood; the presumption was that the mother would keep her baby and the town would support her and her child at subsistence level (and with the most grudging of attitudes) if the father could not be held to account and she could not manage for herself. But in the vast, anonymous city, a desperate mother could simply abandon her baby on the streets without busy neighbors discovering the desertion, as they would inevitably have done in a small town or rural setting. The increase of this phenomenon of deserted children, little "foundlings" as they were called, was a gruesome measure of the hazards that the city could hold in store for young women and their unwanted children.

Orphans as a group grew in number as well. All the dangers of disease were compounded by crowded city life, by filthy tenements and equally filthy and dangerous work places. Children could lose one or both parents to a host of diseases such as cholera, small pox, and tuberculosis. The United States suffered through three cholera epidemics, in 1832 and again in the 1840s and 1850s, and the fact that the disease was waterborne insured that the poor, crowded into tenements and using the foulest of water, were among the hardest hit by the recurring plagues.[9]

"Half-orphans," (the standard term for children who had lost one parent) also claimed the reluctant attention of the state. If the mother died, the children might come to the attention of the larger society because they stood in need of care and nurturing. It was possible that they would turn into some of the little "street arabs" about whom Chicago city officials expressed such concern. But a father's death, on a practical level, was even more catastrophic. Most poor families patched together their meager income from money brought in by fathers, mothers, and children; working men, although they were paid very little, were routinely paid more than women and children, and they made the largest contribution to the family income. Widowed mothers, ill-equipped to provide for their families, might find themselves turning to the city or county for help to support their children. Children were also left "half-orphaned" in fact, although not in law, by their father's desertion of the family. Sometimes this desertion was absolute; but Hull-House resident Julia Lathrop wryly noted "the masculine expedient of temporary disappearance in the face of nonemployment or domestic complexity, or both," contending that "the intermittent husband is a constant factor in the economic problem of many a household."[10]

Natural catastrophes like the Great Fire of 1871 were another cause of dependency in children, and family problems and the stresses of urban life were compounded as well by the labor unrest that characterized the last twenty-five years of the century. In addition, the country experienced a financial panic approximately every twenty years: in 1819, 1837, 1857, 1873 and 1893. In Chicago, the Panic of 1893 was delayed for a time by the Columbian Exhibition, but with the close of the exhibition, jobs disappeared and all the severity of that worst of nineteenth-century depressions was visited on the city. The year 1894 was in many ways a terrible time for the poor of Chicago. Compounding the depression was the violence and bitterness of the Pullman Strike, and the ultimate defeat of organized labor in the prolonged struggle. A smallpox epidemic struck the city; and the winter was one of the worst on record. The dependency rate soared. Families who had never been able to save enough to have a cushion against disaster were utterly destroyed by such compounded misfortune and had to turn to the city and county for help.[11]

The State Response to Dependent Children

Although the vicissitudes of urban life and economic instability throughout the century greatly expanded both the number and types of children in need of help, public officials resisted innovation in dealing with the needs of dependent children, lumping them with the rest of the dependent population rather than addressing their particular needs as did the private organizations that began to flourish in Chicago in the 1850s. In downstate Illinois, dependent children were still primarily indentured through the middle years of the century. An 1854 revision of the apprenticeship law manifested some special attention to children's needs, strengthening their right to basic education and protection by Poor Law officials who were to monitor their treatment and to "defend them from all cruelty, neglect, and breach of contract on the part of their masters." An 1874 law further defined the child's rights to proper care, specifically forbidding "undeserved or immoderate correction, unwholesome food, insufficient allowance of food, raiment or lodging, want of sufficient care or physic in sickness, want of instruction in their trade." Such bad behavior on the part of a master gave the state sufficient cause to end the indentures. These revisions of the original apprenticeship law reflected the state's ambivalence about parental rights. The 1854 revision deleted the clause authorizing the removal of children from parents whom the overseer of the poor deemed unfit. But the 1874 law restored intervention to some degree, allowing the overseers of the poor to apprentice without parental consent any child "who habitually begs for alms."[12]

Although the basic concept of apprenticeship for dependent children was shortly to reappear in social welfare parlance as the innovative notion of "free foster homes," the whole system of formal, legal apprenticeship as a means of caring for dependent children was beginning to die out in nineteenth-century America. In northern Illinois counties, particularly Cook County, poor law officials instead placed children in the poorhouse, and this trend became state-wide by the end of the century. Most often children were in the poorhouse with their mothers, but a few orphans and illegitimate children ended up there as well.

The presence of children in the almshouse was an enduring affront to reformers. In 1853 a Cook County grand jury found the almshouse to be grossly inadequate, noting with disapproval that "the section devoted to women and children is so crowded as to be very offensive."[13] The physical conditions of this particular poorhouse did improve somewhat over time, but those who concerned themselves with child welfare universally accepted the maxim that the poorhouse was no fit place for children. Forty years and much reform agitation later, the situation was not significantly better. Julia Lathrop, who toured the Cook County poorhouse many times as a member of the State Board of Charities, wrote this description of the children there in 1894:

> There are usually from fifty to seventy-five children, of whom a large proportion are young children with their mothers, a very few of whom are for adoption. The remainder, perhaps a third, are the residuum of all the orphan asylums and hospitals, children whom no one cares to adopt because they are unattractive or scarred or sickly. These children are sent to the public school across the street from the poor-farm. Of course they wear hideous clothes, and of course the outside children sometimes jeer at them.[14]

These children, as part of the poorhouse population, were among the most stigmatized and outcast members of nineteenth-century society. Nobody went to the poorhouse if they could help it. These institutions were deliberately set up to be as unattractive as possible, a meager social mechanism intended merely to sustain life in the dependent population. The poor, who could pay with no other currency, were expected to pay with their dignity for their board and room. Lathrop spoke of "the absolute lack of privacy, the monotony and dul[l]ness, the discipline, the enforced cleanliness." Nor was enforced cleanliness always the problem. The poorhouse superintendent in Coles County reported in 1880, apparently without embarrassment, that he could not remember one bath having been taken in his sixteen years in charge. The institution's surroundings reflected his laissez faire approach to hygiene.[15]

It was still possible for poor families to receive some measure of "outdoor relief" in most counties of the state in the mid to late nineteenth century, but such support was very limited. Nineteenth-century economic theory, reinforcing the already parsimonious attitude of Americans, posited that handouts merely increased dependency and led to the "pauperizing" of families, destroying their initiative and drive to do better. Poorhouses were set up to replace most outdoor relief, created with the notion that they must not be too attractive or they would be crowded with shiftless types simply trying to live on the bounty of the town. In reality, authorities need not have feared such a thing. Anyone who could possibly manage it stayed out of the poorhouse. Those who entered were the unfortunate souls who had no one to protect them or find them a tolerable situation in the outside world. Children shared the poorhouse with the chronically sick, the elderly poor, the insane, and the mentally and physically disabled, as well as the "paupers" who simply could not make an economic go of it on the outside. In Cook County, and elsewhere on a less grand scale, the essential misery of the poorhouse was compounded by corruption. The staff jobs were filled by patronage, and those in charge of the various wards were thus unlikely to be much exercised about the humane care of the inmates.[16]

One of the most critical voices raised against the abuses of the poorhouse and the presence of children there was that of the Board of State Commissioners of Public Charities, established by the legislature in 1869 to monitor and coordinate the various social welfare efforts throughout the state. The board's power was originally very restricted. "The duties required of the commission are quite onerous," the First Biennial Report stated ruefully. "The powers granted are very limited. The board has unlimited power of inspection, suggestion and recommendation, but no administrative power whatsoever." Still, the State Board could and did register vigorous disapproval, and it made enough impact so that a bill to dissolve the new monitoring agency was introduced into the legislature almost immediately. The bill failed, but hostile legislators were able to limit inspection dramatically at one point by cutting off all travel funds for the commissioners.[17]

Despite such constraints, the State Board fulfilled an important function as the first official agency in the state to collect and tabulate information about the actual living conditions of dependent members of society, including children. For example, the board reported that in 1880 Illinois almshouses housed 386 children; forty were assessed as feebleminded, twenty-four diseased, fourteen defective, and eighty-three had been born in the almshouse. Of that eighty-three, seventy-nine were illegitimate, a fact pointed to by almshouse critics to illustrate their concern about the inadequate separation of the sexes in the institutions. Some poorhouses had schools or arranged that children should attend the public schools in the vicinity; but in many county almshouses, the children did not go to school at all. Still, there was no doubt in anyone's mind that these children were getting an education, a thorough grounding in the seamier side of life.[18]

In 1879 there was a movement in Cook County to get children out of the almshouse and into private child care institutions. This effort revealed the prevailing attitudes of reformers toward the parents of children who were dependent because of poverty. Much negotiation was necessary to settle which orphanages were to take the children, since religious groups insisted that the children's religious affiliations be respected. Yet in all the negotiations, no one considered that the poorhouse mothers might have an opinion about the removal of their children. The private institutions involved required the termination of parental rights before they would take the children. When the mothers in the Cook County poorhouse learned that their children's well-being was to be bought at the expense of their parenthood, they protested vigorously but without success. Some reformers, in fact, expressed the view that the mothers' unwillingness to give up their children demonstrated their lack of affection for their families. But in the end, the mothers succeeded in making an eloquent statement about these high-handed methods. When the officials from the child care institutions arrived to pick up the children, they found that most of them were gone. To prevent their removal to the orphanages, the mothers had managed to find places outside the poorhouse for all but seventeen out of seventy-five children. The Cook County poorhouse had a rule that no parents who refused to give consent to the adoption of their children could enter the poorhouse, but in 1880, the county agent objected to the rule as inhumane and cruel. He refused to enforce the policy, and his stance meant that children began to enter the Cook County poorhouse again, with and without parents, less than a year after the "rescue operation" of 1879.[19]

The concern that children were growing up in such a wretched setting did not disappear, despite the limited success of the Cook County effort, but it took another forty years for the Illinois legislature to close almshouses to children. In 1895 a law provided that orphan children could be removed from the poorhouse and placed in private homes, but only when a private charity or individual would assume the expenses connected with such placement. By 1900 a dozen states, beginning with Michigan in 1869, had ended the practice of putting children in the poorhouse, but Illinois proved more resistant to thoroughgoing reform. Finally, in 1919 the legislature passed a law limiting the time in the poorhouse to thirty days for girls under eighteen and boys under seventeen, after which other arrangements would have to be made for them. This effectively ended the use of the poorhouse as a child welfare institution. By that time the number of children in Illinois poorhouses had shrunk considerably: to 171 children in 1918 compared to 470 at the peak, 1886.[20]

Child Care Institutions under Public Auspices

Although the county poorhouses provided most of the public care of destitute children in nineteenth-century Illinois, no one made much of an argument to counter the accusations leveled against them of pinch-penny meanness and spiritual demoralization. In reality, they existed as the most frankly minimal of offerings for children in need, with a policy set far more by a consciousness of county expenditures than of children's welfare. Noted social welfare thinker Homer Folks remarked in 1900 that "the states of Illinois and Missouri, notwithstanding their large cities have been singularly backward in making public provisions for destitute and neglected children."[21] In fact, Illinois had only two child welfare institutions under public auspices during the nineteenth century, both far more specialized than the catch-all poorhouses provided by most counties. These institutions were the Soldiers' Orphans' Home and, until 1870, the Chicago Reform School.

The Illinois Soldiers' Orphans' Home, founded in 1865 in Normal, Illinois, was a state-funded institution for the care of children whose fathers had been killed or disabled in the Civil War. An institution with a limited purpose, the Soldiers' Orphans' Home was meant to close once its original population had been cared for. But in the 1870s the eligibility for care was broadened to include children of all Civil War veterans, an act that established the institution on a more permanent basis. Frequently the children were half-orphans whose mothers simply could not feed them any more. In 1872, for example, 532 out of 642 children had living mothers. In 1879, the superintendent gave this description of the newly arrived children for that year: "The class now entering are, for the most part, young and in particularly destitute circumstances—those whom their mothers have struggled long and hard to keep, but who now find themselves, at the commencement of winter, without the means for support, and know they must either send them away to be cared for elsewhere, or permit them to remain at home to suffer. The state must now take these burdens of care and responsibility where the weary mothers lay them down."[22]

The separation of children from mothers unable to provide for them financially was a tragic constant in nineteenth-century children's institutions. At least at the Soldiers' Orphans' Home there was some connection maintained between children and their families; mothers were not required to terminate their parental rights when they placed their children there, and it was not uncommon for the children in the institution to spend time, sometimes whole summers, with their mothers. The population of the home fluctuated with the season and with the economic climate of the times.[23]

This enlightened aspect of the place, however, was not typical of the administration. The Soldiers' Orphans' Home was often plagued by scandals and investigations, and the treatment of the children was very harsh. The fact that it was a publicly funded institution meant that it was scrutinized fairly intensively by the State Board of Charities, and the board found little to praise in the orphanage. The quality of administrators varied widely, since they were appointed by the governor. The first superintendent, Mrs. Ohr, was a Civil War colonel's widow with small children but no business capacity and a rapacious appetite for elegance, furnished at the expense of the state. In 1869, early in her tenure, both the *Springfield Register* and the *Chicago Times* voiced accusations about serious mistreatment of the children. Although Mrs. Ohr and her staff were exonerated, one steward was dismissed on the grounds that he had made sexual advances to a number of little girls in the institution. Mrs. Ohr weathered this upset, kept on because she was "a mother to these orphans," in the words of the investigating committee. But eventually she went too far; a combination of totally ignoring the trustees' instructions, keeping the children from school in order to perform chores around the institution, and thoroughly profligate spending finally ended her career at the Soldiers' Orphans' Home some twenty years after she had launched it.[24]

The two superintendents who followed Mrs. Ohr were more business-like in their approach, but they had no training in the care of children, orphans or not; they were strictly political appointments. The most difficult regime for the children up to the turn of the century was that of a Republican politician named J. L. Magner, who was nicknamed "the cattle driver" by some of the Bloomington/Normal locals because of his harsh treatment of the children. There was consistent criticism that the children were made to work too hard, at tasks that were sometimes beyond them, and they were often kept home from school to work. One particularly distressing instance of work beyond the children's capacity was the scalding death of a three-year-old child, burned while being bathed by some of the older children of the institution.[25]

Nor were the superintendents and their policies the only difficulty. The building, planned by a board of trustees with a poetical turn, was gracefully adorned with turrets and "crowned with a tasteful observatory." But Fredrick Wines, secretary of the State Board of Charities, assessed the building as a thoroughgoing failure on a practical level. There were no closets, no playgrounds, only two bathrooms for over three hundred children, no infirmary, and no private quarters for the superintendent's family. Perhaps worst of all, there was no deep wellspring to supply water. The well went dry after the first year, and water had to be brought in by railroad. The Soldiers' Orphans' Home, beset by scandals and mismanagement, conjured up the worst fears of Illinois citizens about public institutions run badly because of patronage appointments.[26]

The Chicago Reform School, also a public institution, won approval from most critics for efficient management and humane treatment of its inmates. But the school's involvement with predelinquent boys ended with the noted O'Connell decision of 1870, and the institution closed shortly after this (see chapter 4). With the exception of the inadequate provision of the poorhouse, the responsibility for dependent children in Chicago, from 1871 to the end of the century, was under private auspices.[27]

The Growth of Private Institutions
in the Nineteenth Century

The state's minimal response to dependent children was an obdurate problem in the nineteenth century. An equally disorganizing feature of child welfare in Illinois resulting from state reluctance was the proliferation of private agencies to care for children. These institutions mushroomed in the state (particularly in Chicago) in the last half of the nineteenth century, offering a wide variety of services to children, based in part on their religious and cultural identification and in part on the variety of needs that the complex crises of urban life created. These agencies, originally meant to fill the gap left by the inadequacy of state responses, quickly became entrenched in the public life of the city. Their presence contributed to the fragmentation that would plague child welfare efforts in Illinois through the twentieth century, resulting in a lack of coordination that left many dependent children unserved. By the end of the nineteenth century, critics in Illinois and around the country began to see the dominance of private agencies as a negative and talk in terms of a stronger state organization; but in the mid-nineteenth century, the private child welfare institutions were autonomous, both organizationally and financially, not always by their own choosing.

The Chicago Orphan Asylum, founded in 1848 to respond to the crisis of the cholera epidemic of that year, was the first orphanage in Cook County. It was followed in 1849 by the Roman Catholic Orphan Asylum, which aimed to serve Catholic children and keep them out of the Protestant Chicago Orphan Asylum. This carving out of religious turf, begun so early in the history of child care institutions, was to be a major factor in the development of orphanages in Chicago. In addition to a competition among religions for the care of children, a strong sense of ethnicity motivated founders of these institutions. Chicago had institutions representing all nationalities; there were German orphanages, Irish orphanages, Swedish, Polish, Lithuanian, and Jewish orphanages, as well as institutions founded by "native Americans" of English stock.[28]

Besides motives of religion and ethnicity, institutions developed to respond to a variety of needs among children. Many of them took in the children of the poor but insisted that parents relinquish their rights to the children before they were accepted. A few, like the Chicago Nursery and Half-Orphan Asylum, were founded to offer support to working mothers who could not keep their children at home, yet wanted to preserve their families. The children lived at the institution, but mothers were expected to visit them regularly and contribute something toward their children's support. The Chicago Home for the Friendless originally took in homeless and battered women as well as children but soon revised its mission to focus only on children. The Chicago Foundling Hospital specialized in caring for the abandoned infants found with such appalling regularity on the streets and brought by the police to the institution for what care and comfort it could offer. The mortality rate in foundling hospitals was always shockingly high; the babies had frequently suffered from exposure, and feeding them adequately and safely, in the days before infant formula and pasteurized milk, posed a major problem. The desertion of infants was a disturbing and highly visible form of child mistreatment, provoking an 1887 law that made such abandonment a crime resulting in automatically terminated parental rights. But not all children left at the foundling hospital were abandoned on the streets. Dr. William Shipman, founder of the hospital, witnessed a poignant scene in which a mother and her little boy said a heartbroken farewell to their baby before placing it in the champagne basket used as a receptacle outside the foundling hospital. In typical nineteenth-century fashion, Shipman sympathized with a mother pushed to such lengths, yet his assistance took the form only of taking the baby, not of investigating ways that the family might stay together.[29]

One development among private institutions that especially reflected the growing awareness of children and their needs was the Illinois Humane Society, which began its child saving work in 1877. By that time the population of Cook County had begun its phenomenal growth, going from 43,383 people in 1850 to 607,524 in 1880. Both the stresses of city life and its anonymity provoked child abuse, according to Oscar Dudley, director of the Illinois Humane Society, who observed that "what is everybody's business is nobody's business"; and thus children could be terribly treated by parents and guardians even though there were laws in effect to protect them. The Humane Society originally began as the Society for the Prevention of Cruelty to Animals, but in 1877, Director Dudley transferred the society's attention to cruelty against children by arresting an abusing guardian. There was, he wrote, "no reason that a child should not be entitled to as much protection under the law as a dumb animal." The Illinois Society for the Prevention of Cruelty to Animals changed its name to the

Illinois Humane Society in 1881, recognizing that over two-thirds of its investigations involved cruelty against children rather than animals. Dudley asserted that from 1881, when the Humane Society began to keep records, until the time that he was writing (1893), over ten thousand children had been rescued.[30]

The rescue operations were broadened from cases of abuse to the protection of children exploited by their employers, particularly when children were forced to beg or were entertainers or victims of the infamous padrone system.[31] Dudley reported great success in finding asylums and homes for these children, a situation receiving tacit approval from the state, which did not at this point assume responsibility for neglected or abused children or supervise private child placement activities.[32]

State Involvement in the Late Nineteenth Century

The only real state or city involvement with private institutions originally was that the mayor, acting as guardian for dependent children, had the power to place them in child care institutions. The city of Chicago (where most of the children's institutions flourished), the surrounding counties, and the state of Illinois all proved very reluctant to contribute financially to private institutions. The city did give very occasional assistance, in times of real crisis like the cholera epidemics or the Great Fire of 1871, but it was limited in quantity and very episodic. The most the city would do for the Chicago Nursery and Half-Orphan Asylum, for example, was to provide that the city could buy or lease the land upon which the asylum would be built. For the Englewood Infant Nursery, the assistance was even more meager: in 1893 the city provided ten tons of hard coal and burial space for dead babies. For the children who managed to survive, the funding had to come from other sources.[33]

The state did make one major concession in funding when it agreed to provide subsidies for the industrial schools that developed in the last years of the century. The schools were modeled after English institutions made famous by the renowned English reformer Mary Carpenter, who in the 1870s and 1880s enjoyed considerable influence in the United States. The primary point of the schools, reflecting the use of the word "industrial," was to train children to earn their own living in later life, although in fact the training tended to be geared much more toward a traditional agricultural economy than toward anything having to do with industry. Boys learned farming, some shoe and broommaking, woodcarving and academic subjects. Girls were primarily given a common school education and taught domestic skills.[34]

The willingness to fund the industrial schools was traceable to their mission: they were founded to deal with older, predelinquent street children who threatened the public order by begging, consorting with objectionable characters, or living in houses of ill-fame. The law establishing industrial schools added that children in the poorhouse were proper subjects for the schools, which meant that in practice there was a mix of younger children in with more canny and seasoned veterans of the street. The State Board of Charities, which inspected the schools, objected to this mix, but the industrial schools survived this criticism, as well as a series of court challenges ranging from civil liberties concerns to objections that the schools were sectarian institutions and therefore not appropriate recipients of state funds.[35]

The development of the subsidy system, the state funding of private institutions on an amount-per-child basis, was a phenomenon noted by Homer Folks in *The Care of Destitute, Neglected and Dependent Children*, his end-of-the-century assessment of child care trends in the United States. Neither Folks nor other observers of current philanthropic trends, groups like the National Conference of Charities and the Illinois State Board of Charities, really approved of such an arrangement. They urged Illinois to move in the direction of states like Kansas and Iowa, which had converted veterans' orphans' homes similar to the Illinois Soldiers' Orphans' Home to state institutions that served all dependent children, regardless of religion, ethnicity, or parental status. These states and others around the country were moving toward a point where the state assumed primary responsibility for dependent children, not by warehousing them in local poorhouses but by placing them in state-run, central institutions from which they were placed out into foster and adoptive homes. This system of central state control was known as the "Michigan Plan," after the first state to enact the policy. Illinois' neighbors Wisconsin and Minnesota, as well as Michigan, had state institutions for dependent children, winning the approval of child welfare theorists who applauded such centralization. It was, they argued, more efficient and economical, providing children with far better, more consistent care than Illinois' system, where a child might be placed with a superb private agency but might also be made to endure the grim inadequacies of the poorhouse.[36]

"The real contest, if such it may be called," wrote Folks in 1900, "will be between the state and the contract or subsidy systems. To put it plainly, the question now being decided is this—is our public administration sufficiently honest and efficient to be entrusted with the management of a system for the care of destitute children, or must we turn that branch of public service over to private charitable corporations, leaving to public officials the functions of paying the bills; and of exercising such supervision over the workings of the plan as may be possible?"[37] Illinois was seen as nonprogressive in its increasing use of the subsidy system, allowing private agencies to dominate the field while the state remained relatively uninvolved in the care and protection of dependent children.

This minimal level of state involvement offended against another philanthropic tenet, the idea that the state should have a monitoring function over all agencies, public and private, as well as keeping in touch with children who had been placed in families. The State Board of Charities did visit the industrial schools, which got public funds, but it was not until the Juvenile Court Act was passed in 1899 that the State Board was given responsibility for inspection of private as well as public agencies for children.[38]

Another significant change from an earlier view, at least among the more "advanced" thinkers, was a rejection of institutions as the best substitute for a child's family. In the nineteenth century, institutions and asylums of all kinds had sprung up, not only in Illinois but all across the United States. Asylums were not intended to be a dumping ground for society's unfortunates, as the county poorhouses were, but were rather supposed to be a specialized environment in which the needs of a particular dependent population could be met most effectively. But it was not long before a set of critics arose who stressed the negative effects of institutions and urged that institutional life should be resorted to only under special circumstances or on a very temporary basis. For special cases, like the handicapped, perhaps institutions could provide resources and training that they would not receive elsewhere, these critics agreed; but for children whose greatest problem was that for one reason or another their families were not functioning, the negative effects of institutions far outweighed the positive aspects.[39]

According to the anti-institutional analysis, the regimentation in institutions was destructive of initiative and individuality. The qualities that brought rewards in an institutional setting—mindless obedience, dependence, obsequiousness—were the very traits that all agreed were destructive to the forming of a healthy, independent adult citizen. Furthermore, institutions by their nature seemed to foster abuse and bad treatment. Exposés and investigations of various institutions featured accusations of physical cruelty and psychological debasement.[40]

Institutions were expensive, physically and psychologically barren, and downright unnatural for children, according to Charles Loring Brace, a minister who worked for the Children's Aid Society of New York. Brace began a program that took the street children of New York City and sought to improve their lives not by placing them in the highly controlled and contrived environment of an institution but by resettling them in homes in mid-western and western states such as Illinois. He was convinced that the best solution for children in need of placement was to provide homes in the simplest and most direct way, relying as much as possible on the basic goodness that he believed informed the souls of most Americans, especially those who still lived away from the corrupting city in the virtue-producing agricultural heartland of the nation. The methods of the Children's Aid Society reflected the simplicity of Brace's moral equation. Brace and his associates would arrive in a western town with a trainload of city children, and using the medium of the local churches, would call upon citizens to give these needy young people a home. The entire plan of "free foster homes" was really only an updated version of apprenticeship, in which the child agreed to work in exchange for care and training, except that this child-placing organization, aided by such technological developments as the railroads, reached much farther afield than the overseers of the poor had done in earlier times. Free foster homes differed further in that they were based on such a trusting assumption about human nature that there were no legal bonds struck at all between the child and his foster family. Brace firmly believed that a child who brought a willing pair of hands to a family would be valued accordingly and could safely count on good treatment in his new home.[41]

This notion proved, not surprisingly, to be overly sanguine, as the Children's Aid Society came to discover when the accusations began to grow in the later years of the century that New York was not really solving children's problems by the use of its "Children West" program but was merely dumping one of its troublesome populations onto other states. At various times the Children's Aid Society conducted surveys and studies of its "alumni," claiming a very high success rate for the program, but critics questioned the quality of these studies, and opposition to Brace's program continued. The 1899 Illinois Juvenile Court Act forbade any agencies to bring children unaccompanied by their parents or guardians, without the approval of the State Board of Charities. This was partly a protection against the importing of child labor to Illinois, but it was a response as well to organizations like the Children's Aid Society. The law included the provision that any child who became a public charge within five years of arrival in Illinois should be removed to his or her home state.[42]

The notion of placing children in families and the belief that normal family life was a far healthier situation than institutions was firmly entrenched in child welfare thinking by the end of the century. But the earlier, more naive, notion that foster families could be trusted to care for dependent children without supervision had been replaced in philanthropic thinking by a belief that it was important for an outside agency regularly to check on the child and act in his behalf. Coupled with this was the beginning of a move away from "free" foster homes to the belief that boarding homes, foster homes in which a family got payment for keeping the foster child, were most productive of humane treatment. Child welfare theorists and practitioners worried that if a family's greatest inducement to take a foster child was the child's potential economic contribution, there might be a strong incentive for them to over-burden him with work, at the expense of his academic education, which reformers were coming more and more to see as the true and proper occupation of childhood.[43]

One final change in philanthropic theory that saw little reflection in practice but was to bring about a revolution in twentieth-century social welfare was the growing conviction that the best thing that could be done for children was to keep them with their families whenever possible. Students of society came increasingly to regard poverty as a result of a faulty economic and social structure rather than the personal failings of feckless or lazy individuals, and they disapproved of the kind of casual invasion of poor families' lives that could demand the sacrifice of parental rights in return for assistance. This belief in the preservation of the family became a basic underpinning of the social welfare faith as it was articulated in the next fifty years, and the state of Illinois, with its experiment in mothers' pension programs, was to be in the forefront of progressive practice in this area.[44]

In the last decade of the nineteenth century, though, the innovations that would make Illinois notable a few years later were nowhere in sight. Surrounded by vigorous neighbors, Illinois was considered conservative in its reluctance to deal with its child welfare functions and in its willingness to relinquish the charge to private agencies. In fact, the state's attitude toward dependent children had changed very little in the course of the nineteenth century. The first laws and provisions for dependent children had reflected a lack of ardor bordering on indifference, and at the end of the century, the state's engagement in child welfare, despite the crisis engendered by rapid growth and economic stress, was tepid at best. The combination of fiscal conservatism and ethnic and religious tensions meant that state action was regarded with suspicion in many quarters and kept efforts fragmented and inadequate to the need. There was also a fear that the patronage and corruption for which Illinois was already famous might make state administration of programs for dependent children less effective than privately run efforts. Ironically, it was in part this very disorganization and inaction that would lead to the founding of the Juvenile Court and bring Illinois, however briefly, within the pale of reformers' approval.

2

Extending the Boundaries
of Care, 1899–1950

The Progressive reform movement that energized the country for the first two decades of the twentieth century held as key tenets a belief in state action and a rationalizing and ordering of existing services. Chaotic as it was, the care of dependent children in Illinois was an obvious subject for child welfare reformers, who vigorously took up the challenge. Despite the intransigence of much of the child welfare establishment and the penurious attitude of the legislature, the reformers succeeded in establishing two institutions, the juvenile court and mothers' pensions, which would catch on not only in Illinois but virtually all over the country. In addition, the reformers recognized the need for a state administrative unit for child welfare and succeeded in establishing an embryonic unit, though one with far less power than they thought necessary.

The Juvenile Court

The juvenile court, Illinois' great social welfare innovation, is usually thought of in connection with the problem of delinquency, but in reality, it was created as much to exert some coherent state influence over dependent children as it was to deal with delinquents. As early as 1891, Timothy Hurley, of the Catholic Visitation Aid Society, introduced a bill into the legislature that sought to assert some level of state authority over child welfare activities. Hurley proposed that a court, upon finding a child dependent, neglected, or delinquent, could commit him or her to a child care agency that would be required to keep a record of the child's progress and report this information to the court at regular intervals. This bill was opposed by two private agencies, the Illinois Humane Society and the Glenwood Industrial School, on the grounds that it was "advanced legislation," and it failed to pass. Despite this resistance within the philanthropic community, discussion on the best means to offer unified and consistent care to children continued through the decade. The 1898 Illinois Conference of Charities devoted its entire agenda to the question "Who are the children of the state?" emphasizing the crying need for action with regard to the problems of dependent and delinquent children. The conference stressed the state's responsibility to children who could not look to their families for protection and asserted the superior efficacy of such official action over what they called "individual or home effort." Agitation for state involvement did not stop when the charities conference adjourned. Throughout 1898 a coalition of lawyers' groups, settlement house workers, Chicago women's clubs, and agents of private charities worked to produce a bill that would survive a challenge to constitutionality.[1]

The coalition succeeded in their goal with the passage of "An Act to Regulate the Treatment and Control of Dependent, Neglected and Delinquent Children," which became effective July 1, 1899. This act established the first juvenile court in the nation and set the principle, eventually to be followed by every state in the union, that children should have a separate court to address their peculiar needs, or if a county was too small to warrant a separate court for children, at least that the proceedings of the court should be different from those used in adult cases. (In Illinois only counties of five hundred thousand people or more had a separate court; other counties set aside special days for juvenile court procedures.)[2]

At the heart of the juvenile court legislation was the idea of centrality, and this was especially critical in dealing with dependency. The proponents of the law wanted the court to be the central agency that was responsible for children who were dependent or neglected, rather than continuing the current practice of handing a child over to an institution or foster home with no official checks on the child's care and treatment once the child care agency took charge. With the Juvenile Court Act, the child went through the court and was either placed with an agency or put on probation. If he was placed with an agency, that agency had to be registered with the State Board of Charities and was subject to assessment and visitation from the board. If the child was placed on probation, which was possible for dependent and neglected, as well as delinquent children, the probation officer would monitor the home situation and report back to the court. Either way, the reformers hoped, the ungoverned, scatter-shot benevolence to which children had been subject formerly was to some extent supervised and controlled.

Another aspect of centrality in the Juvenile Court Act was its emphasis on childhood as the key to procedures dealing with dependent and delinquent children. The authors of the Juvenile Court Act deliberately set out to blur the lines between innocence and guilt, insisting instead that the essential issue was youth. Youth meant limited judgment and capacity, and therefore issues of culpability mattered less than the fact that all children, whether criminal or merely unfortunate, needed adult guidance and protection. Furthermore, promoters of the law were quick to point out that the distinctions between dependent and delinquent children were never as clear in reality as they were in the written law. According to Timothy Hurley, who became chief probation officer in Cook County, "A child who today is simply neglected, may be dependent tomorrow, truant the next day and a delinquent the day after that."[3]

The downward path for neglected children was illustrated in a Children's Bureau study of the Chicago Juvenile Court in 1922 that seemed to imply that dependent children graduated to delinquency or, at least, were classified as delinquent as they got older. The study noted that between 1915 and 1919, only 7.9 percent of dependent children were fourteen and older (with 38.9 percent under seven years and 53.2 percent between seven and fourteen). By contrast, there were no delinquents under nine in these years, while 68.9 percent of boys and 86.5 percent of girls in the delinquency category were fourteen and older. The amendment of the definition of delinquency to include the elastic notion of "incorrigibility," which encompassed many behavior problems including sexual promiscuity, undoubtedly added to the regrouping of children from dependent to delinquent as they advanced in age.[4]

"The fundamental idea of the Juvenile Court is so simple," wrote Timothy Hurley, "it seems anyone ought to understand it. It is, to be perfectly plain, a return to paternalism, it is the acknowledgement by the State of its relationship as the parent to every child within its borders." Hurley, certainly one of the court's most enthusiastic boosters, rhapsodized about the paternalism thus called forth. In his description of "Dependent-Day in the Juvenile Court" he wrote,

> So intricate are the problems coming before the court to be solved that to an outsider it would seem that the judge must be possessed of the wisdom of Solomon. Sometimes the case should have been

taken to a divorce court rather than to one dealing with the question of child-saving. Sometimes it ought not to have been brought at all. Some cases are worse than mediocre in their commonplaceness, while some are so pitiful they bring tears to the eyes of those who had forgotten they could cry. Being a father, Judge Tuthill is able not only to take up the case from the standpoint of the welfare of the child, but he is able as well to judge wisely of the feelings and real motives of the parent. Some of the children are dressed in silks and show every evidence of wealth and refinement; some on the contrary, are poorly dressed, and the officers of the court tell heartrending tales of finding the little ones with only one garment on their back, filthy with vermin, hungry and deserted. The flotsam and jetsam from the murky ocean of life are cast ashore on the Juvenile Court. Then the good is sorted out from the bad and each case is disposed of in exactly the right way.

Again asserting an almost mystical perception on the part of the judge, Hurley told his audience: "The judge of the Juvenile Court must be looked upon, in a way, as a sort of Recording Angel, who takes all the information at hand, gazes into the past, present and future of the child, and decides to bring into his life just the thing which is needed at that moment to set at work the influences which will produce the desired effect upon his future."[5]

Hurley's confidence in the judge's ability to dispose of cases "in exactly the right way" is fairly astonishing in light of the fact that he had been chief probation officer and must certainly have seen a few bad decisions, or at the very least a heartbreakingly insoluble situation or two. But while he seems a bit more given to florid prose than the other witnesses recounting the early days of the court, he is truly representative of the basic notion behind the new system, that of considerable trust in the paternal wisdom of the judge and a conscious elasticity of procedure to allow for individual decision making.

The juvenile court is one of the most famous creations of Progressive social reform agitation, but in some ways it is very much at odds with basic Progressive thinking. Greatly influenced by the tremendous advances in medicine in the late nineteenth century, the Progressives were optimistic certainly, but their optimism was largely based on their faith in science, on the capacity to order, measure, check and balance their institutions and to make use of "trained experts" to solve life's thornier problems. And while their frequently professed faith in experts may sound naive to a modern audience accustomed to malpractice suits and disheartening revelations about lapsed professionals of all kinds, it is positively hard-headed compared to Hurley's sentimental invocation of paternalism. The benevolent judge of Hurley's piece came by his abilities not through training but because he was a father and therefore presumably the possessor of many virtues and instincts that allowed him to act as Solomon.

Hurley's thinking and that of other juvenile court advocates who were willing to place so much discretion in judicial hands in the name of revived paternalism did reflect a strong current in American culture, however, that of the sentimentalizing of happy family life and the parental role. President Theodore Roosevelt offered an example to the nation of exuberant parenting, and Americans were instructed in their responsibilities by poems like the one from Edgar Guest that urged:

> Be more than his dad;
> Be a chum to the lad;
> Be a part of his life,
> Every hour of the day.

Judge Merrit Pinckney expressed the same sentimental regard for maternal competence in an article on mothers' pensions. He spoke of "this most sacred thing in human life—a mother's love—" and ended his argument, "'God,' said an old Rabbi, 'could not be everywhere and therefore he made mothers.'"[6]

The reliance of the juvenile court on the judge's unassisted human decency was an extreme example of this optimism, however, especially considering that the first juvenile court was established in Cook County, famed for political corruption, where judges were not notable for their probity. Louise de Koven Bowen, a Chicago social reformer and active supporter of the court, acknowledged as much when she wrote in her memoirs of her efforts to have the court's probation officers selected by civil service examinations. "When Judge Pinckney sat on the bench of the Juvenile Court he recognized that the appointment of probation officers was in his power. This was, of course, perfectly safe with him but many of us felt that it might not be wise to give a power of this kind to the judges of the future who might sit in the Juvenile Court."[7]

Despite the possibilities for judicial corruption, the juvenile court movement in Chicago and across the nation did rely heavily on the beneficence and wisdom of the judge.[8] But not all those affiliated with the juvenile court were comfortable with its reli-

ance on judicial discretion. Judge Julian Mack, who served as juvenile court judge in Cook County from 1905 to 1907 expressed
concern about the issue.

> I know—other judges have told me the same thing—that the good
> people of the community think that every judge of the juvenile court
> must necessarily be a fine fellow, filled with the wisdom of the ages,
> capable of dealing with all children that come before him. That sort
> of a genius does not exist. He may in the course of time, through
> unusual experience and opportunity, gain considerable wisdom. He
> may be able, as Judge [Ben] Lindsey [of Colorado] preeminently has
> been able, in addition to being his own chief probation officer, to
> be the counselor of those children that come before him. But few
> judges are really temperamentally fitted, and few are so eminently
> endowed as to be able to do the juvenile work and the probation
> work and all the other work that must be done if the court is to be
> really successful.

In true Progressive style, Mack believed that judges should rely
on trained probation officers, as well as the experts from the newly
established Juvenile Psychopathic Institute who could better in-
terpret a child's situation than the judge who only saw a child and
his family for a brief time.[9]

Problems in the Practical Functioning of the Juvenile Court

Judge Mack's concern about the broad powers assigned to juvenile court judges found an echo in the juvenile court reformers sixty years later who objected to both the judge's broad powers and
those accorded to officers of the court in general. The informality
of procedure in the juvenile court, precisely the aspect that its creators had prided themselves on, was the single greatest issue for
which it was indicted when it became the subject of critical re-
examination in the 1950s and 1960s. But other problems with the
practical workings of the process began to surface fairly early on,
drawing the concerned attention of some child welfare advocates.
As Judge Mack noted, just because the idea of the court was a good
one did not guarantee "that everything connected with it must in
practice be equally fine."[10]

One of the concerns voiced frequently in regard to the care of
dependent children was that despite the general consensus that a
family setting was the best situation for children, in fact many
children were still being placed in institutions rather than being
helped in their own homes or placed in foster families. The 1922
Children's Bureau study of the Chicago Juvenile Court noted that

40.7 percent of dependent children coming through the court from 1915 to 1919 went to institutions, compared to 4.7 percent committed to child-placing agencies for placement in foster or adoptive homes. There was no public money available for boarding children in family homes, and the only institutions that received public subsidies until 1923 were industrial schools. Because they were county funded and relatively simple to incorporate, there was a great proliferation of such institutions, especially in Cook County, where in 1922 there were eighteen schools, ten for boys and eight for girls. The 1920 Child Welfare Committee of the Department of Public Welfare, a gathering of prominent citizens that had been appointed to assess child welfare services in the state, noted this phenomenon with some concern. The committee was reluctant to endorse institutions of any kind in lieu of family placements, but it felt particularly that the law allowing payment only to industrial schools should be changed. Industrial schools, they asserted, should really live up to the purpose of training older children for specific employment, but because they were the only publicly subsidized institutions, they took children who were far too young to profit from vocational instruction. In 1919, 40 percent of all dependent children in Cook County were in industrial schools. A 1923 amendment to the Juvenile Court Act provided that a county could be ordered to pay subsidies to any association to whom a child was committed by the court. This amendment aimed to subsidize children in boarding homes, but, as an unintended consequence, it also encouraged the development of even more institutions.[11]

Another problem in dealing with dependency arose from the "elastic clause" of the Juvenile Court Act, the amendment that had included incorrigibility in the definition of delinquency. The stated intention for including this very broad category was to allow concerned parents and citizens to bring a troubled child to the attention of the court before he or she went seriously astray. But one result of such imprecise language was that children who were clearly dependent, sometimes the tragic victims of adult cruelty, were defined as delinquent rather than dependent. The court lacked the ability to offer restorative treatment to many children and their families, and children were sometimes placed in institutions because the judge and court workers frankly did not know what to do with them. Such was the case with children who were in reality dependent but "have been so criminally neglected [that] even if they have themselves committed no offense, are often con-

taminated by their surroundings. For this reason it sometimes be-
comes necessary to place them in institutions with delinquent
children in order to protect the other dependent children whose
experiences have not been demoralizing." A table showing "Nature of Difficulties Resulting in Commitment" in a study of girls
at the Geneva state reformatory illustrated this point in dreary
detail: Thirty-two girls were placed only for dependency; one girl's
"difficulties" were "rape, venereal disease, St. Vitus dance and
tuberculosis"; for three more, the listing merely read "rape." Another girl's case history provided the information that her stepfather, with her mother's collusion, "compelled me to live with him
as wife. . . . One morning I refused to submit to my stepfather and
they beat me so severely that I had bruises on my face. . . . I was
sent here for protection."[12]

The decision to incarcerate children who were brutalized but
somehow "contaminated" by adult criminality could be justified
with the argument that all institutions for children were supposed
to be nonpunitive and benign in intent, operating without regard
to the child's guilt or innocence. That argument lost credibility
as time passed and such scandalous revelations as those of the
Geneva girls' reformatory become known (chapter 5). But the tendency to place dependent children in reformatories continued long
after the nature of those institutions was revealed. In the case of
children involved in criminal or sexual behavior, there was a therapeutic reason, however dubious, for such placement. For most
dependent children placed in reformatories, the justification was
more egregious; simple stinginess impelled counties to save the
cost of probation officers and other provisions for children in need.
The reformatories were state funded, and as such, assumed all the
financial responsibility for the children. Thus there were real incentives to further victimize children who were already badly used
by sending them to the state training schools instead of caring
for—and paying for—them in their counties of origin. The Child
Welfare Committee of 1920 noted this grim practice, but the committee's call for a stricter definition of "delinquent" and "dependent" went unheeded. The legislative Child Welfare Committee
of 1931 pointed out the same problem, mincing no words in its
summation of the situation:

> The committee cannot close its eyes to the fact that children are
> sometimes brought before county courts whose only offense is that
> they are without means of support, and that such children are now

from time to time committed to correctional institutions, like the St. Charles School for Boys, for want of any other provision. It is apparent that this is highly unfair to the child concerned. No matter how conscientious the management at St. Charles may be, the fact is that it is regarded outside as a correctional institution, and also that any boy received into St. Charles is brought into association with boys of wayward and vicious tendencies by whom his disposition and character may be greatly injured.[13]

Problems of Black Children in the Child Welfare System

Black children were especially vulnerable to inappropriate placement in facilities for delinquents, at least in part because of the limited services for black dependent children. The Juvenile Protective Association, an organization formed to support the juvenile court through investigations of children at risk, pointed out in 1913 that one-third of the girls and young women in the Cook County Jail were black. A 1923 master's thesis from the School of Social Service Administration at the University of Chicago noted that 16 percent of the girls at the Geneva reformatory were black, at a time when black people comprised only two percent of the total population of Illinois. The author contended that the high percentage of black girls resulted from a combination of environmental stresses and a total lack of resources in the community to respond to delinquent and dependent girls without resorting to the reformatory. Because there were few maternity homes or foster placements for unmarried pregnant black girls, they were often sent to Geneva as well, a situation made possible by the sexual misconduct clause in the definition of delinquency. The 1931 Child Welfare Committee found that black boys were greatly overrepresented at St. Charles Reformatory, too; slightly more than one-quarter of the boys in the reformatory were black. Nor did the situation improve after the publication of these studies; in 1946, 29 percent of the girls at Geneva were black, while in the city of Chicago black girls comprised only 8.6 percent of girls ten to seventeen. Black boys in the state training school in the same year comprised 28.6 percent of the inmates, while the black population of Illinois was only 4.3 percent of the state's total population.[14]

In those cases, the juvenile court, far from succeeding at its stated goal of reducing institutionalization, facilitated the incarceration of black children. The court, despite reformers' best hopes, was able to do very little when no placements were available, and the lack of places for dependent black children was a striking feature of the substitute care system in Illinois, a problem aggravated by the closing of the two major institutions for black children in Cook County within two years of each other. The Amanda Smith Home for girls burned in 1919, and the Louise Manual Training School for Colored Boys closed the following year. With the opening of these schools in the early years of the twentieth century, even the five white institutions that had had a policy of taking black children (and then generally only if they were segregated on some level from the white children) had cut down on their intake of black children. The sudden lack of institutional provisions for black children after the double closing was keenly felt in the 1920s. Black children, passed over by most private agencies and offered very little in the way of public support, often got their care and protection from an informal (and unsubsidized) network of extended families and friends within the black community.[15]

Social work professor Sophonisba Breckinridge, who, together with her colleague Edith Abbott, had studied and publicized the effects of the profound racial discrimination under which black children lived in Chicago, chaired the Subcommittee on Colored Children for the 1920 Child Welfare Committee. She pointed out that even black children with families intact faced the most difficult of circumstances. According to the census figures for 1900, 26 percent of married black women worked compared to 3 percent of white women, raising problems of adequate child care and nurture. Black children attended the worst schools in the city, with the fewest resources for technical training and recreation, and housing conditions in "the black belt" were miserable.

When they did get placed, dependent black children were kept in substandard institutions, institutions that were passed over by state inspectors whose job it was to review and uphold decent standards of care. Breckinridge referred in particular to the 1919 fire in the Amanda Smith School, a fire that should have been utterly predictable given the outbreak of several smaller fires previously and the general dilapidated conditions of the school. Two children died in the fire, and at least in part, responsibility for their deaths must rest with the state, declared Breckinridge, since "the deficiencies of this home for dependent children had been repeatedly called to the attention of the authorities responsible for the supervision of such institutions."[16]

Although there were those within the child welfare community who recognized that racial discrimination compounded the problems of some of the most vulnerable people in Illinois, the special problems of caring for and placing minority children was to continue right through the twentieth century. Within Cook County in the 1920s and 1930s, officials attempted to address the special problems of black children, in the 1920s with a demonstration project that used a mix of public and private funds, and during the Depression with the addition of federal funds. But the agencies that placed black children were chronically overburdened. And for black children outside Cook County there were no provisions at all.[17]

Practical Limitations on Juvenile Court Power

Perhaps the greatest problem with the functioning of the juvenile court was the failed hope that it would serve as a central clearinghouse for dependent children. Through the Juvenile Court Act, the court became responsible for dependent and neglected children, but the extent of the court's power was limited. For one thing, children had to be brought to the attention of the court, either by their parents, the police, or "interested citizens." Thus associations like the Juvenile Protective Association and the Humane Society did investigative work to try to uncover children trapped in abusive or neglectful situations. Children could, moreover, be placed in private child care agencies without going through the court and being made wards. In addition, there were jurisdictional problems regarding industrial schools, especially in Cook County, where most of these institutions were located. The industrial school acts, which predated the Juvenile Court Act by a generation, had granted the schools "the exclusive custody, care, and guardianship" of children committed to them. The Juvenile Court Act was established with the expressed understanding that it was to supersede no existing law. Thus, there was a question of guardianship over minors committed from the court to industrial schools. The Juvenile Court Act asserted the court's guardianship and required routine reports on the child's situation if the court requested them. Furthermore, the act required the court to be informed and consulted in any major decision about a child's placement. But many industrial schools resisted the court's assertion of guardianship, maintaining that the earlier law gave them that right and with it the decision-making power in matters of the child's welfare. The court, according to one observer in 1922, often hesitated "to press a claim against the opposition of an important and influential institution." Yet without such pressure, the court's continuing protection for children was essentially nullified. The industrial schools' resistance meant that the juvenile court could not effectively enforce its continuing oversight of all the children who came before it as petitioners. Thus, the centralizing function that the court's founders had envisioned was severely curtailed. At times, the court found even its initial protective function thwarted, since some industrial schools were known to return children almost immediately to parental homes that the court had declared unfit.[18]

In Cook County, the problem was one of coordinating the many scattered efforts directed at dependent and neglected children by a wide variety of institutions and organizations, many with a strong religious or ethnic bias and a powerful predilection for independent action. In the less populous areas of Illinois, where the county court assumed the responsibilities delineated in the Juvenile Court Act, the issue was exactly opposite to the problems of Cook County. In rural regions, the problem was not too many jealous agencies and institutions but rather too few resources of all kinds. Most child welfare responsibilities passed from the overseers of the poor to the county courts in the years after 1899, in particular to the probation department, which acted as the social work agency of the court. In Cook County, the probation staff was large, although generally overburdened and not always of the highest quality. The officers were appointed by the judge rather than being civil-service selected, raising the issue of patronage appointments.[19]

But in many of the rural counties, there were no probation officers at all, and the ones who were hired were often ill-trained. "The quality of probation personnel is almost entirely dependent upon the interest and vision of the county judge, and the willingness or ability of the county board to appropriate the necessary funds," noted a 1940 report on child dependency in Illinois.

> A number of judges and probation officers appeared to assume that they were not responsible for children declared dependent prior to their term of office. This is complicated by the fact that only slightly more than one-third of the counties have full time probation officers and that probation officers usually are so overburdened with current problems that they have no time to think about those which originated before they took office. For instance, in one county the outgoing probation officer destroyed all her records, and such a flow of problems had been brought to the attention of the new officer that she had never had an opportunity to look into the cases of children who were declared dependent before her time.[20]

The Development of a Public Child Welfare Department

Though reformers insisted that the juvenile court was critical in dealing with child neglect and dependency because of the legal ramifications of those issues, social policy analysts had been questioning the administrative capacities of the juvenile court since the 1920s, precisely because of the disorder that was so often evident in the court's practical dealings. In her report to the 1939 White House Children's Conference on "Government's Role in Child Welfare," University of Chicago social work professor Sophonisba Breckinridge argued the need for an administrative agency to work in tandem with the court. For one thing, though "reference was cheerfully made to the juvenile court," Breckinridge pointed out that in most areas of the country, there was no such thing. Instead, county courts with other functions occasionally directed their attention to children's problems. Compounding this lack of expertise was the reality of politics. In general, the judges "were highly political in attitude," and they appointed their probation officers "as an addition to their partisan political facilities." It was a conspicuous feature of the 1930s, Breckinridge declared, to recognize the need for effective administrative units, and she predicted that throughout the country in the coming years, policy makers would have to decide which child welfare responsibilities properly belonged to the juvenile court and which might be more efficiently executed by a state department of public welfare.[21]

By the 1930s, Illinois did have a rudimentary state child welfare agency, although it certainly lacked the power and influence that its proponents envisioned. The state agency had had its beginnings in 1905, not long after the establishment of the juvenile court, when it became clear that, in the typical fashion of Illinois social welfare legislation, the court had been mandated to perform a Herculean task without having been granted sufficient practical power or resources to accomplish the job successfully. Particularly when the administration of mothers' pensions became a court responsibility, the machinery was greatly taxed.

The Department of Visitation, which would become the Division of Child Welfare, began with a limited mission and an even more limited budget in 1905. The department's job was to visit children who had been placed in foster homes by the juvenile and county courts, the overseers of the poor, and the institutions that received money from the state. In addition, the agency was to inspect publicly funded institutions and grant certificates of inspection to those that met with approval. The creation of the department was an acknowledgement that, although the Juvenile Court Act permitted the court to name a group of citizens to inspect substitute care facilities for children, the various courts were not exercising that option on any sort of regular basis. A more consistent unit of inspection was necessary.

The Department of Visitation also reflected a chastened view on the part of those who favored foster home placement over institutionalization. Philanthropists no longer felt that this could be an unsupervised relationship without danger to the child. The breezy optimism of Charles Loring Brace's early placing out experiment had been tempered by experience. Brace, a romantic to the core, had seen institutions as almost invariably corrupting but had enormous faith in the essential kindness of the general populace. This goodness, coupled with a child's capacity to bring a pair of willing hands to a foster home, was a winning combination, according to his thinking. But not surprisingly, in a situation where the balance of power was all on the side of the adult, cases began to surface of children who were worked far too hard, often at the expense of their education, and were sometimes treated with outright cruelty. The Department of Visitation got its start, in fact, after a sensational case of foster care abuse was published in the newspapers.[22]

The Visitation of Children Act allowed for "visitors not to exceed four," but the legislators considerably mitigated the effect of their new law by appropriating only enough funds to pay for two visitors, one of whom had to be let go after the first year. The Illinois State Board of Public Charities urged adequate funding for the department, citing altruism as a rationale and—that classic argument of child welfare rhetoric—"the effect of such children upon the political and economic future of the State."

But the argument that an investment in good child protection would save the public money later on made little impact with the legislature. It was to be an enduring theme of the Department of Visitation to be overworked and underfunded. From the beginning, the visitors' case loads far exceeded their capacity. By 1908 there were approximately 4,747 placements to be reviewed, covering ninety-five counties. Despite the growing responsibilities of the department, the funds for the two visitors were cut; the department petitioned the legislature but received only a modest restoration of funding.[23]

The Department of Visitation was incorporated into the newly formed Department of Public Welfare in 1917, and those eager to develop a vigorous state administrative unit pushed to extend the responsibilities of the department, despite meager funding. In the same year the Juvenile Protective Association published a shocking exposé called "Baby Farms in Chicago," detailing the dreadful conditions—malnutrition, poor sanitation and physical and sexual abuse—to which children were subjected in many boarding situations. The newspapers took up the story, and public outcry about the mistreatment of children in such squalid surroundings resulted in a 1919 state law requiring the Department of Visitation to inspect and license boarding homes on an annual basis. The law specified that the children's physical and moral surroundings had to be acceptable, that the boarding place had to be safe, and that the care and discipline must be "as far as practicable equivalent to that given children of worthy parents in the average normal family."[24]

The Boarding Homes Law extended the supervisory powers of the Division of Visitation of Children. The Child Welfare Committee of 1920 recommended further expanding the department to a general division of child welfare, with the expressed view that the state and the institutions that it ran should not only supervise substitute care settings but should set the standards against which child welfare efforts in the state could be measured. The committee's recommendation to upgrade the Department of Visitation to a child welfare department was implemented; but the hope that had been articulated repeatedly since the nineteenth century—that the state would take the lead in assessing the needs of dependent children and determining the best methods of care—remained unfulfilled.[25]

Elizabeth Milchrist, an employee of the Child Welfare Division in the 1930s who chronicled its development, also believed in the state's responsibility to lead in child welfare efforts, urging innovative programs that would set the tone for private child welfare providers in Illinois. But in reality the state agency dealt largely with strictly administrative matters. According to Milchrist, the 64 percent budget cut in the Depression year 1933 was really a blessing in disguise, because it allowed the department to rid itself of a number of "very inadequate appointments" (her delicate phrase for patronage appointees) that had been made over the years.[26]

The Soldiers' Orphans' Home, condemned by the 1920 Children's Committee as a place of bleak sterility where the children "seem more like little scrubbing machines than human beings," remained the only public institution for dependent and neglected children in the state. For a time it had taken in dependent children regardless of parentage, but in the late 1920s the pressures of veterans' groups again closed the institution to all but soldiers' and sailors' children. The hope that this institution could act as a state orphanage, a clearinghouse through which all the state's dependent children could be placed in family homes, never became a reality. Inadequate funding and staff shortages meant that the child welfare department could not even fulfill its mandate to monitor the care of children, let alone to offer actual care to most of them. Milchrist noted the frustrations of the workers across the years in being asked to do so much more than they could conceivably achieve, given the staff size and funding that was allocated. But, she added (in true bureaucratic spirit, and giving a portent of things to come) at such times the department usually managed at least to devise and send out a form by which to gather information.[27]

The federal government gave support to the concept of public child welfare programs with Title IV-B of the Social Security Act of 1935. Title IV-B was intended to address the desperate lack of adequate child welfare provisions in rural regions. It provided funds for the establishment of county child welfare units and the training of personnel, to be instituted at the request of the judge and county board. In Illinois, five units were established to serve eight counties in the late 1930s. There were some county funds supplied, but the federal government paid a significant portion of the funding, with the double goal of improving children's care and providing a demonstration of how much an administrative unit could accomplish in regions so desperately short of services.[28]

In addition to positive action from the federal government, those committed to strong state efforts in behalf of dependent children continued their work into the 1940s. In 1940, John Kahlert of the Child Welfare Division made the first attempt at a comprehensive description of dependent children in the state. Kahlert found in his review that poor communication still plagued the system twenty years after a child welfare division had been established. He noted that although child care agencies had been obliged to report to the Child Welfare Division on the children under their care since the Child Welfare Act of 1933 had made it mandatory, the agencies' records were often incomplete. Furthermore, the county courts were still relatively autonomous and uncommunicative about the children under their wardship, a critical gap, since in downstate areas the courts took care of the bulk of the child welfare cases. Kahlert, whose task was clearly fraught with frustrations, was obliged again and again to acknowledge a lack of information because recordkeeping in general was at such a primitive level in many agencies and courts. And poor recordkeeping at the very least raised questions about the consistency and continuity of care.[29]

A 1943 Child Welfare Commission, appointed by the legislature to do yet another assessment of the state's child welfare functions, repeated Kahlert's concerns in unequivocal language. The report noted first that its funding from the legislature was so meager that only one part time staff member could be hired to take on the staggering task of assessment. This overworked investigator found no written record of the child welfare functions of the state, nor any bureaucrat with a comprehensive view of "how the taxpayer's money is spent for the benefit of its children." The report described a "bewildering maze" of agencies, many overlapping, while at the same time, there were whole groups of children who were not served at all. Further, "the very act of placing a child under the care of one agency far too frequently automatically deprives him of the services of other agencies." The commission could find no central authority to protect children from such exclusion or to enforce cooperation among the various agencies, whose rivalries "at times thunder so loud that the cries of the children are not heard."[30]

The recommendation to organize and consolidate could hardly be called a new notion, the report noted. Both the 1920 and the 1931 child welfare committees, as well as several other studies, had urged unification and organization of state functions to prevent waste, inefficiency and total failure to provide services to many children. The studies had been careful, and the counsel astute, but their recommendations were not implemented. And in the years since those earlier reports had been issued, the need for organization had increased phenomenally. In the time between the two world wars, state and federal monies had increased from approximately 15 million for the years 1917–19 to 230 million for 1944–45, an increase of nearly 1,500 percent. Yet the scope of these efforts had not even been cataloged, let alone organized, until 1943 when the commission began its work.[31]

Given the level of inertia in a state renowned for appointing superb committees and then ignoring their advice, it is not surprising that the recommendations of the 1940s Child Welfare Commission made little impact on the organization of state services. The commission did continue its investigations through the 1940s, looking especially at the failure of probation services to serve both dependent and delinquent children and urging in its 1949 summary that the 100 million dollar surplus that had built up when war time shortages had prevented expenditures of all kinds "be not diverted but that an adequate portion of it be carefully preserved for the crying needs of Illinois' children." The commission pointed out that the many stresses of the war years—absent fathers and working mothers, for example—had greatly taxed children's psychological resources and had created new needs that would be best addressed through careful coordination and planning of state efforts and attention to children as individuals, rather than warehousing them in large, impersonal institutions where their particular needs were overlooked.[32]

The summary called above all for a single statewide agency that could plan, supervise, and place the needs of children above bureaucratic issues. But, though the commitment to centralization was strong in the 1940s (the state consolidated its many school districts in this decade, for example), it was not strong enough to overcome the chaos and rampant individualism of the state's child welfare system. Despite half a century of effort, child welfare in Illinois was almost as random an endeavor in 1949 as it had been before the founding of the juvenile court fifty years earlier.

Mothers' Pensions

The third major intervention of the Progressive Era in behalf of dependent children was the creation of mothers' pensions, grants given to prevent the breakup of poor families. In his opening address to the First White House Conference on Children in 1909, Theodore Roosevelt gave presidential approval to the notion that the preservation of families should be a main objective of social policy, and other speakers expressed concern both about children institutionalized because of poverty and about the children of working mothers.[33]

Studies of working mothers indicated that the health, education and morals of their children suffered from a lack of attention. The White House Conference advocated an income maintenance program so that mothers could stay at home and keep their children with them, and in 1911, Illinois became the first state to adopt this program on a statewide basis. (Kansas City, Missouri, had inaugurated the first mothers' pension program in 1911, but it was limited to Jackson County only.) The legislation was passed as an amendment to the Juvenile Court Act, and until the late 1920s the administration of the program was the sole responsibility of the juvenile court. The original legislation (which, according to its critics was hastily conceived) was quite liberal in its conception. In cases in which a child was deemed dependent or neglected but "it is for the welfare of such child to remain at home," the law offered funds to either or both parents rather than restricting help to the mother, and it put no limitations on the home situation beyond requiring that the parents be "proper guardians."[34]

A 1913 revision of the amendment proved to be much more restrictive. The revision specifically limited the pension to mothers whose husbands were dead or "permanently incapacitated because of a physical or mental infirmity" and who were citizens of the United States and three year residents of the county in which they had applied. This rewriting not only barred fathers from participation; it also excluded some of the neediest mothers of the state: women whose husbands had deserted them (a common hazard especially among the urban poor); women who were aliens; whose husbands were in prison; who had illegitimate children. The amendment also excluded women who owned any real property, which meant that in order to qualify for help, a family would have to sell their home. Critics of the first legislation argued that its liberal provisions encouraged desertion, and there was the usual concern in refining the legislation that it hit a balance between helping those who were both worthy and needy, without in any way subsidizing the lazy or immoral. There was a strong provincial and moral note in the revised legislation that in fact ended by being punitive in tone. The advocates of mothers' pensions wanted them to go to the worthy poor, and they were concerned to distinguish the grants from ordinary "outdoor relief," although the money was not in fact a "pension" at all but was in reality a form of relief, as critics were quick to point out.[35]

Many private philanthropists were suspicious of mothers' pensions because they feared that traditional supports—relatives, family, churches, and the like—would abandon their responsibilities now that the state (or more properly, the county) was taking the responsibility for support. They criticized the early efforts in Illinois and elsewhere as erratic and disorganized, citing arbitrary decisions about the level of payments being made by untrained probation officers of the juvenile court.[36]

Those who supported mothers' pensions had criticisms, too. The program followed the old poor law tradition of county administration, and many counties, they charged, virtually ignored the program or did the absolute minimum, paying grants far below the maximum payment level to a handful of needy families. The notion of mothers' pensions was that families were not merely to be given money but were to receive assistance in the form of counseling and instruction, as well—instruction in such things as child care and homemaking. One criticism of the program was that probation officers were inadequately trained for such work. In Cook County there was a long list of families waiting for aid, and the administration of the juvenile court bogged down badly because of the mothers' pension program. Private organizations like United Charities were still responsible for funding a great many needy families who were ineligible or who were waiting to be interviewed and approved by the overworked probation officers. And relatives and private philanthropists complained that when they tried to help a family to a few of life's comforts with an extra $20.00 or so, a zealous bureaucrat would subtract the gift from the grant, thereby defeating the purpose of their generosity. The issue became more acute during the First World War when inflation soared and the pensions, always very modest, became totally inadequate for a family's living expenses.[37]

Still, despite the many problems, the notion of mothers' pensions took firm root in Illinois and spread through the nation (a "wildfire spread" according to *Everybody's Magazine* in a 1915 article). The point was, as those who pressed for liberalization of mothers' pensions insisted, they were not intended as a reward for mothers but as an assistance to children. Children did best in their own homes, it was generally accepted, and mothers' pensions were cheaper than putting children in institutions; these two facts, proponents of mothers' pensions kept constantly before the public. Gradually revisions in legislation in Illinois restored assistance to various groups who had been excluded in the 1913 versions of the amendment. Mothers who were not United States citizens were included in 1915; a 1917 revision allowed mothers to own property up to a thousand dollars without being ineligible for help; in 1923 women deserted by their husbands were once more included in the list of eligible receivers.[38]

Twenty years after the first mothers' pension law was passed, the system was firmly entrenched in a majority of states, although administration of the program and the amount of grants varied

Figure 1. Sample Pension

C family: Estimated budget and income

The C family was granted a pension in December, 1916. This family included the mother, aged 31 years, three children, aged 8, 10, and 11 years, and the father, 32 years old, who was in the third stage of tuberculosis, incapacitated for work and living in a sanitarium. The father and the mother were both born in Poland but had been in this country 29 years. The father had been a finisher and had earned $15 a week when he was able to work. The budget for this family included extra diet, for the mother was found to have tuberculosis in the second stage, and the two younger children had had tuberculosis, although it was quiescent at the time the pension was granted. The budget estimates which follow are the original budget and a later budget prepared on the basis of the increased cost of living.

Estimated monthly budget: C family

	Estimated budget on which pension was granted	New estimate
Rent	$11.00	$11.00
Food (extra diet)	22.00	26.00
Fuel and light	4.00	4.75
Household supplies and furnishings	1.75	2.50
Clothing (family)	5.75	6.25
Care of health	1.00	1.00
Total	45.50	51.50

The conference committee recommended a pension of $35 a month, the maximum pension allowed by law for a family with three children, and the committee also recommended that the family be granted "county supplies" (the rations given by the outdoor relief department). The pension grant of $35 was allowed by the court, but the county agent refused the request for county supplies on the grounds that it is against the rules of the county agent's office to supplement pensions when the family is receiving the maximum pension allowed by law. The mother at the time of application for the pension was working in a phonograph office, earning $6 a week, but she is not able to work now. The present situation of this family is as follows:

Income: Pension grant	$35.00
First estimated budget	45.50
Later estimated budget	51.50
Income deficit	10.50 or 16.50

Source: Edith Abbott and Sophonisba Breckinridge, *The Administration of the Aid to Mothers' Law in Illinois* (Children's Bureau Publication #28: Washington, D.C., 1921), pp. 28-29.

widely. Illinois, the first state to institute the program, was the last to provide for state supervision. It was not until 1931, when the state began to contribute funds to the mothers' pension program, that counties were required to report to the Child Welfare Division of the Department of Public Welfare. Even after this administrative change, juvenile court and county judges continued to be involved in the practical aspects of the program in most counties as long as it continued. The uneven quality of county administration and the fact that in many places the most needy families were virtually ignored led proponents of mothers' pensions to advocate more state control rather than relying on the old poor law notion of county responsibility. And the economic crisis of the 1930s further underscored the need for a more central authority as a funding source. The discussion of mothers' aid in the 1930 White House Conference noted specifically that the poor mining counties in Illinois could not afford to fund mothers' pensions and needed assistance from wealthier areas of the state. "The state," insisted the analysts, "has an equal stake in the home life of all its communities and is concerned with securing equal opportunity for all of its children."[39]

But the state's interest in equalizing the distribution of mothers' pensions became more difficult to argue as the Depression wore on and all units of state government faced a desperate financial situation. Instead, those concerned about children in poverty turned to the federal government to save the mothers' pension programs that by 1935 existed in forty-five of the forty-eight states.

The Aid to Dependent Children program, Title IV of the Social Security Act of 1935, was the federal version of mothers' pensions. It was included in the Social Security Act at the insistence of child welfare activists who saw the mothers' pension programs in the various states collapsing in the economic shambles wrought by the Depression. Of all the programs included in Social Security legislation—old-age pensions, unemployment insurance, disability pensions—aid for dependent children roused the least support, according to one political observer of the time. While the federal government subsidized half the amount of old age and disability pensions, ADC originally got only one third of its funding from the federal government. In 1940, the ADC federal matching funds increased to one half, but the grant limit remained at its low 1935 limit ($18.00 for the first child and $12.00 for each additional child). Those advocating the program, notably the Children's Bureau staff, the bureau's former director Grace Abbott, and Frances Perkins, the Secretary of Labor, felt that to push for further financial support would jeopardize the inclusion of the program in the bill altogether.[40]

Thus ADC, which was to become one of the largest federal programs affecting American children, began its checkered career. It always had something of an "also-ran" quality about it, sandwiched as it was between more popular social insurance items in the Social Security Act. Nevertheless, those who pushed for federal support felt that it would keep the grants program from collapsing altogether; they also felt it would encourage more even distribution of funds throughout the various areas of each state.

Ironically Illinois, the first state to provide a mothers' pension program, was one of the last to inaugurate ADC. Arthur Miles, a scholar who assessed public relief in Illinois in 1940, attributed Illinois' failure to pass a state law actuating the ADC portion of the Social Security Act to "downstate" conservatism and political wrangling within the Democratic party, which made their strategies vulnerable and ultimately ineffective. But he gave an analysis beyond the strictly political for the repeated failure of ADC, an analysis that would sound no less convincing fifty years later: "In Illinois, as in many other states, the aged have demanded, and received, preferential treatment from the legislature. Comprising almost 5 percent of the total population and more than 10 percent of the active electorate, the aged have become an effective 'pressure group.' The dependent children, unfortunately, cannot vote."[41]

Washington Post writer Ernest K. Lindley made a similar observation that same year, noting that of the 35 million children under fifteen in the United States, 13 million lived in families earning $800.00 or less. Such children were "a menace to the future of the nation," Lindley argued. They had been shortchanged in the 1935 Social Security Law and would be further sacrificed in 1940 revisions "if the old age vote-chasers have their way. One thing this country needs is more Senators and Congressmen who will give the oncoming generation more than a pat on the head."[42]

Shortly after Miles's study, the Illinois legislature passed the enabling act, and in 1942, ADC began to operate in Illinois. Under ADC the number of children receiving aid more than tripled, according to a 1943 pamphlet assessing the program. In Cook County, six times as many children benefited from ADC as had benefited in September 1941, under the state mothers' pension law. Part of the increase came from the addition of mothers with one child and mothers whose husbands had deserted, two groups frequently cut off aid with the cutbacks of the Depression years. In addition, the goal of achieving more equitable benefits throughout the state appeared to be accomplished as well; the appraisal noted that in some areas of the state, grants had increased two to three times over the old mothers' pensions. (In Cook County, however, grants were slightly lower than before.) The optimistic Public Aid Department appraisal of the ADC program ended with some comments from recipients of the program that illustrated its superiority over the earlier state program:

> I thought I couldn't keep my stepchildren after their father died, for I wasn't earning enough to feed us all. I love them as if they were my own and I don't believe in separating children. We had some relief but no Mothers' Pension because I'm only a stepmother. ADC is keeping us together and the little ones didn't have to be scattered around among relatives who didn't want them.

> I am an old maid aunt trying to rear four orphaned nieces and nephews with no one to help me. I worked at night in a restaurant to get the money to feed us. ADC came to us when I didn't know how I could go on. Whoever invented ADC must have known that an aunt may be just as anxious to rear little children in a home and keep them together as even a mother is. No more night work for me. Time to rest and keep fit for the job of being the aunt-mother.

> One of my babies died because she was not strong enough to live the way we had to after my husband died. ADC and the County Visitor helped me and my four children to move out of our shack by the river where we had chills and malaria all summer and coughs and colds all winter. You have no idea how the move has improved the health of all of us.

> Since we have ADC, life is very different for me and my four little brothers and sisters that I have been trying to take care of since our parents died. The two older ones and I earn a little money each

week. We want to help ourselves all we can. Now we have enough to eat and wear, and time and health and heart to laugh together. I do thank the State for knowing that a sister needs help when she has little brothers and sisters to raise.[43]

In 1940, as Europe went to war and Americans anxiously reflected on the meaning and strength of their form of government, Sophonisba Breckinridge declared that one of the tests of democracy was "a truly integrated national service providing a truly national minimum of well-being below which no one anywhere will be allowed to remain." Breckinridge and her colleagues were well aware that the Social Security Act did not come close to achieving that high principle. It was a beginning, and a limited one at that, as were most of the New Deal social programs. Too many people were left out, the reformers believed, and there was too much emphasis on proof of poverty (or means testing) in assistance programs like ADC. Edith Abbott later declared her support for a general children's allowance, like those in England and Canada, that gave grants to children of all income levels. Furthermore, the goal of a "truly integrated national service" was a long way off, as Illinois' fragmented social services made clear.[44]

Still, the mere fact of federal involvement in social issues was encouraging, and the new programs for children, though limited, could be broadened with determination. It did not seem too much to hope as the country neared mid-century that with federal assistance even child welfare services as chaotic as Illinois' might soon be able to guarantee an adequate level of care to all the needy children of the state.

3

Coherence and Crisis, 1950–90

Though the first half of the twentieth century was a far cry from "The Century of the Child" often predicted by Progressive reformers, the augers for dependent children were good in post–World War II America. The country had survived depression and war and was beginning to enjoy an extraordinary prosperity and growth that would last for fully two decades. Along with the economic boom came the baby boom. From 1940 to 1957, the fertility rate rose an astonishing 50 percent, focusing America's attention on children in a way that would have been unimaginable in the heart of the Depression. In 1964, when Illinois finally established a separate Department of Children and Family Services, it seemed that the Progressive commitment to state intervention and centralization had become a reality.

But the Department of Children and Family Services was born into far more troubled times than was first apparent. By the early 1970s, the country was experiencing a sharp curtailment of economic wellbeing brought on initially by the rising cost of oil and followed by such a spate of shortages that *Newsweek* featured an empty cornucopia on its cover with the apocalyptic headline "Running out of Everything." Increasing economic troubles inevitably meant an austerity in government that policy makers of the 1960s had come to regard as obsolete.[1]

Coupled with fiscal limits on intervention, critics of the Progressive consensus in social policy began to argue that government's capacity to harm children far exceeded its capacity to help them and urged definite limits on state action. Both the revised Juvenile Court Act of 1965 and the Adoption Assistance Act of 1980, the most far reaching piece of child welfare legislation in the era, expressed a wariness of state action and a decided pessimism about the efficacy of the state's dealings with dependent children. That this view was able to achieve no overwhelming consensus of its own was illustrated by the increasingly broad child abuse and neglect laws passed by the state legislature in direct contradiction to the prevailing social theory that government intervention was usually disastrous.

Development of a State Department of Child Welfare

In 1964, child welfare was not the political hot potato it would become in later years. It was primarily the province of professional social workers whose task had changed considerably since the hard times of the 1930s. As Aid to Dependent Children and improved public health reduced the number of children institutionalized because of poverty and orphanage, private agencies looked for new uses for their institutions, concentrating their efforts on such specialties as emotionally disturbed children and adoption. Social work as a profession turned its attention toward the middle class in the conservative 1950s, eschewing the rhetoric and concerns of social reform for an interest in the psychological and therapeutic. And the shift in emphasis on the part of many ethnic and sectarian agencies signaled the reality that their particular clientele was prospering as never before in the postwar years.[2]

As private child welfare agencies became increasingly specialized, the problem of the "left out child" became increasingly more acute. It had always been the bizarre nature of child welfare to be "the craziest patchwork quilt of all services in Illinois," in the unequivocal assessment of one committee studying the problem. Instead of institutions responding to the needs of the child, the child welfare worker had to "shop around, offering the child first to one [agency] and then to another, hoping that the child's particular condition of needs and characteristics enables him to qualify for a particular service." Increasing specialization made this situation worse.[3]

Further straining the existing structure was the shifting demography; the impact of the baby boom taxed all services for children. Another demographic change was the dramatic growth in the black population, particularly in Chicago, as the up-migration from the South, begun in the 1940s, increased in magnitude in the next two decades. Even when they were the state's least populous minority group in the 1920s and 1930s, the neglect of needy black children had been painfully clear to those who cared to see it. By the 1950s, the gap in services to this ever-growing population was impossible to ignore. One observer of the period put the matter succinctly when she declared that the influential head of Catholic Charities began supporting a state child welfare agency "when the problem became too big and too black."[4]

Private agencies concentrating on more specialized tasks viewed themselves as the pacesetters in child welfare, those "in the forefront in the development of helpful treatment processes," as the Illinois Committee for the 1960 White House Conference put it. Thus, in a sense, private child care groups had stepped into the role originally intended to be the special province of the state. When the Department of Children and Family Services was finally created in 1963, it was clear from the definition of its responsibilities that the child welfare turf had been carefully divided. One duty of the new department was expansion of the state's older licensing function; it was to be in charge of licensing and overseeing private agencies. The Department of Children and Family Services would provide direct service as well, emphasizing services that private agencies did not offer. Private agencies specialized in child placement and in running institutions for children. DCFS was to emphasize preventive services: homemaking, day care, and family counseling that could help to maintain families. In addition, the department took charge of protective services, particularly after the passage of the Child Abuse Reporting Act of 1965. And, because so few private agencies would work with minority children, DCFS was to be involved in direct child placement work with minority children.[5]

The new Department of Children and Family Services could hardly have been said to have a clear field in the child welfare arena, balanced precariously as it was between private agencies on the one hand and the juvenile court (still very much involved in child welfare issues) on the other. Nevertheless, there was great hope for this new agency, the product of half a century of recommendations and agitation come to fruition at last. The climate of the 1960s was friendly to the notion of centralization and bureaucratic expansion, and the agency stressed "extending the programs of the department to every part of the state with the greatest efficiency." The early years were a time of growth and energy, what a former director of the agency was to call its "golden age."[6]

Aid to Families with Dependent Children

ADC, poor stepchild of the Social Security System, never experienced a golden age. The ADC program in Illinois and across the country failed to achieve the respectable status of unemployment compensation and especially old-age pensions, which came to be synonymous with the term "Social Security." As time went on, ADC drew increasing criticism, even as it grew in scope and served an ever-increasing population of children. "In the case of most Social Security programs achievement of broader coverage and improved benefits is the cause for national self-congratulation," commented an author in assessing the AFDC program of the 1960s.

> Mounting case loads and costs of AFDC produced only consternation and recrimination. It should be possible to find something good to say about a program which was the only or the principal support of millions of poor people, most of them children, and which allowed dependent children to remain in their own homes instead of being placed in foster care. Testimony, however, was universally adverse: AFDC encouraged fathers to desert and discouraged or precluded marriage of beneficiaries; recipients were exposed to bureaucratic tyranny and humiliating invasions of privacy; benefit payments varied from state to state and section to section to a greater extent than could be justified by differences in the cost of living; and the levels of benefits was so low as to perpetuate rather than alleviate poverty.[7]

The original notion of mothers' pension programs had been to provide an income adequate for a family, but the actual administration of mothers' aid often fell short of that goal, leaving families scrambling to exist just short of destitution. ADC, also meant to provide a decent living for families, failed to keep pace with the cost of living, unlike the old-age provisions of Social Security that were indexed to inflation in 1973. One of the most frequently voiced criticisms about ADC was that the program gave its recipients no incentive to "get ahead," since any money earned by the recipient was subtracted from the base grant. Further, since poor families where the father was unemployed did not qualify for assistance, the program encouraged real or feigned desertion, thus ironically encouraging family breakups when its original goal had been precisely the opposite.[8]

In the 1960s, when the issue of poverty once more began to receive sympathetic attention after the complacent affluence of the 1950s, there were revisions in ADC that sought to make it a more humane and responsive system. There was a program instituted to serve families with unemployed fathers, and work incentives and work training programs were added. The name was changed to Aid to Families with Dependent Children, to emphasize once more the notion that children do better when the whole family prospers and is kept intact.[9]

The 1960s also saw a United States Supreme Court decision (King v. Smith, 1968) that effectively forbade states to refuse AFDC to children because their mothers had male visitors. The Supreme Court, outlawing an Alabama "substitute father" regulation commented that "federal welfare policy now rests on a basis considerably more sophisticated and enlightened than the 'worthy person' concept of earlier times."[10]

The attempts at improvements made in AFDC during the 1960s by no means resolved the difficulties pervasive in the system. The Supreme Court might contend that distinctions between the worthy and the unworthy poor were outmoded, but that distinction was woven tightly into the fabric of American attitudes about social welfare, and both policy decisions and public reaction to public aid continued to support an insistence on "worthiness." Popular opinion grew increasingly hostile to the concept of "welfare," a hostility aggravated by the change in the recipient population, as the mechanization of cotton farming displaced large numbers of southern blacks who migrated North in the 1950s and 1960s. (A 1960 study of ADC in Cook County illustrated the phenomenon of the migration; the table depicting "mother's birthplace" indicated that only 22 percent of the nonwhite mothers had been born in Illinois.) The original ADC legislation was essentially slipped past the public, hidden among other, more palatable programs. This furtiveness was necessary even when the early perception was that the program primarily aided widows and orphans. By the late 1950s, an ADC caseload was more likely to contain children from single parent families because of divorce or illegitimacy than because of a father's death. Dramatically improved life expectancy, resulting from public health measures and the development of antibiotics in the 1940s, meant that nationwide, orphanage as a cause of need for ADC dropped from about 50 percent in 1937 to 11 percent in 1958. In the same year that orphanage accounted for 11 percent, about 19 percent of cases were opened because of a father's physical or mental disability; another 20 percent of cases included illegitimate children. So great was the concern about the rising incidence of illegitimacy that, according to a 1959 Department of Health, Education and Welfare pamphlet, one state (unnamed) proposed psychiatric treatment for a mother with one illegitimate child and sterilization if she had another.[11]

Mothers' aid and ADC had always been aimed at the poor, but

the psychological distance between the middle class and the poor had grown dramatically since the 1930s, both because of racial distinctions and because of the general affluence of the populace. The brief reforming convulsion of the 1960s and early 1970s directed attention and sympathy to the poor. During those years there developed a counterweight to public criticism, a militance on the part of those receiving aid and some of the public officials assisting them reflected in the formation of welfare rights organizations.

The belief—the same belief that reformers like the Abbotts and Sophonisha Breckinridge had voiced a generation earlier—in a family's right to a basic minimum income resulted in a plan proposed in Richard Nixon's administration. The plan guaranteed all families a basic level of income and in addition was constructed to provide incentives to work. This proposal passed the House of Representatives twice but failed in the Senate. In granting an outright income, the bill failed to make distinctions between the worthy and the unworthy poor, the helpless and the able-bodied, thus proving too radical a departure for legislators and their constituents. A similar proposal by President Carter that would have guaranteed a base level income to all families regardless of circumstances went down to defeat a few years later, and by the late 1970s American sympathy for the poor, always a frail entity, had been exhausted. Families on AFDC had to make do with less and less real money; as inflation soared, their monthly allotments increased only slightly, while their real buying power was significantly reduced.[12]

Illinois reflected the national trend toward retrenchment, while remaining significantly less generous to its needy citizens than most northern states. In 1975, the average Illinois AFDC grant was $317.00. By 1980, the grant had increased to $350.00, but adjusted for inflation, the grant would only be worth $227.66 of the 1975 grant. In 1990, The Center for Budget and Policy Priorities issued a dismal assessment of AFDC in Illinois. The study found that benefits had declined to 48 percent of the 1970 level. At the end of the 1980s, an AFDC grant for an Illinois family of three was only $367.00 a month, which—according to the state's own estimate—was only 47 percent of what a family needed to cover its minimum needs. With grants so low, as much as 79 percent of the stipend had to go for rent alone. Though the whole upper Midwest had suffered economic reversals during the 1980s, Illinois' AFDC grants fell well below those of its neighbors. Comparable Michigan benefits were $516.00; Wisconsin, $517.00; and Minnesota, $532.00. "Such findings might be understandable if Illinois were a poor Southern state, with only meager resources to help its low income residents," declared the budget center's director. "However, the opposite is true. Illinois ranks 11th in per capita income, making it better able to afford adequate benefits than most other states. And yet Illinois' maximum AFDC benefit for a family of three is $60 per month below the average for all states and $130 below the average for nonsouthern states."[13]

Though Illinois' comparative ranking on AFDC was abysmal, the AFDC crisis was not only a state problem. As the federal government cut back on nutritional, medical and housing supports in the budget slashing 1980s, benefits shrank nationwide. The conventional wisdom of earlier times, that it was in the common interest of society for mothers to stay home and care for their children, was a much less compelling argument in the 1970s and 1980s when large numbers of women with small children were joining the work force. Thus a 1988 federal law, "The Family Support Act of 1988" sought to address some of the flaws of the welfare system that seemed to perpetuate dependence. As the system was set up, a mother on AFDC who took a job risked losing all benefits, including critical medical benefits, besides incurring major new expenses in child care—often for a job that was barely above minimum wage. Such a situation guaranteed that families would be poorer with a working parent than they had been when living on AFDC. Clearly there was very little incentive for parents to look for work under such conditions.

The 1988 law mandated the states to provide job training programs. These programs, to be phased in over a period of years, would be required of most recipients, with the exception of parents with very young children. There were educational requirements for those under age twenty, and a provision allowing states to require minor parents to live at home or under adult guardianship. There was also a provision to collect child support from delinquent parents of children on AFDC.[14]

The legislation was decidedly aimed at moving people off the welfare rolls and into jobs, and there was a definite element of coercion included in the requirements. But there were some protections in the law, like carefully delineated client rights to information and procedure, as well as exceptions to required job training participation for those who were clearly incapacitated through temporary illness or home responsibilities. In addition, the law provided for a small tax credit for those who got jobs, a year of transitional medical insurance, and transitional child care funding to keep those families who moved into the work force from being overwhelmed by expenses before they could establish themselves.[15]

Significantly, the law provided no funds for increased AFDC benefits. Few could fault the proposed effort to train people so that they might move from the indignity of the welfare rolls to the autonomy of a regular paycheck. But critics worried that implementation of the law, if mishandled, could be punitive and inept, a mere dumping of needy people from the program. One veteran Illinois child advocate neatly summarized the skeptics' anxieties and suspicions when he remarked that he had no doubt that the new law would get people off welfare. What he questioned was whether it would get them out of poverty.[16]

The Issue of Child Abuse and Neglect

Supporters and critics alike feared that AFDC merely perpetuated poverty. Equally discouraging was the program's failure to fulfill its other historic aim, that of keeping children out of substitute care. In fact, by the late 1960s, AFDC benefits for children in foster care were actually higher than for children in their own homes, raising the concern that there might be a bureaucratic incentive to remove children from their homes and keep them out.[17]

Even without such an incentive, the reality was that the children in placement were overwhelmingly the children of the poor, not only in instances of parental incapacity such as illness but also in cases opened under the rubric of protective services.[18]

This was especially true once the terms neglect and abuse began to fuse, losing their distinct meanings in legal and protective services practice. Neglected and abused children had always been included in the child welfare system, and for a time in the late nineteenth and early twentieth centuries, they had received considerable attention from organizations like The Humane Society and The Juvenile Protective Association. In the 1920s, however, and especially in the Depression and war years, official reports on child welfare were much more likely to emphasize dependency in children—the need for care because of poverty, orphanage, or family disintegration due to illness or desertion. Though acknowledged as causes of child dependency, neglect and abuse were not major policy issues at this time. Not surprisingly, in an age when the economic issue overshadowed every other problem of society, dependency—dependency because of poverty—was the chief concern.[19]

Then in the early 1960s, professionals and the public at large experienced a new awareness of the issue of child abuse, originating in the development of pediatric radiology, which allowed physicians to observe abnormalities—subdural hematomas and abnormal x-ray changes in the long bones—that indicated a history of repeated injuries. Abusive parents typically changed doctors frequently, obscuring the recurring "accidents" that should have alerted the physician to the possibility of abuse. Now the technological advances in radiology gave the medical profession hard evidence that considerably more abuse was taking place than physicians had cared to recognize. In 1961, the American Academy of Pediatrics conducted a symposium on child abuse at which the term "battered child syndrome" was introduced. An article on the subject in the *Journal of the American Medical Association* followed in 1962, and the press enthusiastically took up the issue. One major result of heightened public awareness was that most states passed new and more stringent laws regarding abuse.[20]

Illinois passed such a law in 1965, directed particularly at cases of medically confirmed abuse, and mandating designated professionals to report suspected cases. One of the difficulties in dealing with child abuse according to the experts was to get professionals first to recognize consciously what they often did not want to acknowledge and second, to get them to report it to officials. Professionals were reluctant to challenge the privacy of the family, fearing especially the possibility of retaliatory law suits aimed against them. Responding to this concern, the new law specifically granted them legal immunity when reporting suspected cases of abuse.[21]

The frustration with child abuse cases lay in the fact that the abuse was usually a secret act, generally without witnesses; and children, whose credibility as witnesses was easily impugned, were often of limited use in court. The 1965 reporting law reflected a heightened consciousness of the problem, but the operation of the law did not result in a dramatic reduction of child abuse; quite the contrary. The law was not geared to prevention but to prosecution; if anything, the public became more conscious of the issue as time went on and more cases came to light. Violence against children was an act that no one could countenance, and the gruesome details of bad treatment incensed the reading public. In summer and fall of 1972, a sensational case came to light in Chicago in which a child sent back to his biological family from a foster home was killed by his parents. The public was baffled by the series of bureaucratic decisions that had such a fatal outcome. Although social workers argued the importance and possibility of rehabilitating families, even abusing ones, the thrust of public thinking was to concentrate on the first stage, that of removing children from harmful situations.[22]

A 1975 rewriting of the child abuse law reflected the stress on initial action. The law, called the Abused and Neglected Child Reporting Act, made a critical change in the law: it included not only physical abuse cases but also neglect (a much more nebulous category) into the realm of mandatory reporting. It also strengthened the Department of Children and Family Services' role in interceding, changing the language of the law from the instruction to "safeguard [the child's] welfare" to the injunction to "protect the best interests of the child," a term considerably more open to individual discretion and interpretation. The new law specifically included sexual abuse and mental injury as categories of abuse, and it allowed concerned observers who were not professionals to report suspected abuse or neglect with statutory immunity.[23]

A 1980 revision of the Abused and Neglected Child Reporting Act went still further to encourage both reporting and immediate action on such reports. This law mandated the Child Protective Service Unit in the Department of Children and Family Services to begin all investigations of alleged neglect or abuse within twenty-four hours of reporting, unless the matter was of particular urgency, such as the safety of the child or the possibility of the family's disappearance. In an emergency, the investigation was to begin immediately "regardless of the time of day or night." The law allowed a Child Protective Services worker to assume temporary protective custody of a child judged to be in jeopardy. In addition, the law established a twenty-four hour toll-free statewide hot line that any citizen might use to report suspected child abuse or neglect. The law also expanded the definition of child abusers beyond the parents and immediate family members to other people responsible for child care—foster parents, babysitters, day care workers, and so on.[24]

The increasing scope of the law reflected an ever-growing alarm about the issue of child abuse and a general belief on the part of legislators and their constituents that little was being done to protect children against an epidemic of parental violence. The new law, in stressing action and broad discretion on the part of Child Protective Services workers, sought to address situations engraved on the public consciousness where children left in their homes because of legal or bureaucratic complications were subsequently injured or killed.

But by the mid-1980s critics were raising serious objections to child abuse laws like the 1980 Illinois law. One set of critics argued that child abuse provided a convenient bandwagon for politicians of all persuasions, a cause that allowed them to look humanitarian while avoiding the far more pervasive problems that children faced—poverty, poor education, bad economic prospects for the future. Another group of critics expressed more specific concerns about the laws themselves, arguing that increased protection for abused and neglected children, in the words of Douglas J. Besharov, first director of the National Center on Child Abuse and Neglect, "has been purchased at the price of enormous governmental intervention into private family matters." Besharov's concern focused on two groups. On the one hand, he warned that including "neglect" into the reporting laws on an equal basis with physical abuse so broadened the definition of child abuse that large numbers of families were "unnecessarily—and often harmfully—processed through the system."[25]

This was bad enough, certainly, for it obscured the fact that very often neglect was intimately tied to the disorganizing effects of extreme poverty, conditions that could be addressed without removing the children from the home. But the real irony of expanded child abuse reporting laws, according to Besharov, was that abused children were still being passed over in the system designed above all to serve them. The critics contended that a system so deluged with reports, many of which were either minor or completely without foundation, overwhelmed workers, who had to make a discretionary decision with every case. And because workers were overwhelmed and overworked, their capacity to distinguish genuine crises from less serious situations was diminished. Yet the ever-growing public pressure on them to stop child abuse encouraged them, in Besharov's words, "to take no chances. The dynamic is simple: negative media publicity, an administrative reprimand, a lawsuit, even a criminal prosecution are possible if the child is subsequently killed or injured. But there is no bad publicity if it turns out that intervention was unneeded."[26]

The critics worried about state intervention for another crucial reason besides family privacy. Public awareness went only to the point where a child was removed from an unsafe home. What the child welfare community observed was what happened to the children after removal had been accomplished. The expressed goal of every child abuse law passed in Illinois since 1965 was to support families and return children home if possible. But in reality, if this did not happen promptly—at the temporary custody hearing forty-eight hours after the child's removal or soon thereafter—there was a good chance that the family would be separated for a considerable time, at least until adjudication (trial) decided whether or not the parents were guilty of abuse or neglect, perhaps longer. In the crowded Cook County Juvenile Court dockets, child abuse and neglect cases were frequently delayed as much as a year before trial, before culpability was even decided, with the children in foster care, often moving from one temporary situation to another. The longer the family separation, of course, the more difficult a successful reunion became. The number of children in foster care across the nation escalated with the increasingly expanded reporting laws; the national figure for children put into foster care because of neglect and abuse was 75,000 in 1963, compared to 300,000 in 1980. And of those 300,000 children, about half had been in the foster care system for at least two years, and roughly one-third had been in for over six years.[27]

Critics contended that the increasingly militant child abuse laws were seriously disruptive of families without effectively controlling the incidents of severe abuse; they held that the states should rethink the broad classifications that they had set up and return to a much stricter standard for crisis action. Besharov suggested a category of "immediately harmful behavior," which would call for prompt removal of children from the home, as contrasted with a category of "cumulatively harmful behavior," which should certainly be addressed, but not in a crisis mode and not by removing the children.[28]

Illinois critics shared the national concern about increasingly broad child abuse laws. Policy analyst Malcolm Bush, discussing the 1980 Illinois law declared roundly, "This mandate was exaggerated, impossible and ill conceived." He added, moreover, that since control of child abuse was such a popular issue, the Department of Children and Family Services concentrated on it out of all proportion to its size, to the neglect of other child welfare concerns; the child abuse issue was a way of maintaining and even expanding a child welfare bureaucracy in lean times. Child advocate Patrick Murphy went further: "The statute is one of the broad nets of legislation that catch every fish swimming through and allow the fisherman to pick which he wants to keep and which to throw back. Social agencies proposed it and social agencies love it." Murphy and others insisted that a very high percentage of neglect cases were in reality simply cases of extreme poverty; instead of helping parents to deal with domestic catastrophes like unheated apartments, he contended, the state took their children away.[29]

Parental Rights and the Foster Care System

Though expanded child neglect laws threatened parental rights, the 1960s and 1970s was a time when critics of state power sought to limit what they saw as civil liberties invasions, and there had been some efforts to protect parental rights in the child welfare system. The general thrust was a move away from the informality of the older juvenile court toward legal procedures and entitlements, both for children and their parents. For example, the new juvenile court law required that all parties be told of their right to be present at court proceedings, to be heard, to present evidence and to cross-examine witnesses. It also provided that any party to the proceedings who could not afford to hire an attorney could request that the court appoint one.[30]

There were some important court decisions on the issue of parental rights as well. On the state level, for example, in 1971 the First District Appellate Court, in a case involving a ward of the state whose social workers judged that she would be a neglectful mother, ruled that the mere expectation of neglect is not sufficient evidence to remove a child from a parent's custody. But a later court decision, and an amendment to the juvenile court act, did establish that proven abuse or neglect of one minor could be considered admissible evidence concerning possible abuse or neglect of any other minor for whom the respondent was responsible.[31]

Also in 1971 a United States Supreme Court decision, Stanley v. Illinois, struck down an Illinois law that made the children of unmarried mothers wards of the state when the mother died. Stanley, who had lived off and on with the children's mother for years, claimed the right to a hearing on his parental fitness before his children were removed, a judicial procedure required before removing children from married fathers and from both married and unmarried mothers. The United States Supreme Court found that Stanley's right to equal treatment under the law had been denied, making unmarried fathers a part of the court process. One unavoidable result of the decision was the delay of judicial proceedings while the court attempted to notify—first by summons, then by letter, then by publication in the newspaper—missing fathers who had a right to participate as parents in hearings on their children's care and custody.[32]

A 1977 United States district court case involving a class action suit against the Illinois Department of Children and Family Services and other child welfare agencies gave increased rights to Spanish speaking clients. The plaintiffs complained of discriminatory treatment because of the dearth of services to Spanish-speaking people. Specifically they named a lack of Spanish-speaking foster homes; a lack of Spanish-speaking personnel, resulting in limited supportive services; and failure to provide Spanish translations of official instructions and documents, such as those explaining residual parental rights. The case was settled by a consent decree that promised more Spanish-speaking DCFS employees; literature and written communications in Spanish; Spanish-speaking foster parents; and a DCFS ombudsman specifically for Spanish-speaking clients, as well as an annual compliance review to be held by DCFS. The Burgos Decree, as it was known, was an important recognition of one of Illinois' fastest growing minority populations, and was part of the spirit of procedural entitlement that characterized the legal reforms of the 1960s and 1970s.[33]

A 1982 United States Supreme Court decision, Santoskey v. Kramer, strengthened parents' right to due process in termination of parental rights cases by raising the standard of evidence in proving unfitness. The standard required by New York State, a "fair preponderance of the evidence" was rejected by the court in favor of "clear and convincing evidence," the strictest evidentiary standard that could be applied.[34]

But a 1977 United States Supreme Court case, Smith v. Organization of Foster Families for Equality and Reform (OFFER), while on one level concerned with parental rights, raised the complicating issue of a foster family's right to be considered part of the legal process, particularly when they were caring for children for a long period of time. The suit on behalf of the foster parents argued that just as parents had a right to a court hearing before their children were removed, so too did foster parents have a right to due process when threatened with the loss of children who had been in their homes for a considerable time. OFFER argued that foster parents were the child's true "psychological family"[35] if the placement had gone on long enough, and that continuity for the child was the most crucial issue to be considered. The Supreme

Court majority reversed a New York district court ruling that had granted the foster families a court hearing before the children were removed. The Supreme Court argued that although there was likely to be attachment between foster parents and children, foster parents did not have the same right to "family privacy"—and due process against state invasion of that privacy—that natural families did, because they were in a sense creatures of the state, having their origin "in state law and contractual arrangements." The court found that the reviews granted by the state child welfare department upon request were sufficient protection of foster parents' rights.[36]

In explicating the case, the justices expressed some of the concerns that advocates for foster children, poor and minority clients, and foster parents had about the foster care system: despite the state's expressed goal of returning children to their natural families whenever possible, the reality was that children often stayed in "temporary" care for years, drifting from one foster home to another because it suited bureaucratic purposes; or because the turnover in social workers eroded the alertness to the stability of children's placements and resulted in sloppy casework; or because the children were difficult cases who were hard to place and hard to keep in placement.[37]

There was something to offend everyone in the workings of the foster care system. Foster parents argued that they were treated arbitrarily and callously by the child welfare bureaucracy, that while they did the daily care and nurturing of the children (in effect, most of the work), they were deprived of any decision-making power on behalf of the children and were subject to the loss of those children for a whole variety of reasons. It was galling to them to have the standards of their substitute parenting so rigidly monitored, when the children they cared for came from homes that were often inadequate in both physical and psychological terms.[38]

The Foster Family License Compliance Record for the Illinois Department of Children and Family Services, for example, was a thirteen-page checklist that sought to guarantee sufficient space, ventilation, privacy, nutrition, and protection for foster children. It required that each foster child have forty square feet of bedroom floor space, plus a separate dresser and closet of his or her own. It investigated the foster family's source of water, their health, their "outside employment or activities," and their psychological fitness. Arthur Guild, who had done the Juvenile Protection Association's 1917 report on *Baby Farms in Chicago* would surely have rejoiced at the thoroughness of this monitoring, since the regulations were so clearly directed at many of the abuses that he had uncovered and demonstrated the state's concern for the care and protection of foster children. But the many requirements and responsibilities of foster parenting were balanced with few rights and little recognition from the larger society, which in general remained oblivious to foster parents' considerable contribution to the welfare of "the state's children." It was little wonder that organizations like OFFER questioned the reasonableness of a system that asked so much of citizens. On the one hand they were to be loving, nurturing substitute parents, often in very difficult circumstances. On the other hand, they were to remember that "whatever emotional ties may develop between foster parent and foster child have their origins in an arrangement in which the state has been a partner from the outset" and to accept that those emotions were to be suspended at a moment's notice if the child welfare bureaucracy considered removal from their home to be in a child's best interests.[39]

Still, no one could argue that parents fared very well in the system either. They were mostly poor, and, as Justice William Brennan noted in the Smith case, the natural inclination of many middle-class social workers was to place children in higher status foster homes rather than working for reunion with poor and minority families.[40]

It was the broad room for discretion on the part of the child welfare system that caused dismay on the part of both foster parents and natural parents; hence, the two groups went to court to try to limit discretion by specifying legally and exactly what everyone's rights were. Foster parents had limited success with this tactic. On paper, natural parents seemed to have gained significant legal protection in the 1960s–1980s. But in reality many of those gains—for example, in Smith and Santosky—focused on the protection of residual parental rights. At the same time that parents were gaining rights to due process in the courts, new child abuse laws were allowing—and, critics said, inviting—hasty removal of children from the home for less than catastrophic reasons, and this often meant a prolonged separation between parents and children because of crowded court dockets and the general inefficiency of the judicial and child welfare systems.

The legal resort to entitlements and procedural protections had its own traps, as illustrated by the delays caused in publishing for

a long-departed putative father who had a legal right to participate in proceedings. In Illinois the number of professionals involved in a foster care case was sobering; it was possible, if the
case was complicated enough, to have attorneys for the state, for
the state child welfare department, for the child, for the mother,
for the father or fathers; in addition, there could be child protective services workers, state case workers, probation officers, and
possibly social workers from a private agency.[41]

The Progressive commitment to flexibility was condemned by
modern critics because it led to excessively ungoverned decision
making. But the emphasis on procedure that characterized much
late twentieth-century reform could lead to a plethora of laws and
requirements that frustrated those involved and certainly slowed
down the process of settling children into the best permanent situation possible. Neither an informal system, which seemed to sacrifice rights for efficiency, nor a law-bound system, which sacrificed efficiency to procedure, was the magic formula; that much,
most parties could agree on. But it was extremely difficult in an
issue so fraught with conflicting emotions to achieve the right
balance between protecting the rights of the child and the parent,
while at the same time maintaining the interests of society as a
whole.

Permanency Planning

Throughout the 1960s and 1970s, those concerned with the foster care system, both attorneys and social workers, subjected the
system to extensive criticism, arguing that the result of placing a
child in foster care—a result quite different from the stated aim—
was to destroy families without offering children any alternative
but an uncertain and disrupted life. "Drift" was the word used to
describe most children's experience in foster care; because there
was very little long range planning done in behalf of the children,
they would enter the substitute care system with the expectation
of returning home but would instead remain for years—in one
place, if they were the lucky ones, but in many instances transferred repeatedly, so that their childhoods were characterized by
disruption, uncertainty, and a sense of being "nobody's child."

Those critical of the system argued a number of things. One
point was that there had to be a more vigorous effort made on behalf of troubled families so that children could safely be returned
home before so much time had elapsed that successful reunion was

made more difficult or impossible by years of separation. The other essential point was that in cases where the prospects of returning home were unlikely—cases where children had suffered extreme abuse, or had been abandoned or whose parents suffered from chronic mental illness—there should be more consideration of adoption.[42]

There was a strong push in the 1970s to demonstrate that children who had been dismissed as "unadoptable" could in fact be successfully placed in adoptive homes if enough energy was directed to the effort. In 1971, the Illinois Department of Children and Family Services was chosen by the federal Children's Bureau to do a demonstration project on the use of financial subsidies to encourage the adoption of hard-to-place older black children. Illinois was one of seven states to have a provision for subsidized adoptions (passed in 1969), but the subsidy law in itself had not caused great improvements in adoption rates; two years after the law was passed, only 149 subsidies had been approved, only 59 of them for black children. Now the Children's Bureau project demonstrated that adoptive homes could be found for many black children. The subsidy was "a key factor in accomplishing adoptions for a high percentage of older black children," but the project report stressed that "knowing the children well was the core of the service." Merely offering a subsidy was not enough to bring about such adoptions. It required "effort, enthusiasm, and a manageable caseload size." The project had estimated in a survey of 1,962 black children in foster care in Chicago in 1972 that adoption would be possible for 66 percent. Of the 112 children served by the project, almost 70 percent were placed for adoption, with another 11 percent settled in "formalized long-term foster care."[43]

The stress on limiting drift in foster care, in either getting children back to their original homes or into another permanent family, resulted in a national law that had tremendous impact on the practice of child welfare in Illinois. P.L. 96-272, called "The Adoption Assistance and Child Welfare Act of 1980," was an amendment of Title IV-B of the Social Security Act that provided funding for child welfare services. The phrase that summed up the philosophy of this law was "permanency planning," which meant in essence that the law sought to guarantee that no child would enter the foster care system without a deliberate plan being made for him or her, a plan that was to be reviewed periodically. The social service agency was to review and update each child's plan at least every six months, and within eighteen months and "periodically thereafter" the child was to have a disposition hearing before a court or court-appointed body that was to determine whether or not he or she should go home, be placed for adoption, or remain in foster care. The best outcome according to "permanency planning" thinking was for the child to return home. If this was impossible, adoption should be the next goal. In order that "special needs" children (for example, older, minority or handicapped children) might be placed, the law included an adoption subsidy, comparable to the subsidy paid for the child if he or she was in foster care, in order to encourage potential parents who might be unable to adopt a special needs child without financial assistance. (The grant was not meant to be automatic; the law provided that the social service agencies had to have made a reasonable effort to place the child without adoption assistance.)[44]

The inducement for states to become involved in the reform legislation was federal money; the matching rates of Title IV-B of the Social Security Act had been from 33 1/3 to 66 2/3 percent of expenditures. Now federal funds reimbursed 75 percent of child welfare costs. In return for this additional money, states had to make major planning efforts for children in foster care, providing written case plans that justified the wisdom of the current placement and projected a permanent situation for the child within the foreseeable future. There was far more emphasis on adoption for foster children than had existed before, an emphasis that was aided by the lack of the classically "adoptable" white infants who had become more scarce as women exercised other options than adoption. (Abortion was legal in all states after the Roe v. Wade United States Supreme Court decision of 1973, and in addition more unmarried mothers were keeping their babies as the stigma against illegitimacy declined in the socially permissive 1970s.)[45]

Few people could argue with the notion of "permanency planning," with the desire to get children settled in families they could consider their own and end the terrible uncertainty that was so much a part of the psychological baggage of the foster child. But there were critics of permanency planning. One practical complaint (a familiar lament from practitioners dealing with federal funding) targeted paper work, arguing that the institution of case reviews further added to the number of people monitoring one another and increased, at the expense of really effective planning, the checklist of "musts" that had to be run through in order to satisfy the letter of the law.[46]

On a more philosophical plane, critics charged that the rhetoric of permanency planning, by emphasizing the move to permanence from impermanence, deflected attention from the causes of family stress which society and the child welfare system in particular had failed to respond to. And one social worker, defending the legitimacy of foster care, argued that permanency planning made "foster care look like the problem rather than looking at what got the child into the system in the first place." Further, the social worker argued, the emphasis on ends, on getting children placed somewhere permanently, weakened the commitment for caring for them in the interim. Treating foster care as a necessary evil rather than a positive good created, in her words, "yet another impediment to the recruitment of foster parents when, God knows, there are plenty of other impediments already."[47]

Not every child was going to make it home or into an adoptive home, the critics pointed out. DCFS's caseload became more difficult in the 1970s, as legislation to decriminalize status offenders reassigned responsibility for these troubled youngsters from the Department of Corrections to the child welfare agency. DCFS also became responsible for delinquents under thirteen. These and other older children, long-term casualties of the whole child welfare system, were unlikely candidates for "permanency" as it was defined by the Adoption Assistance Act of 1980. The emphasis on deinstitutionalization of child welfare, the stress on the "least restrictive setting available" was in keeping with the philosophy of the 1960s–1970s, which saw the deinstitutionalization of mental hospitals and the mainstreaming of handicapped children in the schools. But in reality, there were not many home environments available to tough, disillusioned, street-wise teenagers. As institutions closed, there were only a few places, such as group homes and independent living programs, left for them to weather their adolescence.[48]

Child Welfare in Crisis

The transfer of children from the Department of Corrections to the Department of Children and Family Services strained the system at a point when DCFS was experiencing other problems. In the wake of economic troubles in the 1970s, social services were facing cutbacks, and the legislature was simultaneously increasing the department's responsibilities and reducing its fiscal capacity. Further, with the growing public interest in child abuse, expectations for DCFS were high and public scrutiny intense.

Agency failures resulting in harm to children received wide press coverage. A particularly explosive issue in the early 1970s concerned five hundred DCFS wards in substitute care in Texas. The Juvenile Legal Aid Society of Chicago, alleging serious mistreatment of children in several of these out-of-state institutions, demanded that DCFS remove the children who were inappropriately placed and justify the placement of the children who remained. The newspapers were intensely critical of DCFS on the issue, and the agency responded ("with a haste bordering on the paranoid," in the judgment of the Juvenile Legal Aid Society attorney Patrick Murphy) by ordering all five hundred children back to Illinois. This precipitate removal of all the children regardless of their circumstances provoked criticism in its turn, not only because of the disruption to their lives but also because there was no advance preparation to receive such a large number of children into Illinois' system.[49]

One focus of attention and criticism was DCFS' most controversial director, Jerome Miller, who took office in 1973. Miller had been in charge of the deinstitutionalization of delinquents in Massachusetts, and he came to Illinois with a radical philosophy that combined a belief in deinstitutionalization, community-based services and in-home services for families, with a hostility to the notion of "professional" social work philosophy and practice. In a sense, Miller was committed to a deliberate disruption of the department he headed, and disruption was definitely what resulted. Miller did battle with private agencies and professional social workers in his own agency on all levels. Many professional social workers left DCFS during Miller's administration and went to private agencies. In addition, in 1974, the Illinois Department of Personnel, following a 1969 ruling of the federal Department of Health, Education and Welfare, lowered its training and education requirements dramatically, so that a clerk-typist of three to four years standing could become a social worker.[50]

Jerome Miller resigned from DCFS in August 1974, but the early optimism about the department was gone. Many felt that the agency, instead of acting as torchbearer for child welfare issues in the state, in fact offered services inferior to those provided by private agencies and inadequate to the needs of the children whom they served. In the late 1970s, the Illinois Humane Association and the Better Government Association produced reports critical of DCFS, citing a major breakdown of communication at all levels. The reports charged that there was poor articulation of policies written

by the department; poor communication between the state department and regional offices (in particular Cook County, the largest
metropolitan office) as well as between DCFS and private agencies; inadequate supervision of workers; and inadequate case
records, an issue that was particularly critical in an agency with
a rapid turnover of workers.[51]

The 1980s, far from bringing improvements in DCFS's perfor-
mance, saw an increased sense of crisis in the state's child welfare system. As federal supports to the states were cut, social service budgets suffered commensurately. DCFS also faced the
challenge of implementing the 1980 Adoption Assistance and
Child Welfare Law, which was meant to reduce the number of
children in foster care substantially.

In fact, the opposite happened, because the 1980s proved to be
a disastrous decade for children. The poverty rate soared. By mid-
decade, one out of five American children lived below the poverty line. In Illinois, the percentage of poor children had increased
from 14.9 percent in 1979 to 21.7 percent in 1989. The connection between poverty and neglect (in cases of homelessness, for
example) brought children into the child welfare system despite
the protests of critics. And two unexpected new public health problems of epidemic proportions, AIDS and cocaine addiction, together with a sharp rise in teenage pregnancy, imposed on DCFS not
only an increased but a distressed population of children in need
of special care.[52]

It was a situation not anticipated by the 1980 child welfare law,
which had looked to families—either the child's own or adoptive
families—to solve the problems of children in substitute care. Both
the flood of children into the system and their special needs overwhelmed an already weak department. Further, the complicated
interplay between the state department of child welfare and the
county-based juvenile court added to the confusion. DCFS might
recommend a disposition for a child, but the final say rested with
the judge, whose decision seemed virtually irreversible.[53]

This perception was challenged in the late 1980s, when both
DCFS and the juvenile court came under fire in lawsuits filed on
behalf of foster children. In 1986, The Children's Rights Project
of the Legal Assistance Foundation of Chicago filed disciplinary
charges against four attorneys from the Guardian Ad Litem's office in Cook County. The Project charged that the accused Guardians Ad Litem, whose responsibility was to speak for the best interests of the child, had had virtually no contact with the children

they were representing and had failed to act in any meaningful way on their clients' behalf. The initial critique was followed by a lawsuit that included the entire GAL office and its chief attorney, as well as the Cook County Board of Commissioners. A year of special investigations, negotiations, and litigation resulted in a major shake-up of the office, with Patrick Murphy, longtime legal advocate for children and head of the Public Guardian's office, named as head of the GAL office. Murphy's arrival resulted in an almost total turnover of attorneys within the office and a much more vigorous advocacy for children. No stranger to the appeals process, Murphy frequently challenged the convention that dependency judges' decisions were final.[54]

In 1991, an Illinois Appellate Court decision on a much publicized case also illustrated that dependency court judges' decisions were not absolute. The appeals court overturned the juvenile court judge's decision to send home a child who had lived for five years in a foster home, decreeing that the best interests of the child overrode the rights of the biological parents. The Appeals Court ordered a new custody hearing and issued a thundering rebuke to the whole child welfare system. "There is no doubt," wrote Judge Dom Rizzi on behalf of the appellate court, "that the DCFS and our juvenile court system are abysmal failures."[55]

The so called Sarah case, made famous by *Chicago Tribune* columnist Bob Greene, caused considerable questioning not only of the institutions that ran the child welfare system but of the 1980 child welfare law and the "permanency planning" that was its essence. In the Sarah case, the appeals court held that DCFS and the juvenile court had violated the 1980 law by failing to develop a permanency plan within the eighteen-month deadline set by law. But the very notion of creating a permanent plan for children implied making some painful and difficult decisions about which families were susceptible to rehabilitation and which were so hopeless that parental rights should be terminated. Public Guardian Murphy contended that judges leaned toward protecting natural families no matter how bad they might be. On the other hand, a successful Legal Assistance Foundation suit against DCFS charged that the system confused neglect and poverty, removing thousands of children from their families unnecessarily. Peter Forsythe of the Edna McConnell Clark child welfare foundation lamented: "We have these wide mood swings or fads. At one time, we're placing everybody. Then, we're reunifying everybody." One thing that everyone could agree on was that an overloaded system in both the courts and DCFS assured that the "Solomon-like decisions" about permanency planning would not be made with anything approaching the wisdom of Solomon.[56]

A 1991 "expert" report confirmed that DCFS was a shambles, in no condition to judge the potential health of families or to plan wisely for such difficult cases as routinely came into their care. The report stemmed from a class action suit, B.H. et al. v. Johnson, filed by the American Civil Liberties Union of Illinois on behalf of the twenty-three thousand children in DCFS custody. The experts, chosen by both DCFS and the ACLU, reported uncompromisingly: "It is the concensus of the panel that the risk to these children's health, development and well-being is not significantly diminished, and is many times aggravated while in DCFS custody. The children remain high risk until they are finally pushed from or exit the system."[57]

The report made dismal but familiar reading to anyone acquainted with the history of child welfare administration in Illinois. In 1990, as in 1940, foster care was still "based on available rather than appropriate settings." A lack of interagency and intra-agency cooperation still impeded good care and placements for children. The courts were still overcrowded and understaffed. Record keeping was still totally inadequate—so bad that one diabetic child was placed in a foster home without notification to the foster parents of the child's imperative need for continuous insulin therapy. Case workers were badly trained and overloaded, with a turnover rate so rapid that it virtually insured chaos. Foster parents were badly treated and embittered, uncompensated for medicine, food, and clothing that they purchased for the children in their care. Emergency shelters were overcrowded and sometimes positively dangerous and kept children long beyond the permissible time limit. Perhaps most chilling of all, DCFS literally could not account for all the children in its custody. The experts decreed that at a minimum the department must develop the capacity "to identify the status and track the progress of every DCFS ward."[58]

There was some promise for the future. After the experts' report, the B.H. case moved forward to a consent decree, emphasizing, among other things, careful monitoring of DCFS compliance. (That this was necessary was illustrated by another report on the 1977 Burgos Decree that had ordered redress for Spanish-speaking clients of DCFS. The court-ordered report found DCFS to be seriously out of compliance with a number of the protections guaranteed by the Burgos Decree.)[59]

A key strength of the B.H. Consent Decree was that it was issued by a federal court. Noncompliance could threaten the state's
funding from the Adoption Assistance Act of 1980, funding that
the state could not afford to lose. Even more to the point, the judge
could find the governor and state officials guilty of contempt of
court for failure to comply with the decree, a possible sanction
with prompt and embarrassing consequences.[60]

But the costs of implementation were considerable. The ACLU
estimated that costs would reach 100 million dollars. DCFS was
granted 37.7 million dollars to begin implementation in 1992.
While some of the necessary funds could be realized by tapping
into various federal funding sources, there was no avoiding the fact
that the state of Illinois would be required to provide a significant
part of the funding to repair a system so long neglected.[61]

Both the plaintiffs and DCFS acknowledged in the consent decree that "the Department's budget and the budget of the State of
Illinois may be subject to pressure and competing priorities." That
much seemed certain. Shortly after the consent decree was final-
ized, the state lawmakers authorized a 54 million dollar cut in
human services for the 1993 year, citing the citizens' unwillingness to raise taxes as their rationale. The decision mandated major changes in DCFS.* How the state would pay for them remained
a compelling question.[62]

Conclusion

Almost one hundred years after the creation of the juvenile
court, child welfare was again in crisis, not only in Illinois but
across the nation. The numbers of children in substitute care were
growing, just as the state's capacity to deal with them was seriously eroded by fiscal constraints and a pervasive "no new taxes"
mood.

In fact, the situation for dependent children had scarcely ever
been out of crisis. It was simply that much of the time the crisis

---

*As of June 1993, the DCFS crisis continued. As July 1 (the compliance date
for increasing DCSF staff) drew near, the B.H. monitor voiced concerns about the
hasty nature of the agency's hiring. Further, the tragic case of three-year-old Joseph Wallace, a state ward sent home by DCFS and the Juvenile Court and later
murdered by his mother, prompted vehement criticism of the child welfare system and a bill in the legislature making "the child's best interest" paramount over
family reunification (*Chicago Tribune*, April-June 1993).

had proven easy to ignore. The attitude toward the other children of the state, delinquent and handicapped children, swung back and forth from fearful to sympathetic, and methods of treatment changed with the changing views. This was not so with dependent children. They were regarded, if anyone was, as the worthy poor, and child welfare appeared to be the most acceptable, the most "white glove" of charities, crossing political lines and tapping a universal interest. But under the surface, the situation was intensely political. Since the early twentieth century, social theorists had argued that a critical response to dependency was to sustain children's families and keep them from coming into care in the first place. That was the point of mothers' pensions, ADC, and the homemaker and other support provisions offered by the new Department of Children and Family Services in 1964. Yet the effort to offer strong support for families was scarcely more wholehearted in the late twentieth century than it had been when Dr. Shipman, of the Chicago Foundling Hospital, regretfully watched the parting of a mother and child a his front door in the mid-nineteenth century. The connection between poverty and dependent children was unmistakable, but to act decisively in that direction took the issue from its safe, neutral territory and into the realm of class injustices—an uncomfortable setting for many philanthropists and for the public at large.

Society's attitude toward dependent children was thus profoundly ambivalent. Public anger was unfocused and unsustained, thwarted by the complicated issues of conflicting rights and conflicting turf that characterized the problem and by the connection with poverty that few wanted to acknowledge. As with most social problems, citizens wanted a "quick fix" solution, and they wanted it cheap.

The 1980 child welfare act in essence acknowledged the inconstancy of public concern and the negative impact of state involvement, aiming to get the state out of dependent children's lives as soon as possible. Like Charles Loring Brace's nineteenth-century "Children West" program, the 1980 law operated on a premise that the natural solution to dependency was family life, an adjustment that need not be too elaborate. And, like Brace's plan, this simple equation had some simple-minded elements. Not only did it fail to provide much for children whose circumstances fell between those two neat categories of a return home or adoption. It also presumed that the same underfunded, overworked state agency condemned as too incompetent to care for children could make the necessary Solomon's judgments about families and could act on those judgments with fairness and efficiency. And, like Brace's plan years earlier, permanency planning was a minimalist solution, looking to a handful of adoptive parents for extraordinary devotion and altruism, while absolving the larger society of its responsibilities for children.

As the century drew to a close, both permanency planning and deinstitutionalization were under fire in some quarters. Many children coming into care seemed to have medical and psychological problems too complex for simple foster care and adoption. Both the nature of children's problems and the simple need for stability led some child welfare specialists to argue for the return of modified orphanages, a solution that would have been unthinkable only a few years earlier.[63]

All of the history of the state's children had a circular quality about it, but none gave the sense of déjà vu more powerfully than the history of child welfare. There had never been much variance in the provisions offered for dependent children: they could be kept in their own homes, they could be put in institutions or some variation of an institution, or they could go to another family. The solutions were wonderfully direct. It was only the implementation that was so fraught with hazards. When the apparently simple mechanism of the family unit broke down, the problems that resulted could be appallingly complex, and it was sadly possible, as one investigatory committee after another had pointed out over the years, for the children of the state to be indicted and punished for their misfortune.

Part 2

Children in Trouble with the Law

Scene in a classroom of the Cook County Juvenile Detention Center, 1988. Photograph by Thomas Classic Photography. Courtesy of the Cook County Juvenile Detention Center.

4

Defining Delinquency, 1818–99

The history of the Illinois's relationship to children in trouble with the law differs in two ways from its treatment of dependent children. First, the state has never shown a reluctance to be involved with delinquent children, as it has in the case of dependent children. Because delinquent children breach the social order, the state's responsibility to deal with them has never been in question. They are lawbreakers and are thus inevitably involved in an intimate, if adversarial, relationship to the state.

It is the adversarial quality of the relationship that is the second distinguishing feature of the delinquent's situation. In all other aspects of child welfare, the state's articulated purpose is to act as benefactor and protector. This theoretical purpose might be belied in actual practice by catastrophic encounters, so that a considerable number of thinkers and practitioners would contend that children are best served when state action is kept to a minimum; but at least in theory, the state's role is meant to be benevolent and helpful. With delinquency, the theoretical case is not so clear. The original relationship of the state to all criminals was a retributive one; criminals had violated the law, and society demanded punitive action against them. By the nineteenth century, the state's original role of determining guilt and meting out punishment was modified to a combined task of punishment and rehabilitation of the criminal; but the theory of rehabilitation was not one that persuaded everyone. There were those who continued to propose that the state's responsibility was the simpler and more ancient role, that of punishing the guilty.

The issue of the state's role, of punishment versus rehabilitation, was a confusing and controversial one in dealing with adult criminals; it was made far more complex by the introduction of childhood into the equation. The notion of rehabilitation rather than simple punishment gained part of its force from the recognition that most criminals did not really act in a genuinely free setting but were instead shaped by circumstances and thus could not be held fully accountable for their fall from grace. If society was prepared, as at least in prison reform circles it was, to speak of limited accountability in adults, how much more compelling that argument became when directed to children. In dealing with adults, the notion of limited responsibility was a statement of belief. With children, it was a demonstrable fact. The essence of childhood was limited capacity, although those limitations changed constantly, since the other essential aspect of childhood was development—physical and intellectual growth and change.

Those who contended that the state's proper role was to help and not to punish children faced critics from two directions. On the one hand, the advocates of punitive justice argued that the special treatment of children was pointless and unwise, that children who committed crimes essentially lost the privileges and protections of childhood and should pay the penalty for their actions just as adults did. A more complex critique of the state as helping parent came from those who argued on behalf of children. This group contended that setting the child aside as a special case where questions of guilt and innocence did not arise might sound merciful, but ironically it often resulted in children being treated more harshly and arbitrarily than adults might be under the same circumstances. Children who were deprived of due process might actually be incarcerated in the name of helping even though they had violated no law; others might be held for much longer than adults for minor infractions. No matter what rehabilitative theory might say, these due process proponents argued, incarceration was still deprivation of liberty; it was prison in reality if not in intention, a contention they bolstered with evidence of the abuse common in reformatory institutions. The heart of the due process argument was that if the state was in part a parental helper toward children in trouble, it was nevertheless true that the element of punishment still persisted, and mere rhetoric could not erase it.

The history of the state's attitude and actions toward delinquents has been complex and circular, owning in part to the unresolved conflict between its role as helper and its role as implacable dispenser of justice. This circularity began in the nineteenth century. Before Illinois had celebrated fifty years of statehood, the pattern of state reactions to delinquency had been established.

The Treatment of Delinquent Children in Early Illinois

In the earliest days of the state, the issue of juvenile delinquency was of minimal concern. In a state with a population of about forty-thousand, the kind of vagrancy, vandalism, and petty theft that plagued more urban settings did not exist as a major problem. Most of the laws regarding children were simply carried over from the laws of the territory, and they decreed a summary justice for juvenile wrongdoers. Children and servants who disobeyed the lawful commands of their parents or masters could be sent by a justice of the peace to the jail or house of correction, "there to remain until they shall humble themselves to the said parent's or master's satisfaction: and if any child or servant shall, contrary to his bounden duty, presume to assault or strike his parent or master, upon complaint or conviction thereof before two or more justices of the peace, the offender shall be whipped not exceeding ten stripes." This law, drawn from English common law and mirroring both colonial and state legislation in the older states of the union, reflected the attitude that the child's behavior and care was chiefly the responsibility of the family, with the occasional assist from the state in case of recalcitrance. It reflected, too, the reliance on corporal punishment as the primary mode of dealing with lawbreakers of all ages.[1]

In the next decade the legislature did give some slight consideration to children. In the 1827 revision of the criminal code, the legislators made some concessions to the vulnerability and limited capacity of youth by explicitly stating the age at which a child could be held responsible for a crime or misdemeanor. Before 1827, legislators did not specifically mention mental competence in the criminal code. Rather, they applied the British common law age of seven as the dividing line between innocence and accountability.[2] In 1827, the criminal code raised the age to ten years. As in British common law, the court made a decision on an individual basis about the capacity of any child above the age of accountability up to age fourteen. An exception was made for the crime of rape; the criminal code of 1827 set the lower age limit at which boys could be tried for this crime at fourteen years, following British common law practice. Also in keeping with the common law the age of consent for girls in statutory rape cases was set at ten years of age. While the 1827 legislature gave some slight indications of a special attention to childhood, it is clear from the age of consent provision—similar to those in force in most states at the time—that society still had extraordinary expectations about the discretionary capacities of its female children.[3]

An 1831 law further addressed the unique situation of children, considering the question of what to do with the child who had been convicted of a crime. It provided that only in cases of robbery, burglary, and arson could children under eighteen be sent to the newly established penitentiary at Alton. Other convicted children were to be imprisoned in the county jail, for a term not exceeding eighteen months. While this provision was intended to some extent to protect children by sparing them the harsh regime in force at the penitentiary, it was in reality a modest reform at best, since county jails were notoriously squalid places, where a mix of men and women, children and adults, were crowded into small, filthy, poorly ventilated rooms and subjected to a whole range of moral and physical degradations. County jails were a chief target of prison reformers, roundly condemned in one report as "public schools, maintained at the expense of the community, for the encouragement of vice, and for providing an unbroken succession of thieves, burglars and profligates, . . . a blot on our civilization."[4]

The Chicago Reform School

Explosive urban growth brought to Illinois, as it had to other states, an awareness of children as a group in need of concerted action. When Illinois acquired statehood in 1818, the older states along the Atlantic seaboard were just beginning to address the problem of the delinquent and dependent children who crowded the streets and bridewells of the larger cities. The efforts of concerned citizens in states like New York and Massachusetts resulted in the opening of a series of houses of refuge or reformation, later called reform schools, for the care of children who were perceived as a threat to themselves and society. The first such institution was opened in New York City in 1825, with Boston and Philadelphia following suit in 1826 and 1828 respectively. It was not until 1855, however, that the Chicago Common Council created a reform school modeled on the established institutions in the eastern states. In that year, the city (moved to action, according to the first annual report of the reform school, by the rising rate of juvenile crime and the deleterious effects of holding children in adult jails) established the Chicago Reform School in the old poorhouse buildings five miles south of the city. These buildings burned down in the school's second year, and the boys were temporarily placed in the local jail and later moved to an old packing house where, together with the superintendent and his family, they spent a freezing winter before eventually moving to a more prepossessing and permanent site.[5]

Despite the initial problems, Superintendent Nichols's reports were cheerful and energetic. The Chicago Reform School superintendent, like the early superintendents of the first reform schools in the East, was an idealistic gentleman with highly progressive attitudes toward children in trouble.[6] He refused to put bars up in the new reformatory building, and the entire reform school administration operated on the concept of an honor system. No physical punishment was allowed; the greatest sanction against a boy was demotion to grade five, the grade of disgrace. The boys were allowed to carry keys to the fence surrounding the buildings, and as time went on, the school developed a "ticket of leave" system that allowed boys to go into the city to visit relatives or to be absent for long periods of time in order to work outside the institution. Superintendent Nichols even established a "cabinet of minerals and curiosities," a museum alluded to proudly from time to time in the annual reports. Nichols clearly saw his institution as a school rather than a place of punishment, a school governed by "parental discipline" and operating from the conviction that the best way to reform boys was through education and moral training, by teaching self-respect, self-reliance, and hard work.[7]

The reform school's government may have been benevolent, but it was by no means indulgent. The boys rose at 5:45 A.M. to face a day filled with four hours of school, six hours in the workshops, and plenty of time for prayers and devotional exercises. They marched to and from work and school to the beat of a drum, and their only time for conversation was the half hour of recreation after midday dinner. At night they slept in hammocks in a common dormitory. Most stringent of all, the institution had control over them until they were twenty-one years old or "until they become good boys," whichever came first. In the first years of the reformatory, the boys had been sent from the courts with definite sentences, but that soon changed to allow the school a more indeterminate period of control.[8]

The Chicago Reform School was lauded in prison reform circles as a model institution. Even after Mr. Nichols retired, sick and exhausted from five years of vigorous effort, the school continued to be run on the principle of the honor code. Unlike the early days of some other institutions, where new superintendents had signaled a disciplinary crackdown ordered by the board of managers, the Chicago Reform School continued much as it had begun. The next superintendents appeared to be only marginally stricter than Superintendent Nichols, despite the institution's rapid growth and the development of new problems, like the need to separate younger boys from older, tougher inmates.[9]

But the institution so warmly praised by child welfare and prison reformers was also a target of vehement criticism and great suspicion from others in the city. One key reason for the resistance to the reform school lay in the institution's basic definition. It was intended above all to be a place where children in need of "proper parental care" were sent. Some of these children had gotten into trouble with the police, but others were simply homeless or lacking proper supervision in the judgment of the police and magistrates. This broad definition of the goal of the school, identical to that of other reform schools around the country, was essential to its mission. The basic point to be stressed in work with children, according to reform school thinking, was not guilt or innocence, but the fact that children were vulnerable and in need of care and guidance. On one level, though, such a position constituted an indictment of the child's parents, and the presence of the reform school represented a major intervention into private family life.[10]

Nor did the reform school do much to assuage parental anxieties about such an invasion. Ordinary citizens were free to visit the institution every Tuesday through Friday from 2:00 P.M. to 6:00 P.M., but visits from "parents, guardians or near relations" were much more restricted and permitted only in the presence of a reform school officer. "And the conversation shall be conducted in an audible tone of voice, and no conversation injurious to the character, feelings, or contentment of the boy shall be allowed." These restrictions implied that parents were at best a dubious influence on their children. The superintendents' reports over the years stated that opinion even more plainly, complaining about criminality, cupidity, and drunkenness in the boys' parents. The reports attempted, as was common in the reform school literature of the times, to assess the causes of the inmates' delinquency, and the list was wide-ranging. Everything from an addiction to circuses, theaters, and bowling alleys to bad companions, and sleeping out in barns, stables, under bridges or in "merchandise boxes" were named as causes of the boys' going astray. But the most basic cause of their problems, clearly stated, was their parents. The reports noted that many of the children had stepparents who made life difficult for them; others had parents who were in jail. One child lived in one room with twelve other family members. Most of the boys came from situations of parental indifference if not outright, deliberate corruption, according to reform school officials. The sympathy felt for the boys did not extend to their parents; typical of nineteenth-century child welfare thinking, the institution did not seek to strengthen family ties but worked rather to detach their charges from their home environment in order to reform them. The school was obliged to put up a fence "as a matter of self-protection," Superintendent Nichols wrote in an early report, "when we were so exceedingly annoyed by the parents, and friends of the inmates, on the Sabbath especially. . . . Some of our boys were told by their parents to escape the first opportunity that offered itself."[11]

The fact that the children were bothered "on the Sabbath especially" was probably no coincidence. Underlying the mutual distrust between parents and reform school officials lay a clash of cultures, the same tension between the immigrant, Catholic population and Protestant reformers that was played out in the public schools of the city. The Chicago Reform School, publicly funded as it was, was ostensibly nonsectarian; but in reality, it was Christian and Protestant in its moral instruction. The bible used was the Protestant bible; the "Our Father" in the school's devotional prayer book ended with the Protestant "For thine is the kingdom and the power and the glory." The Sunday services were conducted by the superintendent, with help from various Protestant ministers; there was no provision for Catholic children to hear mass or receive the sacraments that their church told them were the true means to salvation.[12]

Far from making any provisions for their Catholic children, in fact, the board of managers actively resisted the efforts of Chicago's Roman Catholic Bishop McMullen, who paid the institution an unexpected visit in 1859 to instruct the Catholic children there. The bishop announced his intention to visit weekly, which moved the board of managers to decree that no sectarian teaching could be permitted in their school. The bishop fired back a letter in which he challenged their ability to teach only a noncontroversial, generic Christianity. "What are, I ask, those great fundamental principles of the Christian religion on which the various sects are united? Consider a moment, and you will agree with me that they are a mere nothing. . . . I call anyone to designate any principle, great or small, of the Christian religion, on which the various sects in this country are united, or in which the better instructed boys actually in your school, or likely to enter it, can, in any wise, agree."

He went on to talk about such issues as faith versus good works, the need for sacraments, church organization and liturgy. Notions accepted by "Lutheran and Calvinist sects . . . are rejected by Catholics, Episcopalians, Unitarians, and many others who profess to be Christian believers." And what, continued the bishop, about those who did not believe in Christianity, broadbased or otherwise? Were they to be "excruciated, day after day, with a course of teaching which they reject and despise?" In a neat tactical maneuver, the bishop turned the tables on the Protestants, who so often accused the Catholic hierarchy of attempting to destroy democracy and the republic. "The Constitution," declared the bishop, "provides that Congress shall make no law prohibiting the exercise of religion."[13]

Despite the bishop's vigorous (and published) response to his banishment from the Chicago Reform School, the ban continued. In the year of the controversy, 1859, the annual report of the school did not so much as mention the issue. The report did note donations of such "non-sectarian" reading matter as the *Presbyterian Expositer*, the *Oberlin Evangelist*, and the *Puritan Recorder*, but the bishop's catechisms were not listed. His protest had not succeeded in changing policy; nor did it change in the next decade. The school was uncompromising on the issue of the kind of religious teaching that it would permit. And since a considerable number of the children were of Catholic parentage, this was an enduring source of friction for the institution. The first annual report, for example, noted that of seventy-seven children, thirteen were born in Ireland, and thirty had parents born in Ireland, whereas thirty-four children had parents born in the United States. The fourth annual report recorded twenty-three Irish children and seventy-six children of foreign birth; while the sixth report noted fifty-four children of Irish parentage, and one Italian child—all almost certainly Catholic. In addition, in the latter report, there appeared two children of Jewish parentage, who were presumably "excruciated" exactly as Bishop McMullen had predicted, with the Christian teachings of the school.[14]

A Roman Catholic industrial school for boys was opened in 1864, a clear response to what Catholics viewed as shameless pirating of their children. But immigrant children continued to be committed to the Chicago Reform School as well, and parental pressure on the school continued. Such pressure was clear from the tightening of legal procedures in regard to the institution. In 1861, a special commissioner was appointed to review the appropriateness of commitment before children could be sent to the reform school; earlier they had been committed by a fairly casual decision of the police court. In 1867, the law was amended to require that an allegedly neglected child must be brought before one of the judges of the superior or circuit court of Cook County, who was empowered to notify the child's parent or guardian to appear for a hearing as to the propriety of placing the child in the reform school. Even with these protections, many parents clearly felt that justice had miscarried, and the courts often agreed with them. Responding in 1867 to the question of what protection children had against unjust incarceration, Superintendent Perkins replied, "Only the right of *habeas corpus*. Recourse is not unfrequently had to it; about thirty boys have been discharged this way within a year."

This steady pressure greatly annoyed the reform school staff. Perkins's successor, Superintendent Turner, remarked bitterly that parents went to great trouble and expense to have their children freed on writs of *habeas corpus*, then neglected their care and upbringing exactly as they had done before the child's commitment. But the courts were clearly wary of the reform school's tendency to assess parental unfitness so freely, and this wariness culminated in the 1870 O'Connell decision that was handed down by the Illinois Supreme Court.[15]

The Supreme Court and the Issue of Child Neglect

Daniel O'Connell was a fourteen-year-old boy who had been sent to the Chicago Reform School on the grounds that "his moral welfare and the good of society require that he should be sent to said school for instruction, employment and reformation." His father, Michael O'Connell, petitioned for his release, and the Supreme Court, in a decision that was to have a major impact on child welfare in Illinois through the rest of the nineteenth century, decreed unconstitutional the law that allowed nonconvicted children to be held in the Chicago Reform School. Justice Thornton, delivering the opinion of the court, declared that the progressive management of the reform school was irrelevant. Placement there was still incarceration, and this incarceration was the issue

that the court must rule on. "Even criminals can not be convicted and imprisoned without due process of law—without a regular
trial, according to the course of common law. Why should minors
be imprisoned for misfortune?" Minors, he argued, could be held
responsible for their actions, "are liable for torts, and punishable
for crime. . . . Can we hold children responsible for crime; liable
for their torts; impose onerous burdens upon them, and yet deprive
them of the enjoyment of liberty, without charge or conviction of
crime?" The judges emphatically decided that the state could not.
"If, without crime, without the conviction of any offense, the children of the State are to be thus confined for the 'good of society,'
then society had better be reduced to its original elements, and
free government acknowledged a failure," Justice Thornton stated acidly.

On the subject of parental rights and society's responsibility to
intervene for the good of the child, Thornton argued for great caution on the part of the state. Before parental rights could be abrogated, "gross misconduct or almost total unfitness on the part of
the parent should be clearly proved." The subject of what constituted proper parental care was one that admitted of a wide range
of responses, the justice continued. "The best and kindest parents
would differ, in the attempt to solve the question. No two scarcely agree; and when we consider the watchful supervision, which
is so unremitting over the domestic affairs of others, the conclusion is forced upon us, that there is not a child in the land who
could not be proved, by two or more witnesses, to be in this sad
condition." Daniel O'Connell, the court stated firmly, was held
illegally and must be released at once.[16]

The Supreme Court decision was a stunning blow to the Chicago Reform School. For one thing, it was a surprise, quite out of
keeping with the general thrust of court decisions around the country regarding reform schools and the civil liberties issues concerning them. Virtually all other such decisions had confirmed the interventionist powers of the state.[17]

But most important was the fact that the Supreme Court decision meant the end of the Chicago Reform School as an agent of
delinquency prevention. Henceforth, only children who had actually been tried and convicted could be sent to the school. The 1871
annual report of the reform school was almost entirely taken up
with a critique of the decision. "It is not our intention to deny or
undervalue the recent decision of the Supreme Court of Illinois,"
Superintendent Turner declared unconvincingly, "but we say with

all due respect to that important body that such a decision has fallen upon the youth of Illinois like a blighting pestilence." The very heart of the reformatory system had been to take children in hand before they were hardened by time spent in jail awaiting trial (often as long as four to eight weeks) and by the publicity of the trial. Now, Turner lamented, the boys sent to the reform school were inevitably damaged to some degree by these experiences, and the institution's philosophy of education rather than punishment was completely undercut by the decision. Illinois, the superintendent wrote bitterly, "out of all the Western states, sends her wards to prison as convicted felons."[18]

Turner reported that the reform school was doing its best to remain true to its original principles, but the O'Connell decision was really the death knell for the institution. The Great Fire of 1871 destroyed much of the school, and the city sold the reform school land to the county. These events, combined with the radical curtailment of the school's original mission, discouraged the board of managers and convinced them that there was no point in rebuilding the institution. The boys who had been committed there to serve their court sentences were transferred to the new state reformatory at Pontiac.[19]

The Development of Industrial Schools

The Chicago Reform School staff was not alone in condemning the O'Connell decision. Justice Thornton had put the court's decision in clear civil liberties terms, but for the philanthropic community the ruling was regarded as a backward step for the two key reasons that Turner had suggested. First, it apparently put an end to institutional work with the "predelinquent" street children who were seen as more susceptible of reform than children hardened by both the commission of crime and the judicial process. Second, it forced back on reformatories the very distinction that they had been trying to avoid, that of innocent versus guilty children. In effect, the Supreme Court decision decreed that children were to be treated like adults, a major defeat for the child welfare community. To them, it ordained harsher, not fairer, treatment for children. If Illinois insisted on juvenile prisons, then prisons it would certainly have.

In fact, although the O'Connell decision cast a long shadow over child welfare issues in late nineteenth-century Illinois, it did not in practice have as much impact on events as reformers had predicted. Before the end of the decade that began with the O'Connell decision, the state had reasserted its right to deal with the neglected street children who caused so much consternation to the populace by authorizing the creation of industrial schools. In 1879, a girls' industrial schools act was passed, directed at the child "who begs or receives alms . . . is a wanderer through streets or alleys . . . who lives with . . . or consorts with reputed thieves . . . who is found in a house of ill-fame, or in a poor house." The industrial schools were not, strictly speaking, reformatories; but they were a mixture of reform school and orphanage, and in the law the General Assembly indicated its awareness of the O'Connell decision and the requirement for due process by providing that a jury of six men must assess the child's dependency before she could be placed in an industrial school. The industrial schools act was challenged in 1882 in the Petition of Alexander Ferrier, which claimed that once again, despite the O'Connell ruling, children were being imprisoned for misfortune. The Supreme Court, in something of an about-face from the earlier decision, decided to assess the nature of the school rather than just the fact of incarceration and decreed that the industrial school was "not a prison, but is a school." They did not see the care extended to the girls as imprisonment. "We perceive hardly any more restraint of liberty than is found in any well-regulated school." One point that was not discussed in the decision, but which probably shaped public notions about incarceration, was that both Roman Catholics and Protestants had industrial schools, and some care was taken to place children in schools of their own religion to avoid the sense of cultural and religious invasion that had provoked such hostility against the Chicago Reform School. Another aspect specifically mentioned in the judges' ruling was that in the case at issue the child had expressed a desire to go to the industrial school, and the mother's behavior toward the child had been so violent as to be outright murderous.[20]

After the Supreme Court's favorable decision in Ferrier, industrial schools flourished in Illinois. An 1883 act provided for industrial schools for boys, and with that law, the child welfare community and the state regained their former capacity to deal with the great numbers of street children who were proliferating in the constantly expanding city. The industrial schools were not without further court challenges, but they survived and prospered, taking over one crucial function of the Chicago Reform School, that of dealing with predelinquent children.[21]

The Response to Delinquency in the Late Nineteenth Century

The O'Connell decision's impact on reformatories was significant. "The state reform school at Pontiac is, by the decision of the Supreme Court of the state, a *prison* for juvenile offenders," declared prison reformer E. C. Wines in 1880. "Under the decision of the Supreme Court, the institution fails to meet the design of its originators and best friends." The O'Connell decision meant that the boys sent to the reformatory received fixed sentences, a practice inimical to true reform, according to penologists. It also meant that most of the boys would have been held in jail before trial, and all had undergone the experience of a trial.

Compounding this violation of reforming theory, the state legislature expanded the responsibility of the reformatory to include boys who had formerly been sent to the penitentiary for their crimes. Not only did boys at Pontiac range in age from ten (it had been eight before the O'Connell ruling) to eighteen; they ranged in experience from first time offenders to experienced miscreants. In 1891, the upper age was raised to twenty-one, making the mix of ages even broader. The problem of classification, of how to separate and protect younger, more vulnerable boys from older inmates, was a constant concern. It was a problem by no means unique to Illinois, but it was certainly aggravated by the reformatory's mandate to take the "hardened" boys who would in former times have gone to the penitentiary. The rapid increase of the reformatory population in Illinois increased the problem of classification and contributed to the prison-like atmosphere of the place. The Pontiac reformatory was a great disappointment to prison reformers who had hoped that it would be an experiment in progressive penology. In addition to serious overcrowding, the institution faced accusations of excessive discipline and brutality leveled against the staff. Illinois' reputation as a state enlightened in its care of juvenile delinquents was in eclipse after 1870.[22]

Like Pontiac, the reformatory established for girls at Geneva, Illinois, in 1895 suffered from crowding. Proportionately, the number of girls was much smaller than the number of boys (eighty-nine girls compared with twelve hundred boys), but the superintendent expressed concern almost from the beginning about overpopulation and the institution's inability to take all the girls who might have gone there. She stated the enduring problem of girls' reformatory institutions in 1902 when she declared, "I am now pleading for the good of these helpless girls who seem to be cast in the shade when the question of the boys is to be considered." Girls' reformatories had to battle for funds, because they were invariably smaller than boys' institutions. The same problem had been apparent with the Chicago Reform School. Although the board of managers talked for years about establishing a girls' division, they abandoned the newly established unit after only one year of operation, because they felt the small number of girls committed made the department impractical.[23]

In addition to the problem of size, there was generally a more pessimistic attitude about possibilities for reforming girls. Except for the fact that the girls sent to Geneva had to have been convicted of a crime or misdemeanor, the statute describing the girls who could be sent there sounded much like the law describing the proper subject of a girls' industrial school. But it was clear that one significant cause of placement at Geneva was sexual activity. There were two babies born the year the reformatory opened in Geneva, and the superintendent spoke delicately of "an illness . . . consequent upon the lives formerly led by these girls." The "efficient lady physician" who treated the Geneva inmates was more direct; she noted nineteen cases of venereal disease among the eighty-nine children in the institution. However shamefully exploited these girls might have been, there were still strong Victorian elements in American thinking that accepted the dictum that a woman's fall from the pedestal was invariably fatal. Many prison reformers had long held the notion that once a woman turned to wrongdoing, she was more degraded than a man, because evildoing was more a violation of her true nature. Even an optimist like New York Children's Aid Society worker Charles Loring Brace spoke despairingly of the possibilities of helping "fallen" girls: "There is no reality to the sentimental assertion that the sexual sins of the lad are as degrading as those of the girl," he wrote in 1872. "The instinct of the female is more toward the preservation of purity, and therefore her fall is deeper." Thus the staff and board of managers of the Geneva institution, although they spoke positively and cheerfully about the school's capacity to redirect their girls' lives, faced an extra handicap in soliciting funds and general support from the legislature, because the inmates, children though they were, had already been dismissed as "lost" by a sizable portion of the population.[24]

The reformatory institutions had their critics, but even more devastating for convicted children was a sentence in a city or county jail. As the reformatories got more and more crowded, the use of adult jails for children became a burning issue for philanthropists. All the problems that had led to the refuge and reformatory movement in the first place were evident in places like the Chicago House of Correction and the Cook County Jail. Children there mixed with adult offenders, exposed alike to the harsh conditions that prevailed and to the demoralizing influence of older prisoners. Because there were so few provisions for delinquent children in Illinois, and because of the nature of juvenile crime (according to one assistant state's attorney, the most common cases were "burglary, petty depredations upon freight cars, candy or bake shops, or stealing pigeons or rabbits from barns, hoodlum acts that, in the country, would be considered boyish pranks rather than a crime"), the grand jury regularly refused to indict seventy-five percent of the cases that came before it. Even with that average, however, the number of children in jail was striking. Children unable to pay fines were incarcerated, working off their fines at the rate of fifty cents a day. Those who could not raise bail were held pending trial. In the year 1898, there were 575 children in the Cook County Jail; in the twenty months from March 1, 1897, to Nov. 1, 1898, 1,983 boys passed through the Chicago House of Corrections. Twenty-five percent of the children in jail that year were committed for truancy. The Chicago Women's Club, in company with other child welfare reformers, had succeeded in persuading the board of education to establish the John Worthy School at the Chicago House of Correction in 1897 so that the children had some opportunity for schooling; but there were still no effective restraints on their association with adults when they were returned to their cells at night. When a new boys' building was constructed at the House of Correction in 1899, there were cells as well as dormitories included, underscoring the division between city and prison officials, who still saw their charges primarily as felons, and child welfare reformers, who wanted separate and special treatment for children.[25]

The prison architects might make their statement, but their insistence on the child as criminal was out of keeping with the dominant spirit of the age. Far more than in the heyday of the Chicago Reform School, the notion of childhood as a special stage of development sharply distinct from adult consciousness had great popular currency at the end of the nineteenth century. Children were seen as potential beings who were expected to be in school preparing for future contributions to society rather than at work.

They were perceived as vulnerable, and because of that vulnerability, they were the responsibility not only of their parents but of all adults, through the medium of the state. And above all in pre-Freudian America, they were seen as innocent; no matter how aggravating their behavior, they could not be held accountable for it in the same way that adults could, because it stemmed not from deliberate malice but from developmental limitations.

Gradually in the years following the O'Connell decision, the courts and legislature had been quietly reversing the Supreme Court's decision that children were to be treated like adults in matters of criminal law. The industrial school acts had extended control over a large part of the population once targeted by the Chicago Reform School. In 1891, the boys' reform school act was revised to allow for indeterminate sentencing; and the 1893 girls' reformatory act went even further and committed the girls to the school for their minority, unless they were released earlier by the decision of the board of managers. In addition, the description of the girls who could be committed was almost identical to that of girls sent to the industrial schools of the state.[26] In the judgment of most child welfare reformers, the time had come for a reassertion of the state's responsibility to act as parent to children in trouble with the law. The stage was set for the creation of the juvenile court.

5

Establishing the Juvenile Court, 1899–1925

In one sense it is ironic that Illinois, with such a paucity of effective responses to delinquent children, should have been the first state to establish a juvenile court, ahead of Massachusetts and New York, for example, which had been experimenting with probation and separate children's courts for a number of years. But in another sense, the juvenile court was the logical outcome of all the frustrations Illinois reformers had experienced in trying to work through punitive institutions.

In 1899, the juvenile court theorists essentially took the same stand as that held by the founders of the Chicago Reform School almost fifty years earlier, insisting that the crucial definition in dealing with children was not one of innocence versus guilt, but rather the state of childhood itself. They wanted to side-step the entire argument about criminal versus noncriminal children, which in their opinion had wreaked havoc with juvenile justice in Illinois, and shift the focus back to the issue of childhood and to children's need for parental care.

The theory behind the juvenile court was precisely that of the Chicago Reform School, the idea that children misbehaved because of a want of parental guidance and that the state must intercede and supply the parental care that was missing. And like the Chicago Reform School, the court saw its mission as essentially preventative; the hope was to reach children while they were young and malleable, before they were so steeped in bad habits and the ways of the criminal world that their reformation would be impossible to accomplish.

But though the juvenile court represented a revival of the *parens patriae* assumptions of the Chicago Reform School, the method proposed by Progressive reformers was markedly different from an earlier time and reflected changing American attitudes about a number of social issues. One crucial difference was that the reformation process was not assigned to a specialized institution like a reformatory. Institutions in late nineteenth-century America had lost favor with social welfare theorists, who felt that children should be kept in their families whenever possible.

The key technique of the juvenile court that replaced the nineteenth-century use of institutions was probation. By means of a concerned adult, representing and reporting back to the juvenile court judge, the troubled child and his family were to receive the support and education that they needed to channel the child's activities in a more socially acceptable direction. Reformatories and other institutions were not banished from the field entirely, but the articulated notion was that placing children in institutions was a last resort, to be used only after the possibilities in their own families or foster families had been exhausted.

This acceptance of the child's family as an essential feature in the reformation process also represented a change in social thinking. The inclusion of families was not without some moralistic and critical undertones, but the blatant hostility to parents demonstrated by the Chicago Reform School staff forty years earlier was no longer an acceptable part of reforming rhetoric. There was more expressed sympathy for the poverty of families, a greater sense that their economic condition had less to do with their own incompetence and moral failings than it did with economic factors beyond their control.[1] In 1818 the New York Society for the Prevention of Pauperism had used the phrase "Vice and its attendant, poverty." By the turn of the century, many Progressive thinkers would have argued that that phrase should read, "Poverty and its attendant, vice."[2]

In addition to a less punitive attitude toward poverty, Progressive social reformers argued for a more sympathetic and positive approach to ethnicity. Although it was by no means a universally accepted maxim, Americans were gradually coming to recognize that theirs was destined to be a heterogeneous society. The open hostility toward immigrant cultures and religions that had been so freely expressed in the early and mid-nineteenth century was no longer good form in social reform circles. Greater tolerance for ethnicity caused a shift in the attitude of child savers in their attempts to acculturate the children with whom they were concerned. Earlier work with dependent and delinquent children had concentrated on rescuing them from their environment, including their family environment, and recycling them with ruthless ardor into good Americans—which meant, among other things, good Protestants. By the 1890s although there were still heated struggles between immigrant groups and American Protestants, the coalition that created the Illinois juvenile court saw the immigrant block as a force to be reckoned with and deliberately worked for much greater amity than would have been conceivable to the board of managers that had barred the Bishop of Chicago from the city-run reform school forty years earlier.

Timothy Hurley of the Catholic Visitation and Aid Society, one of the prime movers of the juvenile court coalition, was included not only for his expertise but, as he noted in his reminiscences, because the coalition recognized that it was crucial to have the support of the Catholic church behind the new law, particularly since so many children in trouble with the law were likely to be of immigrant, Catholic families. The coalition further guaranteed sectarian support by stipulating that children were to go to families or institutions of the parents' religion "as far as practicable" when they were placed outside their homes.[3]

The juvenile court coalition consciously sought public approval for their efforts, but they were even more concerned about the judicial response. Julia Lathrop, whose State Board of Charities reports had done much to call attention to the plight of children in adult jails, declared that the proposed experiment had to be more than "a woman's measure" if it was to receive adequate support to pass in the legislature. The sponsors of the idea went to the Chicago Bar Association for consultation, and Judge Harvey Hurd ultimately penned the first draft of the law. The Chicago Women's Club, which had been involved in the project from the beginning (member Lucy Flower had gone to Massachusetts to study innovative techniques there in order to garner ideas for changes in Illinois' procedures) set itself the task of educating and winning the city's judges over to the notion of a special court for children.[4]

The founders of the juvenile court, unlike the reformers of an earlier day, were extremely conscious of the constitutional issues surrounding the passage of the law and the possibilities of consti-tutional challenges. The entire point of the new law was to dis-pense with the notion of adversarial and criminal justice and re-place it with civil procedure and a setting where children needed no special advocate, because every person in the court would be disposed to act on their behalf. But just such an intention to protect children from the rigors of adult justice had been attacked in the O'Connell decision as a violation of basic civil liberties, and even though the O'Connell decision had been virtually reversed in practice over the years, the writers of the new act showed their consciousness of the ruling by providing for a jury of six (like those used for industrial school placement) if it was demanded by "any person interested therein" or ordered by the judge. Still, the jury provision was a token gesture, not much implemented in practice, a vestigial manifestation of civil liberties concerns.

Industrial schools and reformatories, which claimed exclusive wardship over their inmates, posed a more serious concern for the court founders. The final juvenile court law finessed this point. The law provided that if a child was committed to an institution, the court would appoint the institution's superintendent guardian of the person, thus in effect relinquishing court control of the child. It also provided, in an effort to assuage institutions' anxieties, that the Juvenile Court Law did not supersede any existing industrial school or reformatory legislation, laws that had given guardianship of the child to specific institutions. But a contradictory section of the law reserved ultimate guardianship, including the right to return a child home, to the juvenile court. Such a division of practical guardianship withstood the initial test of passage in the General Assembly, but the inherent confusion over which institutions had ultimate control of the child boded ill for the relationship of the court and the entrenched and independent-minded child care institutions of the state.[5]

A further constitutional issue that was to surface in later legal battles involved jurisdiction over children in trouble with the law. The juvenile court act claimed original jurisdiction over children in trouble, with the understanding that a judge could decide to remand a particular child for trial in adult court. This was specifically written into a 1907 amendment of the law. The court claimed the basic right to decide whether or not the child's offense warranted criminal trial procedures and adult treatment or whether the accused child should be treated with the special consideration due to childhood. This set the juvenile court on a potential collision course with the criminal court of Cook County, which also claimed original jurisdiction over anyone committing a criminal act within its domain.

The possible conflict, which indeed materialized in the course of time, lay not only in jurisdictional issues. At its heart lay the fact that the juvenile court assumed control over children up to age sixteen (later changed to seventeen for boys and eighteen for girls) without ever addressing the issue that the age of criminal responsibility was set at ten years. Instead of trying to change that law, they simply ignored it. Instead of tackling the difficult issue of what to do with a child or youth who had committed a violent or otherwise serious crime, they left an escape clause, a possibility of transfer to the criminal court.

It was really not the intention of the founders of the court to deal with children who had committed very serious crimes; rather, they were concerned about the broad range of children held in adult jails for deeds that were more a result of poverty, cultural misunderstandings, or childish misjudgment than of true criminal intent. The provision for transfer to the adult court, like the muddled compromise with the industrial schools and reformatories, helped to deflect opposition from the passage of the law; but it unquestionably left some philosophical contradictions in the founders' argument that children, because they were children, could not be held accountable for their misdeeds. One historian has compared the attitude toward children's justice to that of the treatment of the insane; in essence, she contends that if the crime is bad enough, society is prepared to live with the contradiction of holding accountable and punishing those whom they have designated as not responsible for their actions.[6]

In later years, the convoluted compromises and philosophical contradictions would result in public criticism and constitutional struggles, but in the actual preparation of the juvenile court law, such contradictions did not loom large. The reality of the court's creation was that its founders were dealing with a crisis situation and offering an experimental response. They wanted a mechanism to deal with the problems of large numbers of children exposed to the dreadful conditions in adult jails. In addition, they wanted a mechanism that would monitor and control the ever-growing number of agencies and institutions concerned with dependent and delinquent children; and they wanted to deal directly with troubled children and their families, thus avoiding institutional placement whenever possible. A legal solution was a natural choice because one major group, delinquents, was already involved with the law. Furthermore, on some level, virtually all children's cases involved the legal question of parental rights, and the Illinois Supreme Court had earlier demonstrated such a jealous regard for parental rights that reformers thirty years later could not afford to ignore it.

Another reason for considering the juvenile court a likely mechanism was that Illinois, to the regret of social welfare theorists, had never developed a public administrative capacity. Even if the legal issues could have been disregarded, there was no state agency to build on and little support to create one. So the founders chose a legal institution, county-based and still sufficiently parochial to allow for a sense of local control and civic involvement. They designed an institution that could review legal matters such as parental rights, while also acting as a direct social welfare agency and a monitoring and administrative unit. In retrospect, this combination can be seen to be impossibly ambitious. By the end of the first generation of the juvenile court experience, some critics were coming to the conclusion that the task assigned to the court was too big. But at the time of its creation, the chief concern was not to create the ultimate child care mechanism but simply to establish *some* means of dealing with the child welfare crisis at hand and to write a law that could get sufficient support in the legislature. If the law mandated more than could conceivably be accomplished, it was not the first or last law with this defect to pass the Illinois legislature.

In persuading the lawmakers, the coalition was supremely successful. Some legislators were initially wary, but by the time the bill, embodying its various compromises, came to the floor of the General Assembly, the supporters had achieved a mass conversion. The bill passed the House of Representatives unanimously, and only one lone dissenter in the Senate held out against the law that Timothy Hurley would later call "one of the most beneficient enactments upon the statute books of Illinois."[7]

Challenges to the Court

Twelve years after the juvenile court's establishment, in the midst of a heated political struggle over the court, Julia Lathrop declared that "this is, on the whole, the best equipped and administered court in America."[8] Most of the original coalition that created the court were inclined to agree with her, and certainly if imitation could be regarded as approval, the court had received ample confirmation in the establishment of similar children's courts around the country.

But the first decade of the juvenile court had not been without its problems and missteps, so much so that Lathrop warned readers in an introduction to *The Delinquent Child and the Home*, a Chicago School of Civics and Philanthropy study of the court's first ten years, that "after reading some of the children's histories published in the appendices, the reader may be tempted to exclaim with horror, 'The Juvenile Court is a failure,' though if his eye had first fallen on another group his comment would have been one of approval." What the study of the court and Cook County's delinquent children had uncovered was the enormous complexity of the problem. The extravagant hopes of the first decade had been tempered by experience, and Lathrop admitted that "the contrivances attempted as substitutes for wholesome, orderly, decent family life" were not always successful. Certainly "they never seal up the sources of delinquency."[9]

This tempered view was very different from the effusive enthusiasm of Timothy Hurley, whose book promoting the juvenile court idea had been published a few years earlier. Not only was delinquency itself perceived to be a more complex problem than originally thought. By the time the ten-year study was published, the court had been the focus of some bruising power struggles over questions of technique and jurisdiction.

One major source of conflict was the critical question of probation. The first probation officer of the court was Alzina Stevens of Hull-House, who, together with her Hull-House comrade Florence Kelley, had worked as a factory inspector trying to control child labor. The Chicago Women's Club paid her salary, and as probation officers were added, various Catholic and Protestant organizations assumed responsibility for their salaries. But in 1905, the legislature passed an amendment to the Juvenile Court Act providing public support for probation officers' salaries and making them subject to civil service regulations. A committee (carefully balanced among religious interests, according to Louise Bowen, who headed it) administered an examination to would-be probation officers, with the end result that Timothy Hurley of the Catholic Visitation and Aid Society was replaced as Chief Probation Officer by sociologist Henry W. Thurston of the Chicago Normal School. Added to that blow was the fact that not one Catholic probation officer had qualified to work with the dependent and delinquent children of Cook County, a very considerable percentage of whom were immigrant and Catholic. Within the juvenile court coalition, the delicate balance of civility was tipped. In her memoirs, Louise Bowen insisted that the civil service examination was fair and evenhanded in administration. It is clear, however, that the questions (calling for brief written responses) allowed the committee considerable latitude in their measurement. One example given by Bowen to illustrate ineptitude would probably

have sounded perfectly reasonable to most Illinois Catholics cir-
ca 1905: "Q. Why do you wish to become a probation officer? A. I
seek the position of probation officer because I feel that I am particularly fitted for the work, having had the charge of four boys
who bid fair to be criminals, and made priests of all four." Even
the ingenuous applicant who sought the position "because I like
the uplift business" was perhaps assessed more on the grounds of
infelicitous prose than genuine ability.[10]

The conflict over the civil service exam eventually righted itself, and an ethnic and religious balance continued to be an important factor in the composition of the probation staff. But probation became a point of contention again in 1911 when the Cook
County Board of Supervisors mounted a campaign against the probation department and its chief probation officer, John Witter. Bal-
lard Dunn, the president of the county Civil Service Commission
(which was controlled by the County Board) leveled charges against
the probation department ranging from incompetence and laziness
to child-snatching. A Hearst newspaper (although apparently not
a local one) took up the task of propagating Dunn's view, and an
all-out struggle ensued. The *Chicago Tribune* regarded the accusations with contempt. "The city of Chicago will want to know
what this city, which has Jane Addams, Julia Lathrop, Louise De
Koven Bowen, and hundreds of able, informed, active, high minded women and men, needs of a Hearst rescue," ran an outraged
editorial.[11]

Nevertheless the attack was concerted enough, backed as it was
by the County Board, the probation department's funding source,
to create a major uproar and put the juvenile court on the defen-
sive. The Civil Service Commission appointed its own investigator, and, in addition, a special investigating committee was appointed by the County Board to look into the accusations of family
destruction and child brutalization made against the court. The
Hotchkiss Commission, as it was called, made it clear from the
beginning that it was to be independent of politics, hewing to that
line throughout the ensuing investigation, despite its wry observation that "the atmosphere in which the committee worked has
not at all times harmonized with this calm and impersonal point
of view." The Hotchkiss Commission resisted the County Board's
pressure immediately to increase the number of probation officers, a fairly blatant attempt to gain control of the department. The
commission's assessment of the probation department was that it
did not so much need more probation officers as more clerical and
support staff in order to free the probation officers for actual work

with children and families. And although the report suggested improvements in the juvenile court, their over-all evaluation was favorable.[12]

The County Board escalated hostilities by removing Chief Probation Officer Witter for refusing to fire members of his staff targeted by the County Board. Witter's case went all the way to the Illinois Supreme Court, which decided in 1912 that civil service control of the probation department was an infringement by the executive branch on a judicial function and declared unconstitutional the civil service requirements of the 1905 amendment to the Juvenile Court Act, on the grounds that it violated the separation of powers clause. Because the decision supported the estimable Mr. Witter, the reformers who had worked for civil service control were in the awkward position of having to applaud the demise of what they had created. But the court devised a court-administered equivalent to the civil service test that allayed reforming anxieties, and the County Board was sufficiently chastened to back off from the fray. The hostilities were not completely over, but the scale of warfare was reduced to budgetary struggles after the 1912 Supreme Court decision.[13]

Another Supreme Court decision the next year also proved a victory for the juvenile court, despite the fact that the Supreme Court overturned the particular decision that the juvenile court had rendered in the case. The Supreme Court reversed a juvenile court order that had taken custody from a mother because she and her child were involved in what was apparently a religious cult. But the high court, while reversing the juvenile court's decision, upheld the Juvenile Court Law itself, contending that the act "does not create a new court but delegates powers to constitutional courts already existing." There had been efforts to pass legislation to make the juvenile court illegal, and as late as 1911, the Hotchkiss Commission had declared, "Eminent lawyers and jurists whose loyalty to the Juvenile Court Law is unquestioned have expressed grave doubts of its constitutionality." So the Lindsay decision was a major success, a validation of the juvenile court movement after years of bitter struggle.[14]

The New Court and the Treatment of Delinquent Children

While the juvenile court was enduring these various constitutional and political challenges in its formative years, it had to deal with numerous practical problems as well, chief among them the disposition of children brought to the court. Probation was meant to be the linchpin of the juvenile court system, and court supporters insisted that children should be kept at home whenever possible. But in reality considerable reliance on institutional care both for delinquent and dependent children continued after the court was established. In the first ten years of the Cook County court's operation, for example, 21 percent of delinquent boys and 51 percent of delinquent girls were committed to institutions.[15]

Recognizing the inadequacy of existing institutions for children, the juvenile court coalition worked toward the establishment of institutions that fit the philosophy of the court. St. Charles, a new reformatory for boys, was authorized in 1901 and began operation at the end of 1904. A parental school for male truants was established in 1902 in Chicago, although a similar school for girls was not established for fifteen years. The John Worthy School at the Cook County House of Corrections continued to operate until 1915, when it was replaced by the Cook County School for Boys. However, the John Worthy School was always a stopgap measure, since it was situated on the grounds of the jail and smacked too much of a criminal institution to fit the juvenile court philosophy.

Stopgap measures were often what the court was reduced to, as illustrated by the makeshift provisions for the Cook County Detention Home. Louise Bowen, in the relentlessly chipper prose that characterized the memoirs of her generation, told of the exigencies to which the Juvenile Court Committee was put to house and care for children who could not, by law, be placed in county jails but who had to await their hearings outside their homes. "It was very difficult to get the city or the county authorities to give us any money or necessary equipment for the Home," she wrote.

> The detention home's wagon had fallen apart to the point of losing its floorboards so I went to the county for relief and was told that this was a city matter and I must go to the Chief of Police. I went to his office and stood up against the wall all day; the office was full of expectorating gentlemen who occupied chairs and were rather amused at a woman waiting to see the Chief of Police. When I went to luncheon Miss Lathrop took my place in holding up the wall and we spun the day out that way until at dusk the Chief left by a back door.

Bowen finally saw the police chief, who sent her to the repair department; they sent her to the construction department, which sent her to the mayor, who sent her to the county commissioners. "After six weeks of seeing first one man and then another, in desperation the Juvenile Court Committee bought a new omnibus." The transportation saga continued with the city supplying impossible horses and a barn so small that the horses could not move in their stalls. "The whole thing ended in the committee buying its own omnibus, its own horses, renting its own stable and furnishing its own horse feed," she reported in disgust.[16]

Bowen told her story with cheerful resignation, but it illustrated one of the main objections against institutions—the difficulty of maintaining adequate standards when dealing with tightfisted legislators, city officials and boards of directors. The founders' initial energy and enthusiasm usually sustained an institution for a time— the devotion of the Juvenile Court Committee to the detention home is an excellent example of that—but those energies tended to wane after an institution had been established for a while, or they were closed out by other circumstances. Bowen spoke regretfully of the condition of the Cook County detention home at the gathering to celebrate the twenty-fifth anniversary of the juvenile court. The current staff were political appointees, she said, and as a result "the present Detention Home has every appearance of being a jail, with its barred windows and locked doors. Its attendants do not understand the psychology of childhood; they know very little about dependents and delinquents; their idea seems to be that every child in the institution is there for punishment."[17]

The 1920 Children's Committee, which had been appointed by the Director of Public Welfare to make a comprehensive assessment of child welfare in the state, had reservations about the boys' and girls' reformatories, too, although the committee ascribed the greatest difficulties to understaffing institutions rather than Bowen's complaint about patronage appointments. Both institutions desperately needed relief crews to give the staff a break from their twenty-four hour a day duty, according to the report. The assessors, troubled by a repressed and joyless atmosphere in the institutions, felt that such rigidities as the silence ordered during meals emanated from a staff too exhausted to foster a creative and constructive relationship between the children.[18]

Judge Julian Mack, who was the juvenile court judge in Cook County from 1905 to 1907, had specifically voiced a warning that it was incumbent upon those in charge of institutions for delinquent children to see that they did not fit the description given in the O'Connell decision on juvenile jails. But in circumstances where all services to children were strained by a constantly growing population, institutions were likely to be given short shrift.

Thus despite the insistence of the juvenile court supporters that keeping delinquent children in institutions was only meant to help, in practice it looked very much like an action against a youthful criminal rather than parental care to guide an erring child.[19]

The court supporters originally had great faith in the court's capacity to intervene successfully with children, and in early amendments they had broadened the scope of the law both by raising the age limit and by greatly extending the definition of delinquency. In the 1899 version of the law a delinquent child was "any child under the age of 16 years who violates any law of this State or any city or village ordinance." By 1905, the law read:

> The words delinquent child shall include any male child under the age of seventeen years or any female child under the age of eighteen years who violates any law of this State or any city or village ordinance; or who is incorrigible; or who knowingly associates with thieves, vicious or immoral persons; or who, without just cause and without the consent of its parents or custodian, absents itself from its home or place of abode, or who is growing up in idleness or crime; or who knowingly frequents a house of ill-repute; or who knowingly frequents any policy shop or place where any gaming device is operated; or who frequents any saloon or dram shop where intoxicating liquors are sold; or who patronizes or visits any public pool room or bucket shop; or who wanders about the streets in the night time without being on any lawful business or occupation; or who habitually wanders about any railroad yards or tracks or jumps or attempts to jump onto any moving train; or enters any car or engine without lawful authority; or who habitually uses vile, obscene, vulgar, profane or indecent language; or who is guilty of immoral conduct in any public place or about any school house.[20]

With this sweeping definition, the legislators demonstrated that they were determined to bring all the troubled children of the state within the sway of the state. But the expanded license to intervene did not necessarily mean that children received real help or optimal treatment. Child victims of sexual abuse, placed in reformatories not because of what they had done but because of what had happened to them, were a prime example of the way this expanded authority could be misused.[21]

And if reformers were hard pressed to provide compassionately for the victims of rape and incest, they were absolutely baffled by the problem of delinquent girls. That the juvenile court used its broad definition of delinquency in an interventionist way is illustrated by the story told by Judge Merritt Pinckney at the "Child in the City Conference" held in Chicago in 1911.

> Let me give one case that came to the Juvenile Court, as illustrating what I mean. Two of these girls, the older only sixteen years old and the younger fifteen, were seen at twelve o'clock at night in company with a Chinaman coming out of a chop suey joint down near the red-light district. The sight attracted the attention of one of our probation officers traveling in citizen's clothes; so he eyed the girls very closely. As they approached him, one turned to him and flippantly remarked: "I hope you will know us the next time you see us." He said: "For fear I may not, I will take you into custody now." And so these two girls came to the Juvenile Court.[22]

But once such girls had been brought to court, officials were at loss to know what to do with them. *The Delinquent Child and the Home* reported that from 1899 through 1907, only about 20 percent of boys put on probation returned to court, while 45 percent of girls were brought in again. "The figure suggests how little the court and its officers yet know of the real problem of the delinquent girl," according to former probation officer Henry Thurston. The authors of *The Delinquent Child* heartily concurred. "The subsequent treatment of these girls who have become familiar with irregular relationships if they have not actually experienced them, is a very difficult problem. For it is obvious that even if, because of the conditions surrounding her home life or the failure of the school or of the city to guard her, the girl herself should be held blameless, yet if she has had intimate knowledge of vice or vicious persons and of vicious conditions, she is not a safe companion for the child who is still ignorant and innocent." In the case of girls actually involved in prostitution "not only is there slight hope of rebuilding the body and spirit that they may follow clean ways of living and thinking, but there must be recognized the possibility of both spiritual contagion and physical infection."[23]

The child welfare community of 1910, despite the fact that many of them were avowed feminists, was no more prepared to deal with "fallen" girls than their nineteenth-century predecessors had been. According to *The Delinquent Child*, 81 percent of the girls brought into the court were brought there "because their virtue is in peril, if it has not already been lost." The elastic notion of delinquency allowed the court wide latitude in charging girls. The actual morals charges could range from prostitution to sex delinquencies, which might designate anything from active pro-

miscuity to the girl "who has fallen once." Prostitution was naturally regarded gravely, but in general it was clear that the case
of the girl in trouble was viewed more seriously than that of a boy.
"The delinquent boy . . . is frequently only a troublesome nuisance
who needs discipline but who, as the probation officer says, is 'not
really a bad boy'" whereas the delinquent girl "is in peril which
threatens the ruin of her whole life, and the situation demands
immediate action."[24] The immediate action was usually commitment to an institution, either the state school at Geneva or, for
Chicago girls, the House of the Good Shepherd or the Chicago
Refuge for Girls.

As interventionist as the juvenile court was in sending girls to
Geneva "until the critical years are past," there was very little
discussion or energy directed toward the upkeep of that institution; nor was much creative thought given to a more progressive
remedy for girls. The rhetoric of the juvenile court consistently
assumed that the court was devised for and directed to boys, so
much so that Judge Pinckney protested that "the delinquent girl
is the most neglected, the most important, and apparently the least
understood factor of the delinquent problem."[25]

In part this had to do with the reformers' mentality. A critical
part of their reform rested on the assumption that what was done
by children was not irreparable, that misbehavior was a natural
part of "child life." "A boy's will is the wind's will, and the period of wilful adventure must have its gusty way," wrote Julia Lathrop. But, she continued, it was not possible to take that resigned
attitude toward girls. The loss of purity was still regarded as virtually irreparable. In addition, girls posed two other difficult problems for the court. One was the danger of physical contamination,
the fear that, left on the streets, they would spread the venereal
diseases that so many of them had contracted. (The Geneva physician's report from 1908 to 1910 recorded that of 391 girls admitted, 185 girls had gonorrhea, 3 had active syphilis and 23 had gonorrhea and syphilis.) The other liability was, of course, the
possibility of pregnancy. ("Fifteen girls were sent here pregnant,"
reported the Geneva physician in 1912, "nine had had miscarriages
before coming here, eleven had given birth to children and three
had had two children.")[26]

The question of pregnancy so exercised the Geneva superintendent, Ophelia Amigh, that she spent an entire biennial report discussing it. In the most cataclysmic of terms she declared her belief that many of her girls were the product of bad heredity. "Many

claim that environment does the whole work of helping children towards the downward grade," she wrote, "but brought in close contact with these irresponsibles as we are from day to day, there is no contradicting the statement that heredity plays by far the most important part." She believed that the vast majority of Geneva's inmates were either feebleminded or "moral imbeciles," contending that the best solution was permanent institutionalization "where these poor misfits will not be allowed to become mothers of hundreds more of the same or lower grade of inefficients." She summed up her lament by declaring, "I hope no sickly sentimentality will keep our lawmakers from passing a bill if it is presented again, making the operation of sterilization legal on all who are pronounced by competent physicians and psychologists unfit to bear children or to procreate their kind."[27]

Amigh's report was written in 1909, when she was at the zenith of her influence. As the superintendent of the girls' reformatory, she was the reigning expert on delinquent girls in Illinois, and she vigorously propounded her gloomy message at every opportunity.[28]

She was soon to fall from grace. In 1909, an administrative change transferred the oversight of state institutions from the State Board of Charities to the Board of Administration. Almost immediately, Miss Amigh ran afoul of the new board, which demanded her resignation for a combination of financial irregularities and cruelty to the girls in her care. A former inmate charged Amigh with brutality, and after an intensive investigation, the board agreed. The Geneva superintendent had used a punishment called "the strong chair," "a combination of a ducking stool and the New England stocks," according to investigators. In addition, she had literally worn out rawhide whips on the inmates, charges the board backed by placing the whips on file in their office.

In 1895, before the girls' reformatory had moved to Geneva, Amigh had survived accusations of cruelty and an inmates' riot. Following this early challenge, she had enjoyed virtual autonomy for almost twenty years. Now, though there were some hints that the 1909 attack might be politically motivated (an accusation stoutly denied by the Board of Administration), her credit could not survive the charges leveled at her. She was removed from office, and the scandal surrounding the incident caused the state to forbid corporal punishment in all children's institutions in the state.[29]

The tone at the girls' reform school brightened considerably following this incident. The new superintendent assured her readers of her determination that the Geneva girls should "have every advantage that any modern school for girls can boast of.... And I am happy to state," wrote the new superintendent, "that with very few exceptions the pupils have shown their appreciation of the different attitude towards them."[30]

Professionalization and the Court

The early confidence of the juvenile court creators that a benevolent judge and vigorous and committed citizens could set a child right through timely intervention had definitely waned by 1920. In part, the easy optimism was revised by the heavy caseload the court faced, especially after the 1911 amendment that made probation officers responsible for mother's pensions. In part, too, the enthusiasm was tempered by the enormity of the problems that children faced. The chapter headings of *The Delinquent Child* tell the tale: "The Child of the Immigrant: The Problem of Adjustment"; "The Problem of Poverty"; "The Orphan and Homeless Child"; "The Child from the Degraded Home"; "The Child from the Crowded Home"; "The Child without Play."

The first simple optimism was also supplanted by a greater confidence in experts. Later writings stressed the importance of trained social workers and probation officers, contending that they, and not volunteers from the community, should be in charge of the court's children. The belief in expertise was bolstered by the development of psychology, with its attendant tests and scientific vocabulary, which provided a sense of technique that was missing in the "goodhearted citizen" mode of the early years. (The Geneva biennial reports mentioned in 1910, for example, that the girls were now given the Binet-Simon intelligence test when they entered. The 1920 Children's Committee noted that the girls "suffered from a fear and prejudice against 'having their brains examined.'" But given the draconian measures proposed for the unfit by their former superintendent, Miss Amigh, their suspicion was perhaps a commendable commitment to self-preservation rather than a primitive prejudice against science.)[31]

That the founders of the juvenile court would be susceptible to a "scientific" approach to delinquency was clear from Timothy Hurley's 1907 description of the "investigative and research phases" of the court:

Every Juvenile Court is a laboratory. Every one of its sessions is a clinic—of priceless value to science and society. The causes that produce delinquency, the infantile disease that in later years broadens into crime, are here diagnosed and tabulated. . . . The scientist engaged in his laboratory assiduously seeking some mystic vims to save mankind from physical disease, has not a higher or nobler mission than that which aims to check, and to reduce to a minimum, if possible to eradicate, the germs of child abnormalities which in their development are the scourge of society.[32]

Two years after Hurley presented this metaphor of the court as laboratory, the image became literally true with the establishment of the Juvenile Psychopathic Institute. This institution, which was established in 1909, was privately funded until 1914 and then taken over by Cook County; in 1917 it became a state agency, and in 1920 it was renamed the Institute for Juvenile Research. The agency's role was to study children sent to them by the court, to provide diagnosis and recommendations for treatment. The first director was British-born Dr. William Healy, who became one of the foremost authorities on the psychology of delinquency. Healy's concern was the individual delinquent, and his tendency was to look more at the particular family environment of the child for the cause of the problem than at the broader social setting. This case approach to delinquency, which downplayed the role of poverty, immigration and urban stress, would in later years conflict with a broader social assessment of the issue, but in the early years the two views existed comfortably side by side.[33]

Julia Lathrop contended that the most important role of the juvenile court was that "it lifts up the truth and compels us to see the wastage of human life whose sign is the child in court." *The Delinquent Child* study stressed societal factors that caused delinquency. And Judge Julian Mack at the twenty-fifth anniversary conference of the court declared:

The whole work of the juvenile court and its underlying conception is at best only curative. The court does not get into action until the child has gone wrong. The fundamental duty of society is to prevent the child from going wrong; the fundamental duty of society is to recognize the causes that lead to wrong-doing. The fundamental duty of society is to see what the economic basis is that brings the children into court and correct the economic wrong. Tear down your hovels and your slums. Give your working man the leisure by enforced limitation of hours of work to give thought to the raising of his own family before you step in and say he is not competent to deal with his own children.

This was certainly a call for social action, but the comfortable merger of social thought and psychology was illustrated by the fact that the conference also celebrated the fifteenth anniversary of the Institute for Juvenile Research, and the published papers were called *The Child, the Clinic and the Court*.[34]

Those gathered to celebrate the anniversary found much to applaud, but there were also criticisms about the workings of the juvenile courts throughout the country. Not all states as yet had juvenile courts, and not all courts within a state were equally efficient. Juvenile court effectiveness in small, downstate counties of Illinois, for example, was greatly limited by a lack of probation officers and services to offer children who were brought to court. Furthermore, in areas where there were limited facilities, children were still being held in county jails with adult prisoners, in defiance of the law.[35]

Other recurring concerns were the loss of community interest in the court and the public's desire for punitive action against children. The conference took place in the midst of the country's postwar "return to Normalcy." The hopes that Progressive reformers had had for this new decade which had begun with the triumphant passage of the woman suffrage amendment were fading fast. Louise Bowen noted ruefully, "I frequently said that if women had the vote some of the conditions which then existed would be done away with." In fact, she admitted, some conditions, like those of the Cook County Detention Home, were worse in 1924 than they had been a generation earlier. The millennium reformers had looked for had not come, and by 1924 they were facing a public opinion more conservative than any since the 1880s, overlaid with a patina of hedonism that they found bewildering and repellent. Not only was public opinion more indifferent to social issues than in the years before the World War; in addition, there were outright attacks on reform. Much of the reformers' cherished social legislation had suffered crushing defeats. The federal child labor law had twice been rejected by the Supreme Court, and protective legislation for women workers had been overturned as well, often by using the very suffrage amendment that they had struggled to achieve.[36]

"The court cannot serve its end unless it is sustained by intelligent public interest and cooperation," warned Julia Lathrop. But it was clear that the juvenile court did not compel public interest as it once had done. In part, the stress on professionalism and expertise had closed out the citizen volunteer, but the court was also suffering from the reaction that society was expressing against the reforming energies of the past generation.[37]

Perhaps the most telling discussion at the conference concerned the court's capacity for intervention. Miriam Van Waters, referee of the Los Angeles Juvenile Court and a national figure in juvenile justice, lamented that "the system has already become larded with tradition and encrusted with red tape." She argued that the critical concern should not be the legal mechanism but the ability to attract and keep superior people to staff the court. On the other hand, two judges, Cabot of Boston and Mack of Chicago, worried about the overly intrusive aspects of the court process. Cabot objected that courts held children in detention homes when they might just as safely send them home and allow them to return to court for their hearings. "Here is the state doing a constructive piece of work, showing them what true parenthood is, and it is disrupting the family to start with—taking them away from home for the first time." Judge Mack advocated caution, too. "It is the last thing to do with the wayward child to bring him to court," he declared, urging probation officers to settle as much as possible between children and parents and to use the courts only as a last resort.[38]

In reality, both these apparently contradictory problems were true of the juvenile court system after twenty-five years of development. As Van Waters noted, the court had become bureaucratic and unresponsive, losing the vigor and energy that had characterized the earliest efforts. Yet this rigidity did not limit the court's tendency to intervene. On the contrary, amendments had enlarged the court's powers, posing the challenge to family rights that concerned the judges. This combination of power and insensitivity would, forty years later, cause intense criticism of the juvenile court; but in 1924, there was still a general commitment to the innovation, even by those who expressed reservations. Advocates of the court agreed that it needed fine tuning. They would have rejected the idea that its basic structure was unsound.

The message of the anniversary conference was one of "good news/bad news." The juvenile court was an institution that was firmly entrenched, and those who gathered felt that the court could boast numerous successes. But much work remained to be accomplished, both in preventing delinquency and in treating children already in trouble. And there was a sense that the disorder of the World War and the increasing mechanization of American life exacerbated an already grave situation. "No one can blame the juvenile court," said Miriam Van Waters, "for the existence of these gigantic handicaps to normal child life: broken homes, premature mechanization, and war. Yet none can deny their rise and their influence during the growth period of the court. Surely no humanitarian ideal, no social discovery, ever had more adverse conditions under which to make a demonstration."[39]

Had the members of the conference been permitted a glimpse of the adverse conditions that the next generation was to experience, the mood of the anniversary would undoubtedly have been more sober than it was.

6

Harsh Measures, 1925–49

The Great Depression, despite its shattering effects on family life, health and stability, was a time of great progress in some children's issues. With the Fair Labor Standards Act of 1938, the United States Congress passed a national child labor act that withstood the hitherto unfavorable scrutiny of the Supreme Court and became the major law for the control of child labor in the country. Similarly, the Aid to Dependent Children provision of the 1935 Social Security Act essentially nationalized mothers' pensions and provided the basis for welfare assistance for children from that point forward. New Deal programs offered other possibilities for children and youth: aid to schools, nursery school programs, and job programs like the Civilian Conservation Corps and the National Youth Administration. But in the area of delinquency, the impact of the New Deal was absent, and so was the spirit of reform and optimism that accompanied it.

The 1930s in Illinois saw a return to a punitive attitude toward youthful offenders on the part of the general public, a sharp curtailment of the juvenile court's jurisdiction and a disintegration of the already overburdened state institutions for delinquents, as the dire economic conditions of the early 1930s continued into the decade with no substantial sign of recovery.

The Theoretical View of Delinquency

Even the academic studies of delinquency tended to have a negative impact on the general attitude toward delinquent children and on the view that the juvenile court was the best mechanism for reform. A major 1934 study by Sheldon and Eleanor Glueck, *One Thousand Delinquents,* followed the careers of their subjects for five years after their first encounter with the Boston Juvenile Court and found that 88 percent of the boys studied continued their delinquencies after their initial involvement with the court. "The major conclusion is inescapable, then," ran the sobering assessment, "that the treatment carried out by clinic, court and associated community facilities had very little effect in preventing recidivism." A similar study of the Cook County Juvenile Court showed that of the boys who had one encounter with the juvenile court, 52 percent had a record of adult crime ten to twenty years later. At two encounters with the court, the figure rose to 66.2 percent, and three encounters equaled a 73.5 percent adult crime rate; at four encounters, the figure rose to 89.7 percent.[1]

These studies and others like them did not lead the theorists of the 1930s and 1940s to total despair. On the whole, they firmly rejected the older notions of inherited criminality that had held sway in the late nineteenth century, as well as the idea that the vast majority of delinquents were feebleminded and needed to be controlled by eugenic measures like sterilization.[2] They did not see delinquents as a breed apart from other children. Rather, they argued, these children persistently reappeared in the juvenile justice system because the methods used to help them were not effective.

By the 1920s the older juvenile court vision of the volunteer probation officer who would offer friendship and common sense to children and their families had already been eclipsed by notions of professionalism and specialization. Continuing studies of delinquency emphasized the tremendous complexity of the problems and underscored the need for an equally complex response. Students of delinquency questioned the early view of friendly but nonprofessional assistance. They also questioned such basic assumptions of the early court reformers as the idea that poverty and crowding were invariably productive of crime, pointing out that in some European or rural societies such conditions did not have the same devastating effects as in American urban settings. Further, not all children in crime-ridden areas became delinquents. Scholars insisted that to devise an effective response to delinquency, analysis of the problem must be scientific and sophisticated, including a much broader range of factors than had been previously considered and encompassing both the physical and the social environment of delinquents. The basic analysis and the corresponding studies of delinquency divided broadly into two disciplines: the psychological, which emphasized the particular circumstances of children and their families; and the sociological, which sought to put delinquent youths into a broader social context.[3]

The psychological interpretation of the causes of delinquency was the primary mode of looking at the problem, since psychology in the 1920s and 1930s had become the theoretical base that social work adopted as its own. And psychology, although it generally argued for a compassionate, nonjudgmental and patient rehabilitation of delinquent youths, nevertheless contributed, however unwittingly, to the negative view of delinquency prevalent at this time. One aspect of psychology that modified the earlier, more optimistic view of delinquent children held by the founders of the juvenile court was the view of human nature and child nature proposed by psychologists, particularly by the Freudian psychologists who were in the ascendancy in this era. Americans at the turn of the century had seen children as essentially innocent—innocent savages, perhaps, if they were followers of child development experts like G. Stanley Hall, but innocent—free from sexuality, malice and culpability. It was the progress into life that corrupted people and wrought in them the appalling traits that formed the less lovely aspects of human nature. In contrast Freudian psychology, with its dismaying emphasis on infant sexuality and the rapacious and conflicting character of the young child, described a murky underside to the human character that was not acquired from bad experiences and surroundings but seemed to be present from birth. And granted these conflicting and disruptive tendencies, those concerned with child care in general and the care of delinquents in particular could no longer regard as authoritative the hearty, humorous, common sense approach of the idealized juvenile court judge. They believed that the problem required far more complex techniques.[4]

The most extreme description of what one author has called "Freudian pessimism about human raw material" was expressed by psychologist Joseph Jastrow in 1927. "No child can be permitted to grow up as nature made it and find a desirable place in human society," he wrote. "In this sense the original criminal is the child."[5] This was a far cry from the "angel child" of nineteenth century fiction or the resilient, amoral but malleable little savage described by G. Stanley Hall. Ironically, the up-to-date and modern Freudians, more contemptuous of the notion of sin than any generation that had preceded them, were closer in their view to seventeenth-century Puritans than they were to nineteenth-century romantics or turn-of-the-century child savers in their sense that childhood was not a stage to be applauded and admired but something to be vigorously educated out of the human species.

In addition to this significant change of view about the nature of childhood, the methodology of psychology affected the public debate about delinquency. Freudian psychology proposed a kind of archaeology of the psyche, an examination of submerged fears, anxieties, and desires. Its emphasis was thus concentrated on the individual and his situation, without particular regard for a social setting larger than that of familial relationships. This intensely personal interpretation of delinquents' problems tended to ignore the environmental factors that had so exercised people like Julia Lathrop and Merritt Pinckney. While for the juvenile court reformers poverty, immigration, and child labor were prime causes of delinquency, a psychological reading stressed such issues as unresolved Oedipal conflicts or other personality ailments.

Freudian psychology led away from a critique of society, seeking for causes of maladjustment within much narrower boundaries and, in the very use of the notion of maladjustment, making an implicit assumption that society as it stood was worth adjusting to. Psychologists eschewed the social reformers' interpretation of delinquency and were often suspicious of any social involvement. As one social worker of the time expressed it, "the most daring experimental caseworkers have all but lost connection with social obligation and are quite buried in their scientific interest in the individual as he has evolved through his own growth process."[6]

The quality that was most enticing about psychology was its ostensible objectivity and authority, its scientific perspective. But in reality Freudian psychology played a conservative, not a neutral role by directing attention away from social problems at a time when few families and children were untouched by the harsh economic realities of the day. Furthermore, the assumption of neutrality among Freudians has been sharply questioned by critics of later years who have pointed out that much of what purported to be pure science was in fact an intensely political interpretation. One widely used text book of the 1930s, for example, gave this list of maladjusted personalities: "paupers . . . many unskilled workers . . . dreamers and artistic types . . . deep thinkers—including many writers and novelists . . . moral reformers . . . radicals and agitators . . . peace-loving pacifists."[7]

Many of the more popular discussions of delinquency showed this same obliviousness to the social and economic crisis of the times. Whereas Miriam Van Waters had put the development of the juvenile court into a historical context for the court's twenty-fifth anniversary when she spoke of the stresses of world war, advancing technology, and family instability, in the 1930s the historical context was surprisingly absent. For example, the 1939 Illinois State Senate hearings on the problems of delinquency and the St. Charles Reformatory showed the same disregard for economic conditions that was evident in the psychological assessments of the day. In testimony to the senate's Gunning Commission, experts spoke of the problem of broken families, irresponsible parents and the social maladjustment of delinquents. An appended study of the economic status of the inmates' families gave the salient information that from 1934 to 1937, 55.6 percent of the families were dependent; 24.7 percent were marginal; and only 19.7 percent were self-supporting. Yet, no one mentioned almost a decade of depression as a possible cause of delinquency or as a possible reason for the apparent increase in the seriousness of juvenile crime. Nor did any speaker at the hearings even hint at the idea that some of the hostility expressed toward the reform school's inmates by the citizens of St. Charles and Geneva might be the result of class bias. The hearings took place in 1939; for years there had been labor struggles and strikes going on all over the country and pitched battles between workers and police in Chicago, just forty miles east. Yet no one so much as suggested that the fears about St. Charles delinquents expressed by these middle-class and prosperous citizens might have been connected with general fears about the lower classes. Nor was the issue of race brought up in this context, even though one-quarter to one-third of the boys at the institution were black. No social analysis was proposed nor any recognition of the effects of prolonged depression on family life. From the standpoint of a broader social perspective, the hearings could have been taking place on the moon.[8]

Some, however, did challenge the interpretation that saw delinquency only in terms of an individual's maladjustment to society. This resistance came especially from the Institute for Juvenile Research. The institute, in conjunction with sociologists from the University of Chicago, proposed a theory of delinquency that de-emphasized the maladjustment of the individual youth and saw delinquency, particularly gang activity, as a not unreasonable response to social circumstances. Particularly in disintegrating communities, where more positive community values no longer dominated and where laws appeared to thwart rather than foster individual well-being, it was likely that crime would appear and that what had once been merely group activity would become gang activity. The way to respond to delinquency, argued these sociol-

ogists, was not to see it as a malfunction of the personality but to
recognize it as a logical function of the social self and to replace
malevolent group activity with something more positive. The key
to this approach was that such group activities must come from
the community, not from outsiders intent on shoring up a collapsing neighborhood. The people must decide what measures needed
to be taken and what values their community wanted to promote;
they must further translate these ideals into specific opportunities for their children.

The project that resulted from this analysis of delinquency was
called the Chicago Area Project, begun in 1934 under the leadership of Clifford Shaw with the support of the Institution for Juvenile Research. CAP was a program of community action and delinquency prevention directed at four neighborhoods that were
experiencing extremely high delinquency rates. The CAP staff was
a mix of community people and eager young sociology and criminology students. (Saul Alinsky, one of the most notable and controversial of community organizers, got his start while working
at a Chicago Area Project site in the Back of the Yards neighborhood.) They offered such techniques as "curbstone counseling,"
street work with gangs that sought to meet the boys spontaneously
and on their own turf rather than in a formalized, institutional
setting. A major technique of CAP was to use older youth from
the neighborhood, sometimes young men who had actually been
in reformatory institutions, on the theory that they had standing
in the eyes of the community's young people and could understand
the problems that they were facing. The project worked to keep
issues of delinquency in the neighborhoods, to persuade policemen
and truant officers not to go to juvenile court with a case but to
work out a more informal settlement and a community solution.

Emphasizing as it did community control and the avoidance of
official intervention, the Chicago Area Project encountered considerable hostility from both police and professional social workers. While it continued for many years as a notable Chicago experiment, its principles were not incorporated into statewide
policies on delinquency until CAP itself became part of the Illinois Youth Commission in the late 1950s.[9]

Still, the CAP approach won the wholehearted approval of the
1943 committee that had been appointed to study the best way of
coordinating the various state functions in dealing with delinquency and delinquency prevention. One member of the committee,
Ernest W. Burgess, was a University of Chicago sociologist and

philosophically kin to the Chicago Area Project; and the report reflected this affiliation. The committee recommended that the state embark on a program of delinquency treatment and prevention that stressed the development of community-based programs for delinquency prevention, involvement between reformatory institutions and the communities from which incarcerated youth came (the report went so far as to suggest that the institutional and community staff should be rotated periodically), and clinical services for those children in need of specialized treatment. The report made it clear, however, that not every delinquent youth needed psychiatric or psychological counseling. The tension between the fields of sociology and psychology showed in the committee's criticism of a study of the Institute for Juvenile Research done by two psychiatrists. The psychiatrists had contended that only psychiatrists had the breadth of qualifications—education, experience, and sensitivity—to govern a heterogeneous staff like that of IJR. The committee criticized this "air of amazing arrogance" and noted icily, "Statements such as these may be good propaganda but their validity is not scientifically demonstrable and they certainly are not conducive to an effective coordination of the efforts of persons representing different disciplines." Further, they added (voicing the CAP heresy against the creed of the age), expertise counted for nothing if it could not be translated into terms that lay people and community leaders could understand.[10]

The Jurisdiction of the Juvenile Court

In legal circles, there was an even more virulent struggle over issues of delinquency. Psychologists and sociologists might argue, but both groups assented to the notion that delinquency prevention and treatment should be nonpunitive, and in that narrow sense, they were heirs to the juvenile court ideal. Such was not the case in legal circles. There the battle lines were drawn much more starkly between those who felt children should be treated differently from adults and those who felt that children who had committed infractions of the law had lost their right to special protections.

The argument for special treatment versus a renewed "get tough" attitude toward children in trouble centered on the proper jurisdiction of the juvenile court, an issue that was left so unclear in the original law that constitutional struggles were almost inevitable. In 1912, in the case of Lindsay v. Lindsay the Illinois

Supreme Court had affirmed the juvenile court's standing, but the real problem lay in the jurisdictional conflict between the juvenile court and the criminal court, an issue the Lindsay decision did not address. A 1907 amendment to the Juvenile Court Act had given the juvenile court judge the discretion to transfer a case to the criminal court, but the situation was unclear if the child was originally arraigned before the criminal court. Juvenile court judges Mack and Pinckney both contended at different times that the juvenile court law had in effect changed the age of criminal responsibility from ten to seventeen (eighteen for girls), which would imply that all children below that age properly belonged in juvenile court.[11] But the age of ten remained in the law, and the prosecuting attorneys of Cook County never acknowledged the juvenile court's claim of primary jurisdiction over juveniles, continuing instead to exercise concurrent jurisdiction with the juvenile court. If the police brought a case to the state's attorney rather than sending it to the juvenile court, and if the case seemed serious enough to prosecutors, they would institute proceedings instead of transferring the child to the juvenile court.

This practice was protested in 1920 by the chief probation officer, who pointed out that the most frequent conclusion of such prosecution was that the children, after spending time in the Cook County Jail, were either transferred to the juvenile court for disposition (sentence) or were put on adult probation. Despite this fairly benign outcome, complained the probation officer, the role of the juvenile court in protecting children from contaminating association with the adult criminal system and especially the jails had been thwarted by such a process.[12]

Juvenile court proponents hoped that a Supreme Court decision would put an end to such concurrent jurisdiction, but in the 1926 case of People v. Fitzgerald the Illinois Supreme Court confirmed concurrent jurisdiction rather than denouncing it. The court asserted that because the age of criminal responsibility was still set at ten years old, "the criminal court and the juvenile court have concurrent jurisdiction over persons charged with a criminal offense who are below the age of seventeen years." The Supreme Court did leave some specialized jurisdiction to the juvenile court, adding that if a child was already a ward of that court and committed a second offense, the juvenile court had continued jurisdiction in regard to the second offense.[13]

In 1935 the juvenile court of Cook County lost even this limited jurisdiction through an Illinois Supreme Court decision that came on the heels of a campaign to amend the Juvenile Court Act. "In Chicago, the cradle of the juvenile court idea," according to one dismayed proponent of the juvenile court, "certain forces in the community were attempting to abolish the court. Led by *The Chicago Tribune*, there are groups in that city aiming to remove the juvenile court from the roster of agencies which deal in a fundamental and effective manner with serious social problems."[14]

The enemies of the court did not succeed in the legislature, but they experienced a victory in the Supreme Court. The case at issue concerned Susie Lattimore, a fifteen-year-old ward of the juvenile court who was accused of murder. In fact, the juvenile court had transferred her case to the grand jury, but on a technicality the state's attorney presented the case to the Supreme Court as if Susie Lattimore were a juvenile tried in criminal court without permission of the juvenile court. Legal fiction though it was, that was the issue upon which the Supreme Court deliberated, and their decision was a stunning defeat for the juvenile court. According to the Constitution of 1870 the Cook County criminal court had jurisdiction over anyone ten years of age or older accused of a crime or misdemeanor. The juvenile court was a court of limited jurisdiction, said the Supreme Court, and the legislature did not have the right to confer on such a court powers that had been reserved to the criminal court by the Constitution. In other words, that section of the Juvenile Court Law that asserted jurisdiction over delinquent minors in Cook County was unconstitutional.

The Supreme Court decreed that, while the juvenile court and criminal court might continue to have concurrent jurisdiction in other regions of the state, the juvenile court in Cook County essentially existed by permission of the state's attorney. The juvenile court could deal only with those children accused of lawbreaking whom the state's attorney did not choose to prosecute. Lest there be any doubt about the mood of the Supreme Court that issued this major reversal, the justices declared: "It was not intended by the legislature that the juvenile court should be made a haven of refuge where a delinquent child of the age recognized by law as capable of committing a crime should be immune from punishment for violation of the criminal laws of the State, committed by such child subsequent to his or her being declared a delinquent child."

Whatever the Supreme Court might assert, it had assuredly been the intention of the juvenile court reformers precisely to create a haven for juvenile offenders. This goal was now in serious jeopardy and in People ex rel. Malec v. Lewis, a decision handed down on the same day, the court confirmed the stand it had taken in Lattimore.[15]

Juvenile court advocates in Illinois and around the country were badly shaken by this decision. A speech to the American Sociological Society in late 1940 lamented: "At the present moment, the Cook County Juvenile Court, the first of its kind to be established anywhere in the world, stands divested of all jurisdiction in relation to juvenile delinquents. It exists by the sufferance, so to speak, of the criminal court of that county. At any time they may care to do so, the judges of that court can remove from the juvenile court all children over ten years of age who are charged with any infraction of the law, including any misdemeanors."[16]

Some reformers proposed a constitutional amendment, while the Central Howard Association, a prison reform group, argued for new legislation to set the age of criminal responsibility at seventeen. Neither of these reforms came to pass; but the assessment in the fiftieth anniversary history of the juvenile court in 1949 gave a fairly cheerful reading of the situation. Although it had originally appeared that the juvenile court of Cook County was utterly undone by the 1935 Supreme Court decision, the history noted that in practice, the state's attorney had moved cautiously, prosecuting as adults only children accused of serious crimes.[17]

Nevertheless, the Lattimore and Lewis decisions were a measure of how far the mood of the state had swung from the days when only one dissenter had prevented unanimous approval of the Juvenile Court Act. At a time when Chicago (or at least the *Chicago Tribune*) was trying to present an image of cracking down on crime, at a point when the have-nots seemed to be more threatening than pitiful to many middle-class people, there was to be no quarter given to offenders because of their youth. The notion of kindly treatment to children in trouble lost ground with much of the public in the 1930s and 1940s, and with a Supreme Court that reflected those public values.

Institutional Care of Delinquent Children, 1930s and 1940s

The institutions that cared for delinquent children had always been the weakest part of the juvenile court reformers' new approach, and these institutions degenerated badly in the stressful years of depression and war that characterized the second quarter of the twentieth century. Economic troubles, staff shortages occasioned by the Second World War, and a general pessimism about children in trouble with the law contributed to the decline of facilities that had been assessed as less than satisfactory almost from the point of their construction. Two outside experts assessing the girls' and boys' training schools for the 1920 Child Welfare Committee investigations had commented—tactfully but pointedly—on the repressive atmosphere in both institutions, the overworked staffs and the general failure of the schools to offer much genuine retraining of the children placed in their care. In 1931 another child welfare committee, this time under legislative auspices, inspected the institutions again and returned an even gloomier assessment, without the cushion of tact and professional bonhomie that had characterized the 1920 report. The 1931 report expressed explicit concerns that the institutions were at best custodial rather than rehabilitative. The buildings were badly overcrowded, the atmosphere was repressed and stultifying, and only half of each day was devoted to education, a particularly grievous lapse in dealing with these children, so many of whom were contending with educational disabilities that contributed to their problems. The assessors found the staff to be overworked and underqualified, primarily patronage appointments, untrained in work with children. Living as they did so exclusively on the grounds of the training schools, they became "institutionalized" themselves, so used to thinking of boys as delinquents that "they cannot understand a boy's problems in normal life, nor help him attain a better adjustment."

One major concern about the training schools was a problem that had dogged reform schools for over a century, the issue of adequate and appropriate classification of inmates to insure protection of the more vulnerable children. At the St. Charles training school this constant problem was compounded by the fact that, according to the staff, perhaps one-fourth of the boys should never have been committed at all. Generally, this class of inmate came from downstate counties where there were no probation services and few foster homes or institutions for dependent children. Lacking other options and eager to save the county money, judges sent dependent boys and girls to the state training schools, thereby relieving the county of their expense. Such dependent boys shared St. Charles with older boys from Cook County who were sent to the reformatory after all other possibilities (such as probation and the Parental School) had been exhausted. Thirty-four percent of downstate inmates were under fourteen, compared to sixteen percent of boys from Cook County in that age bracket. The 1931 report gave this description of the consequent mix of population: "At one end of the scale we find older boys with established criminal records (one boy claimed 200 successful robberies before commitment) and at the other, mischievous, truant or disobedient lads who may never have committed an overt act. The combination is highly unfortunate."

The assessors were also concerned about the capriciousness of sentences that placed one boy at St. Charles for armed robbery while another youth whose crime might in fact be less serious could be placed in the prison at Pontiac. In part, they contended, this was due to a "get-tough" attitude on the part of criminal court judges and state's attorneys who tried the boys in criminal court; but it also resulted from a lack of placement space at St. Charles and the shortage of probation officers in many counties. To illustrate the need for probation services, the delinquency section of the 1931 child welfare report closed with the story of a boy "who broke into a filling station and stole $12 worth of merchandise and of whom the state's attorney wrote, 'Has no previous record. Father dead. Court believes he can be reformed.' The court gave that boy a one year to life sentence at Pontiac."[18]

The 1931 Child Welfare Committee had concluded that more and better facilities as well as better trained and better paid personnel were needed at the state institutions. None of these suggestions were implemented. As the Depression wore on into the decade of the 1930s, the issue became one of funding existing services of all kinds, rather than improving services to incarcerated children. The public schools suffered, the mothers' pension fund shrank and St. Charles School, isolated from public view and caring for a population less likely to elicit sympathy than other groups in need, steadily declined in quality. Overcrowding was a major problem in 1931. By 1937 the institution had 783 boys, while its stated capacity was for 677. As a result, boys who had been sentenced were held at the Cook County Detention Home until an opening occurred in the reformatory. In a masterpiece of understatement the Detention Home's 1937 annual report declared, "The boys resented being held in the Detention Home for months without having the time count on their period of commitment to St. Charles." The boys in fact resented their situation so much that they took two modes of action: they rioted and they launched a letter-writing campaign to friends on the outside to protest their situation.[19]

The large number of children housed in the Cook County Jail

was a further measure of hard times and the general indifference to the laws protecting children. The Central Howard Association found that 308 boys and girls of juvenile court age had been admitted to the Cook County Jail from 1938 to 1942, some awaiting trial in criminal court, some to work off fines for disorderly conduct or other minor infractions at the rate of a dollar a day, and some held for "safekeeping" on the authority of a parole officer or sheriff. (These were generally children waiting to be returned after escape from state institutions for the retarded at Lincoln or Dixon.) Black children, the study noted, were greatly overrepresented proportionately and were held for longer periods of time than white children.[20]

But the clearest reflection of a changing attitude toward delinquents was the Gunning Commission's hearings on the boys' reformatory at St. Charles. By 1939, there had been so many escapes at St. Charles that the citizens of the adjacent towns of St. Charles and Geneva were up in arms. The problem of runaways from the training school, together with other concerns voiced by a variety of constituents, occasioned the creation of a commission chaired by Senator Thomas Gunning to investigate and remedy the myriad of problems that the school was experiencing.

The commission hearings were a pastiche of views on delinquent youth, from the most punitive to the deeply sympathetic, and they demonstrated how grave the problems of the institution had become. One great concern of the citizenry in the surrounding towns was their perception that the school housed dangerous boys who posed a threat to the community. Community representatives insisted, vehemently and inaccurately, that St. Charles had been constructed as a home for dependent boys but had gradually turned into an institution for delinquents through careless placements. Another contingent asserted that the boys themselves had gotten tougher over the years, particularly since a 1919 juvenile court amendment permitted boys who had been tried and sentenced by the criminal courts to serve their sentences at St. Charles. The remedy of this latter group, a solution supported by a minority committee of senators at the hearings, was to build a maximum security prison for juveniles and to use St. Charles for dependent boys and those guilty of minor offenses.[21]

At the opposite extreme were testimonies concerning the inappropriate placement of dependent children, especially from downstate counties where there were few facilities for probation or foster placements and virtually no institutions for dependent children. This group argued, as had the 1931 Child Welfare Committee before them, that the worst possible treatment for these naive, often very young boys was to place them in an institution with older, tougher boys from the city. They objected to the use of St. Charles for the care of dependents and urged the Gunning Commission to devise community and county supports for the care of these unfortunate young people.[22]

A third aspect of the hearings had to do with the conduct of the institution, particularly with regard to the quality of personnel. The staff was almost wholly untrained and made up of patronage appointments. The gist of many complaints was that civil service procedures should be enforced to upgrade the quality of work with the inmates. The Urban League added another complaint, that of discrimination against black inmates and staff members. Testimony objected to the segregated cottages of the institution. Further, ran the argument, in a school that had a quarter to a third black inmates, there was not a single black housefather. The testimony charged that black staff members were dismissed capriciously and given inappropriate tasks, such as assigning a black recreational instructor to the job of garbage collector. With a handful of Jewish boys in the institution, the superintendent had enlisted the services of a rabbi; but black youths never saw a minister of their own race. And the black inmates were closed out of some of the most advantageous occupational training that the school had to offer. The superintendent of St. Charles denied these charges at length and in writing, but it was clear from Urban League testimony as well as other opinions presented to the Gunning Commission that the racial situation was far from healthy at St. Charles.[23]

The legislative response to such a range of problems was varied and contradictory, a jerry-built solution that attempted to satisfy everyone. One piece of legislation provided for Sheridan, a maximum security prison for young offenders deemed too dangerous (or too fleet-footed) to be kept at St. Charles. The new institution was everything that the most hardline critic could desire. It consisted of cells, stacked in two stories and outfitted with two machine gun turrets trained on the cells to control possible insurrections. According to the psychiatric social worker who was given the unenviable task of making the Sheridan facility an appropriate setting for juvenile rehabilitation, he and other workers promptly converted the gun turrets to storage bins for athletic equipment. But the message of Sheridan was clear, as much at odds with the thinking of the original juvenile court reformers as anything could possibly have been. Appalled at the frankly punitive philosophy conveyed in the prison's architecture, a 1941 special commission to study St. Charles remarked bitterly of Sheridan, "The committee felt that the present unit of Sheridan has no service to offer any inmate body which is expected in time to be returned to live in a free community."[24]

Responding to the concerns that dependent boys were sent to St. Charles because downstate counties would not fund their care in more appropriate settings, the 1943 legislature passed an act that reimbursed counties for half the cost of caring for dependent children. But they had at least in part undercut the motivation to implement this cost-sharing when, in 1939, they had amended the wording of the act establishing St. Charles as a school for delinquent boys to redefine it as a school for dependent, neglected, and delinquent boys. Faced with a policy that violated the law, the legislature chose not to stop the practice but to legalize it. At the same time that the lawmakers changed the law to include dependent children, they extended the upper age limit to nineteen, two years beyond the previous limit, to address concerns about first offenders who were sent to Pontiac when a more rehabilitative setting might have been tried.[25]

Thus the end result of the Gunning Commission hearings was the redefinition of St. Charles to make it, in effect, an even more unworkable setting than it had been, a place that was supposed to deal humanely with a whole assortment of boys from eight-year-old dependents to nineteen-year-old delinquents. Beyond elasticizing the inmate description, little was done to address the serious operational problems of the school that had surfaced in the senate hearings. It was not until 1941, when a boy was beaten to death by two housefathers, one of whom was drunk, that newspaper coverage and a public outcry forced a thorough investigation and reordering of the school.[26]

A blue ribbon committee of distinguished citizens, assembled to consider the problems at St. Charles, found little to justify the institution's designation as a training school. The issue that had brought them there was brutality, which they found in every aspect of the institution's environment. The staff was overwhelmingly made up of patronage appointments, untrained, poorly paid and overworked. The citizen committee disapproved generally of the harshness and repressive quality of the punishments meted out, but they were especially dismayed at the exhausting and futile physical labor that was calculated to engender a hatred of work in precisely that group of boys who should be learning the joys of honest labor. One punishment outlawed after the committee's reorganization efforts took effect was called "swabbing." It consisted of filling a basement half full of water and ordering the boys on punishment duty to soak it up, hour after hour, with buckets and burlap bags. They got no food and no respite; they worked until they finished or until they dropped.[27]

The committee also moved to improve the better classification of boys. So little information came with a boy upon commitment and so little time was given to assessing him that the policy until 1941 had been to place boys in cottages strictly on the basis of size. (The committee noted that in terms of record keeping, "The most accurate history of activities within the institution is the history of violations of rules or depredations.") The reorganization committee ordered recreation programs and combined the educational and vocational departments, emphasizing in-service training of the teaching staff and stressing the critical need for education in a children's institution. They replaced the superintendent and introduced five child guidance workers, although the vast majority of the staff was left over from the earlier regime.[28]

The 1941 reorganization of St. Charles did not cure all the ills of reform schools in Illinois, of course. The advent of war caused dramatic shortages of goods and personnel; it also increased the incident of juvenile delinquency because of disordered families (mothers working sevens day a week, fathers away at war) and, in the opinion of at least one expert, because of the emotional disorder engendered by the progress of the war itself.[29]

But certainly the 1940s saw a more sustained legislative examination of the problems of institutional care than had been true in the 1930s. The legislative child welfare commission active throughout the 1940s ordered reports on probation needs as well as intake studies of both Geneva and St. Charles. Among other things, studies found a disproportionate number of black youths incarcerated compared to their numbers in the general population; pointed out the use (and misuse) of Geneva as a maternity home and venereal disease treatment center; and urged the commission to order further studies as to the general workings of the institutions. But it was clear from the 1949 child welfare commission's assessment that although the commission had sustained an interest in the institutions for juvenile delinquents over the decade, mere legislative concern and study had not done much to resolve the significant problems there. In fact, one of the greatest improvements for girls came not from law but from medicine. With the advent of new drugs in the late 1930s, the annual report of the Cook County Juvenile Court remarked, it was becoming possible to keep girls at Cook County Hospital for the treatment of venereal diseases rather than sending them to Geneva until the disease was under control.[30]

The 1949 commission report spoke especially about the impossible assortment of children and youth at the institutions—inmates who were feeble-minded, psychotic, or dependent mixed with older, more sophisticated and aggressive delinquents, making individual rehabilitation virtually impossible. They urged the creation of a state administrative board that would oversee the actions of the individual reformatory institutions and make initial screening decisions to eliminate the inappropriate placement of children. They further urged a revision of the law that placed dependent children in reformatory institutions. (The legislature enacted such a law in 1949, reversing the 1939 law and outlawing the placement of dependent boys at St. Charles.)[31]

The spirit of the commission's report contrasted notably with the embattled note of the 1939 Gunning Commission hearings. The postwar report called for reform in all children's services and reflected an energy and sense of possibility appropriate to a victorious and newly prospering nation. But the commission was not prepared to gloss over the problem of institutionalization or to downplay the size of the task that lay before those concerned with child welfare. The summary of the state's activities in child welfare and juvenile justice on that fiftieth-anniversary year of the founding of the juvenile court was terse and uncomplimentary: "In the over-all picture, we must face the tragic facts of neglect, of suffering, and of the waste of opportunities and money which could be prevented. . . . Conditions exist which reflect grave discredit on a state which had the vision, the progressive motivation, to enact the first Juvenile Court Law in our country."[32] In short, said the commission, the state of Illinois was in a state of disarray.

Conditions at midcentury looked less promising than would have seemed possible to the optimists who felt themselves to be presiding over a benevolent revolution in 1899. Their concept of childhood had been sharply redefined by psychologists in the 1930s and 1940s, and concern for children subordinated to more pressing national and international issues on a practical level. "The Century of the Child," which writer Ellen Key had so confidently predicted early in the century, had turned out to be a misnomer for the years of international tension and economic upheaval that had characterized the first fifty years of the twentieth century.[33] At midcentury the fortunes of Illinois children in trouble with the law seemed as tenuous as they had been in 1899.

7

Rejecting the Parental State, 1950–90

As Illinois moved into the second half of the twentieth century, the focus on children's issues voiced by the 66th General Assembly continued, reflecting postwar confidence and prosperity and the primacy given to children and families during the baby boom.

In the 1950s, the rhetoric of intervention and psychology prevailed in the state's discussion of delinquent children. But the second half of the century was to see a replay of the whole spectrum of attitudes toward delinquency. In large part because the reality of intervention with troubled young people never agreed with the benign rhetoric of the official literature, theorists and reformers in the 1960s began to stress children's rights to due process and criticize the rhetoric of "helping" put forth by the traditional juvenile court advocates. These challenges to an earlier view of troubled children brought about some critical changes in law and treatment. But the sympathetic stance toward young offenders that characterized the reform efforts of the 1960s and 1970s was itself overshadowed by a sharp swing to the right both nationally and statewide and a much stronger public persuasion about the need to crack down on juvenile crime.

The Interventionist Phase: The 1950s

A major concern in child welfare was to systematize and order the scattered services provided for children in need. One step toward improving services for delinquents and delinquency prevention was the 1953 creation of the Illinois Youth Commission, born of the suggestions of the 1943 Coordinating Committee of the Department of Public Welfare, which had urged that the treatment of delinquents and efforts at delinquency prevention be linked in practice for more effective functioning of both services. This goal the Youth Commission sought to achieve, taking over the care of the state reformatory institutions for young people from the Department of Public Welfare and expanding placement for boys to include an intake and diagnostic center at Joliet and a number of forestry camps for boys with less serious behavior problems. In addition, the delinquency prevention arm of the agency, the Division of Community Services, sought in general to emulate the principles set forth by the Chicago Area Project in regard to community action; the Chicago Area Project itself became part of this agency in 1957.[1]

The point of the Youth Commission was to coordinate efforts in behalf of young offenders and potential offenders and to impose some control and planning on the scattered efforts of family courts, the staffs of the various institutions, the parole staff, and other aspects of the care of delinquents. This was a sizable task, as the assessments of the 1962 Governor's Commission made clear. The commission had been appointed because of trouble at Sheridan, the juvenile prison authorized in 1939 at the height of the "get tough" fervor in regard to juvenile crime. Since Sheridan was built like an adult prison and was intended as a maximum security institution for delinquents, it was hardly surprising that charges of brutality should surface there. Despite the Youth Commission's efforts to put a positive construction on the institution ("Boys of any age requiring close supervision and a great deal of help in developing self-control are committed to the Illinois Industrial School for Boys at Sheridan," a 1969 article on the Youth Commission stated euphemistically), those interested in a rehabilitative program for youth had condemned Sheridan from the beginning and continued to feel that it functioned merely to punish. A 1955 Chicago study of the reformatory institutions, for example, made a fairly upbeat presentation about what a mythical "Johnny" and "Jane" could expect from their respective experience at St. Charles and Geneva. But the terse comment about Sheridan was that such a cell block structure "is extremely expensive to construct and most penologists agree that it is unnecessary for any except perhaps the most desperate criminals."[2]

The scandal at Sheridan involved charges of brutality against the boys incarcerated there. In February 1961, the superintendent, the assistant superintendent, the school principal (the superintendent's cousin), the chief guard, and three other staff members were dismissed after a Youth Commission investigation substantiated charges of boys being beaten, confined naked in unlighted cells, and put on bread and milk rations. The Governor's Commission appointed as a result of this incident was asked to assess the entire Illinois Youth Commission, and although the commission concluded that the IYC should continue, and in fact should be upgraded to code department status in the state governmental structure, the report cited numerous problems both with the correctional and delinquency prevention functions of the agency.[3]

Many of the institutional problems had a familiar ring. At Sheridan, where conditions had triggered the investigation, things seemed to have improved under a new administration, but the commission objected to the prison mentality that still reigned there, objecting that the staff, frankly called guards, were there merely for security and did not participate in constructive recreational and other activities with the boys. Further, the investigation pointed out that 37 percent of the boys in this maximum security lockup were fifteen years old or younger; one was only twelve, and fourteen boys were thirteen years old. There were 302 boys at Sheridan on April 30, 1961, ranging in age from twelve to twenty-five. The younger boys in such a mix were both physically and sexually abused, stated the investigating committee staff person; such an impossible mix of boys "requires considerable rethinking of patterns of classification and institutional care provided in Illinois." A glimpse of the institutional mind at its most rigid was the eating schedule: the boys ate their "evening meal" between 3:15 and 3:45 P.M. and went without food until 7:15 the next morning, a sixteen-hour fast that the Governor's Commission regarded as "much too long a period between meals for adolescent boys."[4]

St. Charles, Geneva and the diagnostic center at Joliet all got somewhat higher marks than Sheridan, but the commission lamented the torpor of the institutions and their lack of creative or effective programming, especially considering the extraordinarily high ratio of staff to inmates (267 staff positions for 294 girls at Geneva). School was generally available only to those under sixteen, in part because of crowding, and the vocational training was limited. Crowding was a perennial problem, not improved by an increasing number of commitments to the IYC. There were, for example, 4,384 young people under its jurisdiction in 1961, compared to 2,147 in 1954. The Illinois legislature, ever-obliging, once again amended the law to fit a less-than-desirable reality when they removed the upper limit of forty boys per cottage at St. Charles in 1961. Consequently, some cottages had double the number of inmates that they were built to contain. Geneva suffered similarly, and the commission was particularly exercised about such overcrowding since it felt that the institutions, even if kept at optimum capacity, were too large for effective rehabilitation.[5] Running throughout this critique was a sense of frustration at the inertia and lack of engagement displayed by officials in dealing with institutionalized young people. The "convict haircuts" at St. Charles reflected this. So did the chilling description of Geneva girls turned away from the Illinois Research Hospital because they had delivered their babies en route from the reformatory and thus had "no further need for prematernal assistance."[6]

The findings of the Governor's Commission in regard to the Division of Community Services (delinquency prevention) were less dramatic but salted through with the same lack of ardor. The most effective community organization groups were in well-established ethnic neighborhoods and the suburban community of Rolling Meadows, while the Cabrini-Green housing project and the Lawndale area, which had experienced an almost 100 percent ethnic turnover from Italian and Jewish to black between 1957 and 1961, had only minimal success with delinquency prevention.[7]

The Governor's Commission thought that the IYC needed strong central leadership and stronger backing from the state in the task of rehabilitating youthful offenders. But though they criticized, they felt the Youth Commission should be retained. The IYC did in fact continue to operate throughout the 1960s, and in 1969 became the Youth Division of the newly created Department of Corrections.[8]

The same urge to unify and centralize that had inspired the creation of the Youth Commission had also moved the legislature in 1949 to write the Family Court Act, although this was in fact merely a renaming of the old and much amended Juvenile Court Act. The aim was to bring all the cases concerning children, such as adoption, and prosecution of adults contributing to the delinquency or mistreatment of minors into one court. In 1963, a year after the report on the Illinois Youth Commission was issued, the newly formed Citizens Committee for the Family Court released a study of the Cook County Family Court done for them by the National Council on Crime and Delinquency. Like the Governor's Commission, the National Council on Crime and Delinquency decided that the institution that they scrutinized was viable but in dire need of repair. The court did not function as a true family court, the study found. The change had been a change in name only. The court shared concurrent jurisdiction with the circuit and criminal courts on matters like adoption and prosecution of adults in child-related matters, and the family court exercised this jurisdiction very rarely. It had no jurisdiction over issues like divorce and child support. The assessors felt that the court as it functioned was in reality a juvenile court and not a family court, although they contended that a family court for Cook County was a plausible notion. Further, they were concerned that the family court lacked exclusive jurisdiction over delinquent children, since the Lattimore decision of 1935 had given original jurisdiction to the criminal court.[9]

In addition to jurisdictional questions, the assessors insisted that the family court law needed a thoroughgoing revision. Cook County had the distinction, they pointed out, of having the first juvenile court and the more dubious distinction of having the oldest juvenile court law in the nation. It was full of anachronisms and contradictions and needed to be overhauled and modernized.[10]

The study also examined the practical functioning of the court and found much room for improvement. It noted many staff problems, from judges who were overworked and who stayed too briefly in the court to master its complicated legal procedures to an overburdened and underpaid probation and detention home staff. The old issue of patronage appointments surfaced again, especially among the clerical staff. The study recommended unequivocally that such "political sponsorship" should be abolished. It pointed out as well the need to coordinate and unify the scattered functions of the court, to place the administration of the detention center and the family court under one general authority, rather than having the detention center responsible to the Cook County Board of Commissioners.[11]

As to the detention home (or Audy Home) itself, its philosophy might have been humane, but the conditions were so bad that the effect was punitive and repressive. The operation of the institution was geared to the conforming child, likely to be in rather short supply among delinquents. (The study noted wryly that "a child who can conform to the detention program without difficulties usually does not belong there.") The isolation cells especially appalled the reviewers. "The old solitary confinement cells at Eastern State Penitentiary are larger," they noted in dismay, "and in addition they had a small exercise yard available. Such facilities were condemned by Charles Dickens."[12]

The Dickensian quality of this punishment was underscored by the fact that dependent and neglected children, for whom the Audy Home served as an emergency shelter, could also find themselves in the isolation cells for misconduct, even though they were under the ostensibly benevolent protection of the state. The presence of neglected, dependent, and retarded children awaiting placement in state institutions complicated the running of the detention center and almost guaranteed abusive treatment for such wards of the state. No one approved of it, but it was a practice that persisted until 1968, for the simple reason that other existing facilities were so limited.[13]

The Audy Home staff were overwhelmingly patronage appointees; many workers were over fifty-five years old, lacking a high school education and with no training in the care of children. Both morale and the quality of work were consequently low, and the final assessment of the reviewers was that "the Audy Home staff, particularly the Superintendent and Assistant Superintendent, have been attempting a Herculean task against impossible odds. . . . They have not been given the means that would make success a possibility."[14]

The Due Process Reforms of the 1960s and 1970s

The family court study strongly recommended a major revision of the Juvenile Court Law, a revision accomplished in 1965. The new law was influenced not only by those seeking effective treatment for young offenders but also by a growing number of lawyers and judges who challenged the very notion of helping as it had been laid down by the juvenile court founders. So much criticism had been leveled at the concept of the court, according to one author, that the 1950s was tagged "the fearful fifties" by juvenile court defenders. Critics' objections focused on the miscarriage of justice that was possible when too much discretion was allowed to the court. They pointed out that because children were unprotected by due process rights, they could, in fact, be dealt with more harshly than adults. They could be detained without any kind of hearing for an indefinite period of time, they could receive longer sentences than adults for the same offenses, and they were deprived of the right to counsel and the right to appeal the court's judgment.

The heart of the matter was the notion of the state as benevolent parent, an idea that was open to wide variations in practice and highly dependent upon the judge's competence, the court's caseload and the available facilities. "Nobody wanted then [in 1899] and nobody wants now, to detract one iota from any child's existing rights," declared one juvenile court defender. Certainly not, agreed the more moderate reformers; the original juvenile court founders had believed that they were enhancing the child's protections. But the reality over more than fifty years showed clearly that in practice children's basic civil rights were sometimes jeopardized by the informality of the system.[15]

A more radical contingent of those who criticized the court was unwilling to grant the benevolence of the juvenile court reformers, however. These critics argued that the court had been set up for far more cynical purposes than those professed to the public. Though the creators may have argued their concern for children's welfare, they were in reality acting out of a sense of self-interest— out of the desire to preserve the influence of the private child care community, as one author argued, or out of a deep fear of social disorder that led them to seek to control the children of the poor.[16]

Although not everyone was prepared to accept a conspiracy theory of the juvenile court's creation, the evidence that the contemporary system operated harmfully rather than protectively toward children was mounting, and a particularly distressing feature of the issue was how effectively bad treatment could be masked by paying lip service to interventionist ideals. The 1962 study of the Audy Home gave such an example, quoting this bland description of the discipline techniques there: "Behavior problems within the institution itself are handled in such a manner as to lessen anxiety of the children, to prepare for the eventual release of the children from the institution, and to keep a well balanced and peaceful atmosphere in the living sections," ran the annual report of the detention home. "It is highly debatable," snapped the reviewers who had just inspected the grim isolation cells, "whether extended isolation lessens anxiety."[17]

In 1967 the United State Supreme Court in the landmark Gault decision summed up the argument against uncontrolled state intervention in regard to children in trouble with the law. The Warren Court, which had insisted on a number of procedural protections for adults (such as the right to counsel and the right to remain silent) gave a ringing denunciation of the juvenile justice system as it operated in practice.

The Gault case was a perfect example of due process violations in the name of helping. Gerald Gault was a fifteen-year-old boy accused of making a lewd and obnoxious phone call to a neighbor. He was on six months probation at the time of this accusation, because he had been in the company of a boy with a stolen wallet. He was arrested and detained overnight at the Children's Detention Center. His parents, who were not notified of his arrest, had to learn from neighbors of his whereabouts. At a hearing the following day, the complaining neighbor was not present, no formal complaint was made, no sworn testimony was taken, and no record of proceedings was kept. Later, there was conflicting testimony about whether the boy even admitted to the actual offense. After another brief hearing a week later, and with no access at any time to legal counsel, Gerald Gault was committed as a juvenile delinquent to the Arizona State Industrial School "for the period of his minority unless sooner discharged by due process of law." Gerald had in effect received a six-year sentence for a misdemeanor that could at a maximum have cost an adult two months in jail and a five- to fifty-dollar fine.[18]

In response to this tremendous disparity of treatment, Justice Fortas wrote for the court: "So wide a gulf between the State's treatment of the adult and the child requires a bridge sturdier than mere verbiage, and reasons more persuasive than cliche can provide." The essence of the eight to one Supreme Court decision (and in fact much of the spirit of 1960s reforms involving women and minorities as well as children) was captured in Justice Fortas's epigramatic contention that "unbridled discretion, however benevolently motivated, is frequently a poor substitute for principle and procedure."[19] In a sense, the Gault decision was the judgment of the second half of the century upon the first.

The Gault decision did not destroy the juvenile court nor completely equate the position of minors and adults under the law. In fact, later Supreme Court decisions such as the 1971 decision that a minor before the juvenile court did not have a constitutional right to a jury trial curbed to some extent the initial thrust of the Gault decision. But there could be no question that it had a major impact on the juvenile court. Gault was the spiritual descendent of the much condemned O'Connell decision of one hundred years earlier, with the notable difference that Gault was more in tune with the temper of its times. Whereas O'Connell had been roundly condemned, there was considerable agreement among those engaged in juvenile justice pursuits that the Gault decision was wise and necessary.[20]

The 1965 Illinois Juvenile Court Act reflected this consensus in the protections it accorded to juveniles two years before the

Gault decision made such protections imperative. According to a League of Women Voters assessment of the new law, it sought to preserve "a delicate balance between the social aspects of the court and the legal requirements of due process and fundamental fairness in hearings."

The law guaranteed "the right to be present, to be heard, to present evidence material to the proceedings, to cross-examine witnesses, to examine pertinent court files and records and also, although proceedings under this Act are not intended to be adversary in character, the right to be represented by counsel. At the request of any party financially unable to employ counsel, the court shall appoint counsel."[21]

In the ensuing years these rights were strengthened on specific points, such as the provision of the Public Defender to represent minors needing counsel and the 1973 amendment that specified, "The procedural rights assured to the minor shall be the rights of adults unless specifically precluded by laws which enhance the protection of such minors." The new law made a point of using the term "minor" rather than "child" in recognition of the fact that the term child was inappropriate for older adolescents. Originally, the law had preserved the distinction in age between boys and girls. Despite a general acknowledgement that girls mature more quickly than boys, practical considerations had persuaded the lawmakers to declare boys adults at seventeen, while extending the court's protection to girls for another year. This inequity was removed in 1972, when an amendment standardized the age of delinquency at seventeen for both sexes.[22]

The Question of Status Offenders

One of the most important changes in the new law concerned status offenders, those young people who violated laws or ordinances merely because of their age—truants, runaways, children considered "incorrigible," or beyond the control of their parents. Such young people provoked agonized and heated controversy among the experts. From the time of the Chicago Reform School there had existed an argument that these were the children most susceptible to help. According to interventionists, predelinquent children who were on the brink of lawbreaking could be stopped and trained into good behavior and a more socially responsible attitude. In 1870 the Illinois Supreme Court temporarily halted involvement with predelinquents, but the first Juvenile Court Act, especially through its early amendments, greatly extended the interventionist power of the state on the grounds that an assessment of delinquency was not an indictment of the child but a recognition of the need for help. But the reality was, as critics of this broad definition of delinquency pointed out, that an encounter with the state rarely edified. Once young people became involved with the system, their troubles escalated rather than improved, and adolescents with relatively minor offenses could find themselves incarcerated in the state's training schools.[23]

The 1965 Illinois Juvenile Court Act deliberately separated status offenders from minors who had committed delinquent acts, seeking to retain some state capacity to intercede but in essence decriminalizing the new category "Minors in Need of Supervision." The creation of the MINS category required a tacit and somewhat uncomfortable admission that the issue of delinquency was indeed an issue of guilt versus innocence; but the thrust of the procedural reforms of the 1960s was away from wishful thinking and toward a confrontation with unpleasant realities. Furthermore, the youth movement of the 1960s caused a reassessment of older societal values, designating such virtues as sexual purity and filial obedience as strictly private matters, beyond the scope of the court. During the turbulent times of the 1960s and early 1970s the phenomenon of runaways increased as well, bringing home to the middle class some of the hazards that young people faced not only when they were on the streets but after they had been "rescued" by the authorities. So strongly did the issue loom that the federal Juvenile Justice and Delinquency Prevention Act of 1974 provided a federal assistance program "to deal with the problems of runaway youth."[24]

It was one thing to talk about decriminalizing status offenders; it was quite another thing, as those who dealt with runaways and MINS discovered, to keep young people out of punitive entanglements with the state. The difficulty was that a minor classified as MINS (or PINS, JINS, YINS, CINS in the acronyms of other states) was noncriminal until he or she defied a court order. But a runaway who was told by the judge to stay put or a truant ordered back to school could become delinquent by defying that court order. And since a court order was just one more adult command, it was not unlikely that the young person would run again or skip school or defy a parental order and find that he or she was a delinquent after all.[25]

It was this insidious slide into delinquency that caused such frustration to juvenile justice practitioners and theorists. The Chicago Juvenile Legal Aid Office had made the issue of runaways a cause célèbre during the early 1970s, pointing out that one boy who was kept in solitary confinement at maximum security Sheridan and regularly dosed with Thorazine had originally found his way into the Department of Corrections as a runaway. The unfavorable publicity of the Legal Aid lawsuits gave impetus to the further decriminalization of status offenders; in 1972 the legislature amended the law to provide that even a MINS who had defied a court order was to be kept out of the Department of Corrections and dealt with by the Department of Children and Family Services instead. A 1979 law sought further protection for status offenders in prohibiting the preadjudicatory detention of status offenders in secure facilities.[26]

But in a 1981 assessment the Chicago Law Enforcement Study Group asserted that, despite Illinois' progressive approach to the problem (it was one of a small group of states that distinguished status offenders from delinquents), the juvenile court in Cook County was still failing to deal effectively with MINS. "We cannot expect the court to provide effective treatment in all MINS cases," ran the conclusion,

> but less than half the MINS actually received service, less than a fifth showed evidence of substantial positive change, almost three quarters returned to court after an initial MINS petition, and only slightly more youth received services during court involvement than before. In addition, multi-problem youth did not receive services as frequently as less needy youth with fewer identified problems, and less than five percent of the parents received services separate from their MINS children. With this sort of evidence, it is hard to argue by any standard that the court is fulfilling its mandate.[27]

The report suggested three possible modes of action:

1. To maintain the current level of intervention in dealing with status offenders
2. To remove status offenders completely from the purview of the court
3. To reserve the interventionist power of the court, while also including the minor's family within the court's jurisdictional authority and regarding court intervention as a last resort after all voluntary means had failed.[28]

The Illinois legislature, when it once again took up the vexed

question of status offenders in its 1982 session, opted for the third
choice as a compromise between those who felt that relinquishing the state's ability to intervene would be a betrayal of children
in trouble and those who felt that the only minors who would
profit from professional intervention were those who sought it
voluntarily and not through court coercion. The compromise created a new term, MRAI (Minor Requiring Authoritative Intervention) and set up an elaborate series of procedures to be followed
before "last resort" cases might find their way to court. The MRAI
legislation was posited on the presumption of plentiful and vigorous voluntary agencies to assist the MRAIs and their parents, but
this presumption was largely wishful thinking in that second year
of the "Reagan Revolution" when plentiful funding for social agencies was decidedly missing from the federal or state agenda.

Critics a decade later raised questions about the effectiveness of
the MRAI legislation, charging that in practice it might be self-de-
feating. Although no formal studies had assessed the program, observers asserted, based on both the low number of MRAI cases state-
wide and the increasing number of delinquency petitions, that
officials were sidestepping the complicated provisions of the MRAI
legislation and filing new cases under simpler and more punitive
delinquency charges. Status offenders were often involved in alter-
cations or petty thefts, making delinquency charges relatively easy
to file. Both because there were so few resources for MRAIs in the
community and because of a growing "get tough" mentality toward
young people in the state's attorney's office, critics charged, the legislation that should have further decriminalized status offenders had
ironically resulted in recriminalization instead.[29]

The Conservative Temper of the 1970s and 1980s

The reform years of the 1960s and 1970s had brought a growing awareness of children's rights to both professionals who worked
with young people and to some extent to the public consciousness. But the reform years had been a polarizing time, full of hostilities between the demographically dominant younger generation
and a contingent of older Americans bewildered and offended by
the criticisms leveled against them and against a society they felt
had helped them to prosper. While the 1960s was on one level a
celebration of youth, it was also a time of resentment toward the
disorder and disruption that came with changing times. This seg-
ment of the populace demanded "law and order," electing Richard Nixon (who was to prove in the long run an unlikely choice)

to bring a semblance of law-abiding tranquillity back to their protest-ravaged land.

The growing demand for law and order was also a result of the baby boom moving through its crime-prone years. The increase in delinquency as a result of the birth rate was an event that had been predicted by the experts, but it was also accompanied by an increase in the level of serious and violent crime. Between 1960 and 1967, according to FBI statistics, 49 percent of those arrested for serious crimes were under the age of seventeen. During the same years, the percentage of juveniles arrested for murder increased 56 percent; forcible rape, 38 percent; robbery, 96 percent; and aggravated assault, 121 percent. In Illinois where there was a sizable population of juveniles (Illinois, along with six other states, claimed 44 percent of the total juvenile population of the country in 1969) such statistics caused consternation.[30]

Pro- and anti-youth arguments continued throughout the 1970s, with the pro-youth contingent arguing that children fared worse than adults in the justice system and a growing proportion of anti-youth spokesmen, sounding uncannily like their forebears of the 1930s, arguing that the time had come to stop the coddling of young criminals and "crack down" on troublemakers. The movement gained in strength as the decade wore on, despite the protests of their opponents that since the last of the baby boom was moving out of adolescence, the crime rate among juveniles was in fact declining by the end of the decade.[31]

In 1979, in response to public pressure for sterner measures against juveniles, the Illinois legislature passed the Habitual Juvenile Offender Act, which provided that "any minor having been twice adjudicated a delinquent minor for offenses which, had he been an adult, would have been felonies . . . and who is adjudicated a delinquent minor for a third time shall be adjudged a Habitual Juvenile Offender." This law was only applicable if the third offense was "murder, voluntary or involuntary manslaughter, rape, deviate sexual assault, aggravated battery causing permanent injury, burglary, home invasion, robbery or armed robbery and aggravated arson." Minors found to be Habitual Juvenile Offenders were committed to the Department of Corrections to age twenty-one without possibility of parole.[32]

In 1982 the legislature made further revisions directed at increasing the penalties for crimes of violence. The most critical of these was the automatic exclusion provision, which declared that any youth fifteen years old or older who was charged with murder, rape, deviate sexual assault, or armed robbery when the armed robbery was committed with a firearm was excluded from the jurisdiction of the juvenile court and would automatically be prosecuted in criminal court. The history of the juvenile court had swung full circle once again. The Juvenile Court Act of 1965 had reasserted the juvenile court's right of original jurisdiction over minors and had specified that minors were to be sent to the criminal court only at the juvenile judge's discretion. This in essence reversed the apparently antiquated Supreme Court decision in Lattimore, which had given the criminal court the power of waiver. In 1982, the legislators went further than the Lattimore decision, creating an absolute situation by specifying the crimes that were adult in nature and removing discretion altogether from the courts.[33]

It was "among the most dramatic changes ever made in the history of the court," according to the annual report of the Cook County Juvenile Court.[34] But it was legislation in keeping with the spirit of the times. "National Trends Indicate Growing Hostility Toward Young People," warned a headline from *Youth Law News*, the publication of the National Center for Youth Law, a few years later. The writers cited among other things the fact that a fifteen-year-old murderer had been sentenced to death in Arkansas in 1985.[35]

Whether proponents of harsher legislation would have agreed with the center's generalization about hostility, they were clear about their intention to reverse what they saw as the soft and ineffective treatment of the "serious, violent, chronic delinquent." A report of the National Advisory Committee for Juvenile Justice and Delinquency Prevention appointed by President Reagan to review the Office of Juvenile Justice and Delinquency Prevention founded in 1974 argued that the effectiveness of the agency's first ten years had been vitiated by the tendency to concentrate on the wrong problems: "Over the past ten years the Federal government has funded or undertaken a wide array of programs ostensibly designed to deinstitutionalize so called "status" offenders, separate juveniles from adult offenders and prevent juveniles at risk from becoming delinquents. Much of what was done was good; some was not." Good or bad, argued the report, the efforts missed the crux of the problem, the serious, chronic juvenile offender. Almost entirely abandoning the language of rehabilitation, the report argued that officials needed to improve the ability to "identify, apprehend, prosecute and treat or incarcerate these juveniles."

The "runaway youth" of the 1970s, uncomfortable symbols of family stress and social disorder, had in the 1980s been neutral-ized into "missing children" whose faces haunted the populace from milk cartons, grocery bags, and subway placards. The issue of delinquency prevention, the president's advisors opined, "when perfected, might be the only effective means of controlling juvenile delinquency. However, until then, our urban society cannot continue to suffer at the hands of the vicious juvenile." The federal government's role, according to this advisory committee, was to concentrate on "vicious juveniles" and otherwise "to limit its role and to restructure its priorities and programs so that states and localities may be helped to set their own priorities and discover their own solutions."[36]

This report was very much in keeping with the philosophy of the Reagan administration, both in its argument against federal involvement in standardizing principles of juvenile justice and in its emphasis on getting tough with juvenile crime. (Alfred Regnery, the Reagan-appointed director of the Office of Juvenile Justice and Delinquency Prevention had, in joking recognition of this stern approach, sported a bumper sticker that read, "Have you slugged a kid today?" until he was forced by public outcry to remove it.)[37]

The president's advisory committee declared that their assessment of the nation's needs in regard to delinquency "evolve from no exotic view of delinquency, nor from some strange new theory about what needs to be done."[38] In this they were precisely correct. Their view was a very old one and had always been espoused by a portion of the population. What they proposed was a return to retributive justice, a persuasion both ancient and persistent. Like citizens of a much earlier age, they believed that the only way to deal with criminals of any age was by stern measures, and they refused to absolve children from wrongdoing because of youth and limited capacity. The state of Illinois had begun its official existence with this common law notion but had revised it thirty-seven years later in favor of a system that emphasized the child rather than the offense. In the course of the state's history the two sides of the impossible description, the child who is also criminal, had teetered up and down, with one era emphasizing accountability and the next generation stressing childhood as the critical factor to be considered. In a sense, the emphasis on the non-guilty condition of the status offender in the 1960s and 1970s carried its opposite, the concern for the guilt of actual miscreants, in its train. It was just as likely that the emphasis on retributive justice would in its turn be revised. Each new phase of juvenile justice was shaped by the conditions of its particular time in history, but the circularity of the argument came from the essential contradiction with which the actors had to contend. The basic element of child-hood was innocence, or, for the less romantically inclined, limit-ed capacity and vulnerability. The basic element of crime was will-ful malice against another. The essence of justice was to hold such a deliberate malefactor accountable for his or her actions. This could never successfully be done with children, because of the lim-ited capacities even of minors old enough and big enough to be extremely threatening. Thus those who argued for retributive jus-tice avoided the question of capacity and emphasized the "here and now" and the public's right to protection. Those who stressed the limitations of youth in determining the just and proper way to deal with a child in trouble emphasized the individual needs of the particular minor and the way the future would be shaped by present treatment. Each position had its pitfalls, logical and practical; each was built on a certain amount of unreality. And the public acceptance of such views was especially affected by the broader attitude and recognition of childhood that society espoused at a particular time.

In the late twentieth century, the country's mood was conser-vative, and the importance of children was reduced by the dramatic decline of their numbers in the population. To some they seemed expensive, unproductive and downright menacing. Yet American society had long paid lip service to the notion that children were the hope of the future, and the age showed a decided ambivalence about youth. On the one hand, Americans agonized publicly about violence done to children—by their parents, by lurking strangers. On the other hand, society was prepared to consider even execu-tion of a youth if he had been the perpetrator of a vicious crime. In 1989, the United States Supreme Court underscored the coun-try's unrelenting mood, upholding the states' right to execute mi-nors sixteen and older.[39]

The Illinois Senate, that microcosm of public emotion, ex-pressed these ambivalent feelings toward children in two votes of the 84th General Assembly in 1985. The senators unanimously passed an Infant Mortality Reduction bill; and they unanimously passed a bill expanding the list of charges that would automati-cally transfer a youth from the juvenile system to the adult crim-inal court.[40] The senators were prepared to give children a chance at life, it seemed; but if, somewhere along the line, things went awry—clearly, they were making no promises.

Part 3

Disabled Children

Tilton School Group, Chicago, c. 1885. Special Collections of the
Chicago Public Library.

8

From Hope to Fear, 1838–99

Like all the children of the state, handicapped[1] children
have experienced a wide range of official treatment over the years,
from the state's benign intervention in the mid-nineteenth century to the stark coercion of institutionalization and involuntary
commitment laws in the Progressive Era. Like other children subject to the *parens patriae* actions of the state, the story of handicapped children is a circular one, moving from the exuberant optimism of the first reform efforts to policies made in fear, then,
by the mid-twentieth century, returning to a belief in individual
rights and possibilities uncannily similar to the vision held by reformers a century earlier.

The history of handicapped children in the state illustrates especially the erratic nature of Illinois' response to children in need,
the lack of a coherent policy able to recognize and respond to every child requiring help. The state's support has been highly selective, determined more by random circumstances than by any
rational program. Historically, children desperately in need of assistance have been totally ignored while other groups, blessed with
powerful advocates or interested legislators, have fared much better. This scatter-shot approach, which has caused such a curious
imbalance in the state's response to disabled children and such
unevenness of treatment, was in evidence from the beginning.

The Origins of the Special Schools

It might be expected that the state of Illinois, which took such
a reluctant approach to its dependent children in the nineteenth
century, would have totally ignored the needs of handicapped children; but this speculation would be far from the reality. In fact,
the state took an early and energetic interest in its "afflicted" children, priding itself on setting the standard for activity in what was

then the northwest region of the country. Handicapped children were given their earliest legal recognition in the Pauper Law of 1833, which sought to fix responsibility for the needy firmly with their families and, failing that, with the township or county in which they lived. But it was not many years before the state legislature moved away from this parochial view of care to a far more energetic and experimental involvement with the handicapped. In 1839, the same year that the Pauper Law was strengthened to instruct overseers of the poor actively to seek out any handicapped children in need of aid, the state legislature approved the establishment of the Illinois Asylum for the Education of the Deaf and Dumb.[2]

The genesis of the school was different from that of the Chicago Reform School or the various institutions for dependent children that would be created a few years later, in that it did not emanate from a pressing need, but rather from the interest and benevolence that characterized the pre–Civil War reform movement that was in full force by 1839. The school owed its origin to the Honorable Orville H. Browning, a member of the state senate. Browning became interested in the possibilities for helping deaf children when he encountered an educated deaf man on a steamboat journey in 1838 and learned of the possibilities for educating a group who were otherwise doomed to isolation and to the legal status of infants, because they were so thoroughly cut off from communication with society. Intrigued, Browning corresponded with the superintendent of the Kentucky state school for the deaf in order to learn more about the prospects and requirements of creating such an institution in Illinois, and later that year he proposed his idea to the General Assembly, where it met with a warm reception in both houses.

The bill was signed into law in 1839, but after the first burst of legislative energy, the project languished. It took 2½ years before the board of directors acquired a site for the institution in the city of Jacksonville, and the school did not admit pupils until 1846. The biggest problem facing the board was financial. The economic troubles that began with the Panic of 1837 had hit the state with full force by the early 1840s and caused the board real difficulties when it sought to implement the legislature's instructions. Nor were their troubles over when the buildings were finally erected and open to students.

The first superintendent, Thomas Officer, found that he had to do some vigorous recruiting to convince parents to send their chil-

dren to the new school. Even after he had devoted his best energies to the task, the opening enrollment only numbered four pupils. The number of students increased slowly, hampered to some
extent by the requirement that families too poor to pay tuition
had to make a declaration of impoverishment to a justice of the
peace before the state would cover their children's tuition. This
experience was generally felt to be humiliating, and the school for
the deaf, as well as the other institutions for handicapped children
that were established later, eventually dispensed with such proof
and made tuition free to all state citizens regardless of ability to
pay.[3]

In addition to small enrollments, Mr. Officer's school had administrative problems as well. Although Officer was superintendent, the board of directors had established the position of steward to handle all the institution's arrangements beyond the school
room. This dual administration was anything but successful; the
warfare between the institution's two chiefs became so fierce that
Officer resigned in 1855, along with several members of the board
of directors.

The board, after a number of unsuccessful attempts to hire a
new principal, finally chose Phillip Gillette, a young minister who
was employed at the Indiana School for the Deaf. By the time
Gillette arrived, only 22 of the 107 students remained at the
school, and confidence in the institution was at an all-time low.
One of the local papers, reflecting the prevailing cynicism, remarked on Gillette's arrival that "acceptance under such circumstances was proof positive of incompetence and untrustworthi-
ness." Despite this unprepossessing beginning, however, Gillette's
superintendency proved to be a major force for the institution. The
state legislature abolished the dual administration that had been
so productive of hostility, and Gillette settled down to a tenure
that would last thirty-eight years and make the Illinois School for
the Deaf one of the foremost institutions in the country.[4]

Notwithstanding the internecine warfare that was going on at
the school for the deaf, the state increased its philanthropic commitment by establishing a school for the blind at Jacksonville in
1849. The school for the blind, like the institution for deaf education, began more from an aroused interest on the part of Jacksonville's citizens than from any crying need in the community.
Its beginning was fortuitous. A young blind teacher named Samuel Bacon arrived in Jacksonville in 1848 seeking employment. He
had been misinformed and believed that the newly constructed

institution there was a school for the blind; it was, in fact, the state's first insane asylum. Bacon visited with community leaders, who urged him to start a private school for the blind in Jacksonville with the aim of persuading the state to take it over. Within a year, Bacon and his supporters had won over the legislature, and the state school for the blind was established. Although the school for the blind did not appear to experience the growing pains endured by the school for the deaf, Bacon did move on shortly after the school became a public institution, replaced by Dr. Joshua Rhodes, who spent the next twenty-four years as superintendent.[5]

The Antebellum Reform Mentality

The mission of the two schools, as propounded in their respective enabling legislation, expressed clearly the mentality of antebellum philanthropists toward the handicapped. The purpose of the institution for the deaf, according to its creators was

> To promote, by all possible and feasible means, the intellectual, moral and physical culture of the unfortunate portion of the community, who, by the mysterious dispensation of providence have been born or by disease become deaf, and of course dumb, and by a judicious and well adapted course of education, to reclaim them from their lonely and cheerless condition, restore them to the ranks of their species, and fit them for the discharge of the social and domestic duties of life.[6]

The legislation creating the school for the blind gave a similar rationale:

> To qualify, as far as practicable, that unfortunate class of persons for the enjoyment of the blessings of free government, obtaining the means of subsistence, and the discharge of those duties, social and political, devolving upon American citizens.[7]

Both declarations show the strong consciousness of the republican experiment that permeated the American mentality in these early years of the country's growth and development. The sense of possibility dominated the antebellum years, the notion that in a republic all people had a right to develop to the limits of their abilities, not only for the sake of society but because all of them, even the most limited, had individual rights that were due to them. American George S. Sumner, writing from France to his compatriots in Massachusetts about the techniques and methods of Edouard Seguin, a French doctor who pioneered in work with retarded people, put the case for responsibility in a succinct and memorable paragraph. "For other nations," he asserted, "the education of the deaf, the blind, the infirm in intellect, may be regarded as a philanthropic provision, a complement to civilization,—for republics, it is an imperative duty—the necessary result of the principle on which they are founded, and by which they are sustained,— the principle of justice, that accords to everyone—not as a privilege, but as a right—the full development of all his faculties."[8]

In addition to the sense that even the most infirm people in a republic had a right to the fullest possible development, enthusiasm for care of the handicapped was given impetus by the fact that there were new and specific techniques to be tried in their education. In the same era, the care of dependent children in Illinois and around the country generally suffered because caretakers clung to the simpleminded position that for a child whose family had failed, all that was needed was placement in another family—any family—to right the loss and obliterate the catastrophe. But those who worked with the handicapped proposed no simpleminded solutions. What impressed philanthropists about the new experimental institutions was that they had something new to offer an age-old problem. Not only were they proposing kindly treatment for the children sent to them; they were also arguing that by means of new teaching techniques, their pupils would be able to learn, to break the isolation in which their disabilities had imprisoned them and go further than previous ages had imagined possible toward becoming self-sufficient individuals.

Only a year before the founding of the Illinois School for the Deaf, Dr. Samuel G. Howe of Massachusetts had first written in the Sixth Annual Report of the Perkins Institute for the Blind of his amazing success in reaching Laura Bridgman, a child who was blind, deaf and dumb, and almost wholly lacking a sense of smell. Howe continued the story of Laura's education with each succeeding report. She learned to communicate by means of a finger alphabet devised by Howe and eventually learned to read and write, knit, and play, to the gratification of a watching world. She was the first American child so thoroughly to transcend her limits, and she gained great renown. Everything that was written about her, according to Howe, was promptly translated into several languages. She met the governor of Massachusetts, as well as other notables, and she furnished a shining example for philanthropists of what was possible in the new age.[9]

Illinois might not have had such spectacular successes with

which to woo the legislature, but by means of the same techniques used in more established institutions, educators were able to send home for summer vacation blind children who could not only care for themselves but who could also read by means of a raised alphabet and deaf children who could communicate using a manual alphabet and sometimes even achieve oral communication. The improvements were visible and impressive. It was by giving student demonstrations before the legislature that Samuel Bacon had convinced lawmakers to convert his private school for the blind into a state institution.[10]

Because of the striking nature of their achievements, the experimental schools occupied a special status in the state, which the boards of directors and superintendents were careful to maintain by steady pressure. The boards for both the experimental schools reminded the legislature with each biennial report that their expenses were bound to be higher than mere custodial institutions. First and foremost, successful teaching institutions for the deaf or blind required skilled instructors, who were expensive and difficult to come by. Good will was not enough, they insisted, Superintendent Gillette going so far as to declare that a new teacher of the deaf was destined to ruin at least one class of students before perfecting the necessary teaching skills. The institutions argued the need for special equipment, ample space, even traveling funds so that the staff and administration might communicate with experimental schools in other states.

Each school had its own set of problems, unique to the disabilities of their students. Blind students needed far more uncluttered space for navigation than sighted students, an added cost to any institution; they were also less likely to be able to help out with domestic chores around the school than boarders in other circumstances. Deaf children could be expensive, too. In their silent world, they received no notice of impending accidents and tended to be very hard on the furniture and equipment of the school, Gillette noted ruefully. (Eventually, the school required parents to post a yearly bond covering any possible property damage that might occur that term.)

The funding of each school had originally been provided by allocating a percentage of the state common school fund for their upkeep, but this was changed to require the General Assembly to pass a special appropriation every two years. While this mechanism provided a needed measure of accountability, the superintendents acknowledged, it also caused irksome delays in building pro-

grams and made efficient planning difficult. Undoubtedly it resulted in a less than candid presentation of the schools' difficulties as
well, since it could hardly be expected that the institutions would
seek appropriations from the legislature with a story of mistakes
or failures, however much the school officials may have learned
from such errors.[11]

The Special Status of Handicapped Children

Despite the somewhat aggrieved tone used by the superintendents to describe the crying needs of their schools, the schools for
the blind and deaf were obviously the recipients of special treatment by the legislature when compared to children seeking education in the public schools of the state and certainly when compared to dependent children. There were, in fact, a number of
differences between the care of handicapped children and dependent children, both of whom, as a last resort, were cared for by
the provisions of pauper laws. The experimental schools for the
handicapped enjoyed prestige and aimed not merely to survive but
to distinguish themselves among schools for the handicapped nationally and internationally. They recruited talented staffs and
enjoyed immunity from political interference, despite their dependence on the legislature.[12] By contrast the Soldiers' Orphans'
Home, the only state funded school for dependent children in Illinois, was politicized from the beginning. The superintendents'
qualifications always had more to do with their political affiliations than their training in child care, and the maintenance of the
children furnished a perfect study in parsimony.

Another striking difference was that the schools for the handicapped did not vie with private schools to serve their populations
of children. For a variety of reasons, the state from the beginning
willingly took on the responsibility to care for handicapped children, and there was not the development of fierce rivalries that
characterized the various homes for orphaned and dependent children. In part this was because the founder of the first school was
a legislator and took his case directly to the legislature, thereby
setting the standard for state involvement. In part it had to do with
the fact that the institutions upon which the Illinois schools were
modeled were state supported. Perhaps another influence was that
so many pioneers in the field of special education were French-
men, operating out of a revolutionary mentality and rooted in the
notion of the state's responsibility to its citizens. Whatever caused

the precedent, the care of the handicapped in Illinois was early seen to be an issue of state responsibility, compared to the care of dependent children, which was generally left to the county or private agencies.

Religious sectarianism and ethnic consciousness produced a plethora of private child care agencies in the nineteenth century. But, as powerful as these factors were, both in public education and in the care of dependent and delinquent children, they do not appear to have caused much upheaval in the special schools. Blind students were taught a generic morality in their classes and encouraged to attend the churches of their choice on Sunday. Mr. Gillette of the School for the Deaf was not so broadminded. In fact, had his school been nearer Chicago, he would probably have done battle with angry parents at some point, since he was unabashedly evangelical in his point of view. At the Tenth Convention of Instructors of the Deaf, which was held at the Illinois institution, one of the school's teachers read a paper in which she insisted that "we have conceded more on this Bible question than opposing forces had a right to ask." She further challenged the opponents of religion in the schools with the ringing declaration that "if it be bigotry to say that all that is grand and glorious and progressive in our national life is the result of the hold that the Bible has had upon us, then we glory in our bigotry."[13]

She could not have gloried in bigotry with such impunity had she done so in a more populated area. But, despite the fact that the school statistics through 1886 counted 271 German, 161 Irish, 25 French, and 13 "Hebrew" children, along with numerous other nationalities that were typically Catholic or Lutheran, no religious controversy of the sort that dogged the caretakers of dependent and delinquent children troubled the staff of the School for the Deaf. Dr. Gillette, tucked safely away in southwestern Illinois, was allowed to have his way religiously, free from legal upheavals and private schools that might challenge his hegemony.[14]

Handicapped schools' attitudes toward parents also distinguished the special schools from institutions for dependent and delinquent children, though it would be too much to say that the superintendents' attitude toward parents was genuinely cordial. Gillette included the daunting information in one report, for example, that "persons accompanying or visiting pupils are not furnished entertainment at the Institution." And on the whole it cannot be said that the staff working with handicapped children was very sensitive to the anguish that was the cruel concomitant of a family's love and devotion to an afflicted child.[15]

The lament of teachers was that families were far too protective of handicapped children, anticipating their needs and waiting on them to such an extent that the children failed to develop independence. Teachers complained also of a tendency to indulge the conduct of a handicapped child, to permit much worse behavior than would be tolerated in a child with no disability, so that children frequently were very badly behaved by the time they arrived at the special schools.

The superintendents were impatient with the reluctance of parents to send their children to school, arguing that it was selfishness and sentimentality, not tenderness, that kept children home instead of at a school where they might experience real growth and learning. "No parents are more chary of entrusting their children to strangers than the parents of deaf-mutes," remarked Gillette, noting that "the ordeal of committing a deaf child to strangers is one of the most trying that ever comes to a parent." After forty years of witnessing such partings, he said, they still affected him. But he was not always so compassionate. In other reports, he spoke of the "gross selfishness" of parents, calling them indifferent and unnatural, unable to rise above their mere animal natures to provide opportunity for their offspring. "The pang of early separation is short," blithely asserted Gillette, who had only to witness, never experience, such a parting.[16]

By the 1880s, both the schools for the blind and deaf had moved to advocating compulsory education of handicapped children, looking to "the strong arm of the law," in Gillette's combative phrase, to secure for children the education that their parents would not see to.[17]

Yet despite the element of criticism and the growing note of coercion toward the end of the century, the special educators of the deaf and blind treated parents with considerably less hostility than did the philanthropists and staffs who worked with dependent and delinquent children. Berate parents they might, and regret their tendency to spoil their children; still, the educators of handicapped children, especially in the early days, bore in mind that these children were to return home and take their place in the community, generally under the family's aegis. Children from all the institutions, including The Experimental School for Idiots and Feeble-minded Children founded in 1866, went home for summer vacations in the schools' first years. Parents were asked their opinions of various innovations at the schools, and favorable replies were printed in the biennial reports. To be sure, there was a certain critical element, sometimes close to a note of contempt that sounded in the superintendents' reports when they talked about parents. But there was never the clear indictment expressed by the reform school superintendents, who flatly decreed that their charges' parents had failed in their responsibilities and had lost their right to govern their children. Nor was there the ruthlessness toward parents too poor to keep their children that characterized the nineteenth century child-saving movement and led the State Board of Charities to decree at one point, regarding a little girl found in an almshouse with her sick mother: "This is an example of a case in which the child should be rescued from pauper surroundings, even if the feelings of the mother must be sacrificed."[18]

Parents of handicapped children were on some level partners in the enterprise of education. Unlike the unfortunate mother in the almshouse, most of them had not sunk to pauper status. In fact, one point that the superintendents made frequently and proudly was that their institutions cut across class lines, serving the children of the prosperous as well as the children of the poor. An important aspect in the treatment of handicapped children that gave their parents a measure of protection against the overzealous intrusion of the special schools was that parents could, at any point, remove their children if dissatisfied. Thus, to a limited extent, the schools had to court them. And because the handicapped were not perceived to have the taint of poverty that so shaped relations with dependent and delinquent children, they were given the highest accolade that American philanthropic language could award: they were dubbed "deserving."

Repeatedly, the superintendents of the schools for the blind and deaf voiced their insistence that their schools were not asylums or charitable institutions. Their goal was education, and the children there were not to be pitied but enabled, so that they could return to the community and take their place as functioning citizens.[19]

They were, in the words of the trustees who oversaw the school for the blind "the most meritorious class of those who are public beneficiaries."[20]

The Experimental School for Retarded Children

The retarded, another group of handicapped children who gained recognition in Illinois in the years immediately following the Civil War, at first shared the experience of special treatment that the blind and deaf enjoyed. In fact, their supporters insistently compared them to other groups, pointing out that the state provided assistance to the insane, the blind, and the deaf while retarded children were "a class equally abject, equally deserving, and in all respects equally entitled to our care and support."[21]

Like the other schools, the Experimental School for Idiots and Feeble-Minded Children was the product of conscious philanthropy. The first building used was the former governor's mansion, generously provided by the governor's widow at a nominal rental fee, and the board of directors was composed of men of affairs. Like the older special schools of the state, it was experimental, insisting on the right to select only students who could genuinely profit from education. The stress on expertise and professionalism that characterized the older schools prevailed here as well. The first superintendent was Charles Wilbur, whose brother, Harvey Wilbur, had opened the first school for the retarded in the United States. Like the other special schools, the new experimental school was located in Jacksonville, although "retired and protected from the gaze of idle spectators" and all who might exhibit "offensive curiosity."[22]

The school for retarded children did differ in one way from the older schools. More than the schools for the deaf and blind, this special school arose from a sense of need. Both the state insane asylum and the school for the deaf had reported for some time the presence of retarded children sent to their institutions who required treatment elsewhere. There was a considerably larger population of retarded children than of other afflicted groups, judging from the census reports and the superintendent's estimates. It was hard, complained the experts, to get a reasonable estimate, because Americans regarded the presence of a retarded child as a disgrace and tended to hide them from the larger society.

The experimental school for retarded children could not hold out the hope that it would restore children as thoroughly to functioning citizenship as the special schools for the deaf and blind. But they hoped to make dramatic strides in teaching retarded children to care for themselves and learn decorum and cooperative behavior. The school aimed to educate all of its pupils to some extent, some even to the point of earning a livelihood.

Although the school was founded immediately after the Civil War, the spirit that prevailed was antebellum. Superintendent Wilbur, in arguing the need for the school's continuance to the legislature, expressed a reforming mentality very much in tune with an earlier age. He was profoundly optimistic, insisting that his work was feasible, and making the appeal to human rights that characterized antebellum reform: "But it should be remembered that they have human origin; that however they may differ in physical or mental or moral organization, they are yet human beings; that their degradation in the scale of humanity, however it may modify, constitutes no absolute release or outlawry from the duties or rights which belong to them as human beings; and finally, that they have a human soul—a human destiny."[23]

From the beginning there was an implication in the reports of the superintendent and board of directors that their school was treated by the legislature as something of an "also-ran" institution. Superintendent Wilbur's optimism was tempered by this and by the public's lack of faith in the enterprise, a skepticism fueled by misconceptions about the nature of the handicap. Retarded children did not evoke public compassion as blind and deaf children did. But nothing in the founding philosophy of Wilbur's school foreshadowed the change that was to come only a few years later when not only the populace but the professionals dedicated to the care of retarded people moved from the language of compassion to the language of anxiety and fear in calling for their care.[24]

The Hierarchy of Status among Handicapped Children

On some level there had always been a hierarchy of status in the attitudes of philanthropists toward the handicapped. Blind children, despite their disability, were not cut off intellectually from the rest of society, and it was this ability to communicate freely that made blindness, in a sense, the most reparable of all handicaps. The educators of the blind worried that blindness isolated children socially, turning them inward to an unhealthy degree. One of the later superintendents of the Illinois school repeatedly stressed the danger that the education of the blind could be too abstract and theoretical, leaving them totally unequipped to manage in the ordinary world or find employment.

Nevertheless, both teachers and the public clearly admired the intellectual prowess that blind children often demonstrated. The blind, asserted their well-wishers, were avid for knowledge, so much so that one superintendent assured his board of directors that such eagerness was "a usual concomitant of blindness. If the blind appear indifferent to any lesson, the teacher may rest assured that the lesson is at fault, not the pupils." The Illinois School for the Blind tried to offer a high level of intellectual stimulation to its students, to which end such illustrious speakers as Jane Addams, Edward Everett Hale, and Booker T. Washington participated in the institution's lecture series.[25]

Blindness was a disaster easily imagined by a lay person. Deafness, argued philanthropists, was in reality a far more disabling affliction, although it was perceived to be less devastating in the popular imagination than blindness. Superintendent Gillette of the school for the deaf complained that "the isolation of a deaf-mute in society is very inadequately comprehended." Yet both he and the State Board of Charities occasionally minimized the disability, Gillette by his assertion that deafness, which had once been "a calamity is now only a serious inconvenience" and the State Board in their rather facile attempt to assess the suffering experienced by various groups of disabled people. They felt that the insane suffered most, the retarded not much "however great the anxiety of their friends," the blind suffered solitude, "and the deaf and dumb did not appear to suffer at all."[26]

This surprising analysis underscored the double silence to which the deaf were condemned. Not only could they not hear; they could not speak, and therefore whatever anguish they felt was a matter for more subtle perception than most observers could achieve. Perhaps part of the reason for the cavalier attitude expressed by the State Board of Charities was the fact that in the nineteenth century, deaf people did not face the difficulties that the blind encountered when looking for work. The general expectation was that the professions and commerce were closed to them because of intellectual and communication limitations. But, according to a State Board of Charities report, "they nearly always are able to pay the cost of their living, by their labor, even without special training."[27]

The blind, on the other hand, although in a sense the aristocrats among the state's handicapped children, faced extremely limited prospects in the outside world. A few of the students became musicians. Others became piano tuners. But for the most part, work was very difficult to find for male students and harder for females. Those who counted on using the skills they learned at the institution (such as broommaking and caning) could find a return to the larger world a shattering experience. One outspoken superintendent, Professor Frank Hall, went so far as to declare that sending students out of the school to earn their keep was "a hollow mockery" unless there was some attempt to provide them with the capital and resources that every small business needed to succeed.

Because the blind had so much difficulty finding work in the larger society, and because blindness could strike at any age through accident or illness, the state school began to admit students over the age of twenty-one. Gradually a policy developed of accepting older "shop hands" who were not so much students as permanent residents. Various superintendents expressed doubts about the wisdom of this practice over the years, urging instead that a separate institution be established as a facility to care for the adult blind. Such an institution was opened in Cook County in 1896, receiving from the beginning more applications than it could accommodate. Despite evidence of popularity, however, the State Board of Charities took a stand firmly opposing the Industrial Home for the Blind. The board objected to a number of things about the institution, one issue being the unwarranted special treatment to the blind over other needy groups. But the board's strongest objection was to setting up residential and custodial enterprises when they were convinced that the blind did best when incorporated into the larger society.[28]

The State Board of Charities took the same attitude toward the deaf, insisting that they should be integrated into the community even if they themselves might feel a certain reluctance. To some extent, Mr. Gillette, the long-time superintendent of the school, agreed with them. The introduction of the oral method into the school, the training of children to read lips and to speak rather than to rely on signing, reflected a commitment to ultimate integration.

The controversy over the efficacy of the two methods was (and continues in the present day to be) a heated one, in part because of its underlying implications. Proponents of the oral method stressed the greater accord that a deaf person would have with the hearing world in being able to speak and read lips, thus using the common language of society. Those who expressed skepticism about teaching the oral method, as Dr. Gillette came to do after some years of offering the method at his school, pointed to the massive amount of effort necessary to achieve even minimal success with the oral method. Granted, opponents of the oral method said, sign language might cut off communication with the larger society; but with deaf students, whose disability limited their basic information so profoundly, it was critical to spend as much time as possible in learning. The emphasis was on giving information efficiently, not on what they saw as cosmetic touches to make the deaf socially acceptable.

Gillette continued to be a moderate on the issue of the oral method, including it in his curriculum and discussing the issue in a balanced way in his reports. But his writings reflected his sympathy for the tendencies exhibited in the deaf to draw together into an exclusive society. Gillette had some spirited exchanges with inventor Alexander Graham Bell, whose wife was deaf and who was a champion of the notion that the deaf must be included in the larger world. On the whole, the State Board of Charities agreed with Bell, applauding the establishment of a school for the deaf within the Chicago school system (the first of its kind in the country) and urging as much deinstitutionalization as possible to ward off a clannish spirit that they called "deaf-mutism."

The board also took Gillette to task frequently for what they saw as his empire-building tendencies (although they never put the matter quite so bluntly). Gillette insisted that there was an urgent need for expansion at his institution, and he regularly importuned the legislature for additions to the school. The State Board of Charities held to a view that if space was needed (an assertion of which they were not convinced), that space should be in a new institution, located in another part of the state. The board, which saw its mission not only to monitor the financial and administrative aspects of state charity, but also to engender a spirit of "scientific philanthropy" in the whole process, frequently reminded the legislature and their other readers what a disaster overgrown institutions could become—tyrannical, unresponsive, and all-around inefficient.[29]

The Growing Hostility toward the Retarded

When the State Board of Charities spoke of the retarded, however, the board's suspicion of institutions and desire to integrate special populations into the larger society evaporated completely. In the first days of the Experimental School for Idiots and Feeble-minded Children, the school was committed to teaching its pupils by the methods developed in older institutions for the retarded, methods that aimed to stimulate the senses and that were built on the premise that even severely retarded people had "human attributes of intelligence, sensitivity and will," which were "not absolutely wanting but dormant." Like the schools for the deaf and blind, the school for the retarded sent children home for summer vacation (both for economic and demonstration purposes) and assumed that ultimately their pupils would go back to their families or some other situation in the community.[30]

This assumption about the child's ultimate reintegration into society began to change fairly early in the institution's history. Within a decade of its founding, the school's board of directors and superintendent were talking about the wisdom of establishing a custodial department for people who could not profit from education but were in need of humane and intelligent care. By 1880, shortly after the school had relocated to Lincoln from Jacksonville, Wilbur was arguing against sending his pupils home for vacations, asserting that "they are permitted to be without restraint at home" and that all their training disappeared over the summer. He quoted the superintendent of the Ohio state institution, who argued that "a large proportion" of retarded people "ought to be all their lives in an establishment where their work can be utilized, their evil tendencies repressed and their weaknesses protected."[31]

Wilbur's change in attitude away from the earlier aim of integration and acceptance by the larger community was a phenomenon that was taking place almost universally among teachers of the retarded. Only Samuel Gridley Howe of Massachusetts, one of the grand old men in the special education field who worked with the retarded as well as the blind, remained fiercely anti-institutional and committed to an integrationist view in the care of the retarded. Upon his death in 1876, his successors in Massachusetts moved rapidly toward a custodial point of view.[32]

The rise of the belief in custodial care for the retarded and of the state's need to intercede vigorously in their lives arose from a complex of circumstances and attitudes. One practical matter that moved philanthropists toward a belief in custodial care was the grim fact that the care of retarded people was often appalling. As one of its allotted tasks, the State Board of Charities inspected the almshouses of the state, reporting on conditions in the various counties. Some counties still followed the old practice of giving care of the poor and needy to the lowest bidder. This was certainly the most dismal provision, since it invited every form of cruelty and mistreatment without even the perfunctory check afforded by the county poor law officials' inspection.

But most of the almshouses were not a great deal better than the "lowest bidder" arrangement. The almshouse in most counties held the rejected of society, the old, the sick, the insane, and the retarded. Although the State Board of Charities would occasionally note with approval that an almshouse was clean and run in an efficient manner, more often their remarks were negative, ranging from the mild remark that, although the keeper of the

DeKalb Poorhouse seemed kind enough, "both he and the matron have mistaken their calling" to the vivid descriptions of almshouses so crawling with bedbugs and other vermin that the State Board inspectors advised that the buildings be burned. The insane and retarded, harder to care for than other inmates, were usually treated most callously. The inspectors noted a case where a retarded man was kept tied to a tree like a dog, with a collar around his neck, the tree dead from his circling and pacing. In one place, a retarded man was kept in a stall and only given attention on the rare occasions when the stall was washed down. Frequently the retarded and insane were kept in unheated outbuildings at a distance from the rest of the poorhouse, exiled and virtually ignored. At best retarded people in poorhouses were maintained; at worst they were treated with a casual brutality that made their lives a misery.[33]

On the care of retarded children in their family homes, opinion varied widely. Samuel Howe had contended to the Massachusetts legislature that in poor homes especially the retarded were badly treated. The Illinois State Board of Charities and Superintendent Wilbur did not repeat that accusation; both the superintendent and the State Board remarked that families often behaved kindly and protectively to their retarded children. Their greatest concern was that the care of a retarded child could so consume a family's time and resources that they would be left destitute. "Especially heavy is this affliction in the families of the worthy poor," according to the trustees of the state school for the retarded. The proponents of state involvement argued that care at home was the most expensive form of treatment and that county care (the poorhouse) was virtually worthless; care in state institutions was not only the best and most judicious treatment for the retarded, they insisted, but by far the most economical. (This assertion was made frequently but never demonstrated or elaborated at any length, perhaps because in reality it was so unlikely. Even in the nineteenth century, institutions were criticized as too expensive, a criticism entirely familiar to late twentieth-century ears.) Just as Superintendent Gillette had talked about using "the strong arm of the law" to enforce attendance at the school for the deaf, now those concerned with the retarded argued that because retarded people remained in essence children for life, the state had special interests and rights regarding them.[34]

The combined argument of providing better treatment for the retarded while showing solicitude for their weary families appeared frequently in philanthropic literature of the late nineteenth century; but this benevolent motivation was by no means the only rationale for permanent institutionalization. A far more pervasive argument was posited on the threat to society that the retarded were believed to pose if they were allowed to remain at large.

American society had never been noted for its compassion for the mentally handicapped, but in the early days, the institutions for the retarded had insisted on their pupils' basic rights, as well as their rightful place in the ranks of the "worthy" to whom charity could be administered without demoralizing effects. In the years after the Civil War, this basic perception of worthiness changed to a kind of indictment of the retarded. No one suggested that they were consciously to blame, but blamed they certainly were for many of society's gravest problems.[35]

More than any other cause, the change in attitude toward the retarded stemmed from the emphasis on science, especially the impact of Darwinian evolutionary thought, that pervaded late nineteenth-century thinking. At the heart of evolutionary theory was the notion that life was a struggle to survive. The species that survived and evolved in a brutal universe were those that were strong and able to adapt. The strong mated with the strong, a phenomenon that Darwin called natural selection. The weak, unable to adapt, died out. If by some unusual force of circumstances the weak managed to survive and reproduce, their weaknesses would be perpetuated, to the ultimate destruction of the species.

This rough description of a complex theory was the nub of the matter for nineteenth-century American society, which promptly applied the logic of evolution to the human race. Nature, as social theorists explained, had produced the human race in its present form through the same remorseless sequence of evolution that occurred among the lower animals. The finest product of evolution, they unabashedly proclaimed, was Western Civilization, particularly "Anglo-Saxon" civilization, that is English and American society. That society was in jeopardy, warned Social Darwinists, if the unfit were allowed to contribute their hereditary taint to this highly evolved race.

What constituted "the unfit" was to some extent a matter of opinion. The most extreme racial supremacists included all blacks, Asians, and most Southern and Eastern Europeans in their indictment. Certainly, the massive immigration that began in the 1870s greatly affected American fears about the future of their race and the future of their republic; and the popular notions of evolution

and the decline of the species gave a legitimizing argument to in-
choate fears in a society beset by anxiety about a rapidly industri-
alizing economy and flagrant and pervasive corruption in politics.[36]

Not everyone concerned with social policy was a Social Dar-
winist to the extent that they were prepared to exclude all immigrants or refuse to succor the poor. But the rhetoric of evolution
was as powerful in late nineteenth-century America as the rhetoric of the revolution had been a century earlier. Frederick H. Wines,
Secretary of the Illinois State Board of Charities, showed the impact of Darwinian thinking in 1870 when he wrote in the board's
opening report that by addressing the problems of the unfortunate
directly and efficiently, the state would be helping to dry up the
"fountain of hereditary taint, which otherwise may, in time, work
for the destruction of the race." "A struggle for existence characterizes society as it characterizes nature," he wrote in 1872, "and
the termination of the struggle must ever be the survival of the
fittest. But the struggle, while it lasts, is marked by individual
hardship and misfortune, which we may alleviate, but which we
cannot prevent."[37]

Wines and philanthropists generally were not prepared to abandon the notion of charity, but unquestionably, evolutionary con-
victions and fears wrought changes in their approach, especially
toward the groups that were deemed to be blatantly unfit. The retarded led the list of unconscious polluters of the race, and a major concern of late nineteenth-century philanthropists in regard to
them was to keep them from procreating. Dr. William Fish, superintendent of the Illinois institution for the retarded, wrote of
retarded girls: "This large class, unprotected and uncared for, are
a constant menace to society: adrift in the world, they recruit the
large army of fallen women who are social outcasts. They add to
the burden of the tax-payer by bringing into the world other unfortunates to be cared for."[38]

Speaking at the Illinois "Children of the State" conference in
1898, Alexander Johnson of the Indiana School for the Feeble-
Minded elaborated this notion, warning that the retarded were
naturally prolific and that they would inevitably produce offspring
defective in some regard. Their children "although not quite all
idiotic or imbecile, are never normal. Some defect of body or mind
will be theirs. They will be idiots, epileptics, insane, tramps, paupers, prostitutes or criminals."[39]

The most influential expression that retardation was inherited
and had to do with long-term decline within a family was Robert

L. Dugdale's famous work *The Jukes: A Study in Crime, Pauperism, Disease, and Heredity*, written in 1875 as an appendix to the thirty-first annual report of the New York Prison Association. Dugdale studied the Juke family from the early eighteenth century to the 1870s and found a story of criminality, pauperism, disease, and prostitution passed on through the generations. Although Dugdale himself emphasized the importance of environmental factors, his work seemed to confirm late nineteenth-century America's worst fears about bad blood in the body politic, and it resulted in a vigorous effort to contain what was perceived as faulty stock.[40]

The issue of hereditary disabilities was not only directed at the mentally handicapped; it came up in discussions of the intermarriage of the deaf as well. Mr. Gillette, who insisted that only a very small proportion of deaf people passed the trait on to their children, felt that in any case it was worth the risk, because of the profound need that deaf people had for love and because deafness, in his view, was no longer the disaster it had once been. In opposition to Gillette's view, Alexander Graham Bell and the Illinois State Board of Charities encouraged intermarriage between deaf and hearing people to reduce the threat of hereditary deafness.[41]

Regarding the deaf there was a spirited controversy in the late nineteenth century; with retarded people, there was never a sense that the hereditary threat might be reduced. Social thinkers, with a conviction far in excess of scientific information, devoutly believed that a defective tendency could be contained only by being stopped, not diluted. In a sweeping generalization that would make a modern geneticist wince, Indiana's Superintendent Johnson asserted that only 30 percent of retarded people were affected by some accident before or after birth; the other 70 percent "are as they are, because their parents had the same or some other physical or mental defect." No other trait, these specialists insisted, was so certain to be reproduced in a child as mental defects.[42]

The use of the word "defect" and "defective" summed up the essential change in the attitude toward the mentally handicapped from the antebellum reforming mind to the "scientific charity" of the late nineteenth century. The early word for all handicapped people had been "afflicted," with its connotations of randomness, innocence, and the mysterious actions of Providence. Reformers were fond of quoting the Bible passage in which Christ's disciples ask him to explain the reason for a man's blindness. Who had sinned, they asked, this man or his parents, that he should be born blind. No one sinned, Christ answered; the man was blind so that "the works of God should be made manifest in him."[43]

By the late nineteenth century, the retarded, as well as the epileptic, were called defective, no longer the personification of an inscrutable message from God to man, but merely lacking in the necessary qualifications for full humanity—not a product of a mysterious Providence but of the inexorable dictates of heredity.

It was not that the popular attitude had changed; that had always been hostile and frightened of mental disabilities. What changed so dramatically was the tone of those who styled themselves the protectors of the mentally handicapped. The board of directors of the Illinois State Institution for the Feeble-minded, in what they apparently regarded as a winning metaphor, sought to demonstrate the utility of their institution thus: "If in the material world it is considered good policy to utilize waste products, to labor with refractory metals, to bring all the powers of human ingenuity to bear in solving the chemical and mechanical problems involved in reclaiming waste material, is it not worth our while to labor with the waste products of humanity, to turn to account the talents they possess, to elevate them in the scale of humanity and to throw a ray of light into the darkened minds of those created in God's image."[44]

The mention of God and humanitarian concerns jockeyed for space with strident warnings about the threat of the retarded in much of the rhetoric of the time. Dr. Hugh Patrick, speaking to the 1898 "Children of the State" conference on the need for a colony for epileptics, revealed an extraordinary mixture of hostility and humanity:

> If it is ever the duty of the strong to care for the stricken, there is a very flower of charity to pluck, and if it is the duty of the state to protect itself from degeneracy, there is a seed to be rendered innocuous by isolation. The unknowing victim of ancestors and progenitors, sinned against in his birth that allows such matter to propagate its kind, the child belongs by right to the commonwealth, and has every claim upon it; the claim of retribution, the claim of pity, the claim to be protected from himself. Just as valid is the claim of the people for freedom from physical and moral pollution, and above all is that higher claim, "In as much as ye have done unto one of the least of these my brethren, ye have done unto me.[45]

The State Board of Charities, with less ambivalence and less concern for a humanitarian note, spoke about the debilitating effects of epileptic seizures on families and associates thus: "An epileptic and his attendant are perhaps never together equal to more than one full man, often not so much as that."[46]

The solution that was offered to spare society both the hereditary taint of retardation and epilepsy and the unpleasantness of these disabilities was institutionalization on a massive scale. For epileptics, philanthropists suggested a separate colony where people of all ages could live in their own society, free from the hostility of the larger community and safe from any possibility of procreation. For the retarded, enlargement of the badly overcrowded school was the proposal. The State Board of Charities, which vigorously fought Phillip Gillette's attempt to expand the school for the deaf, agreed with every increase requested by the institution for the retarded. There should be no rest, Indiana Superintendent Johnson told the 1898 conference, "until every imbecile man and woman and child in the State shall be gathered into a safe home, and the dreadful increase of vice and pauperism and crime of which these poor people, the innocents, as the kindly Scotch folk call them, are the unconscious cause, shall stop."[47]

Especially striking about this determined move toward institutionalization was that proponents of child welfare condemned the use of institutions for virtually every other group of children, urging foster care for dependent children, probation for juvenile delinquents, and special schools within the school system for blind and deaf children. Frederick Wines of the State Board of Charities acknowledged this apparent inconsistency but posed the rationale for segregating the retarded and epileptic in these terms: "The advance of civilization in which civil liberty plays so large a part, has been secured, as history teaches us, by no means or agency than by the development in civilized and enlightened communities of the power of self-control. In proportion as the human race has acquired this power, the bonds of despotism have been broken. Mankind, or any portion of it, which is incapable of self-control, requires the strong hand of extraneous control, for the preservation of social order and the peace and security of the community."[48] The retarded and epileptic, offending, however blamelessly, against this imperative of self-control, were to be set apart, to be philanthropically excised from society.

An earlier State Board of Charities report had warned against such segregation. Two disadvantages of charitable institutions, according to that report, were "the aggregation of the victims of misfortune in large numbers, and their withdrawal from the bosom of the community. Their withdrawal from our midst is felt,

perhaps selfishly, to be a relief. Out of sight, they are out of mind."
Such withdrawal, the report insisted, was bad for both the unfortunate, who lost the normalizing influence of society and for the
broader society, where the crucial sense of benevolence was blunt-
ed by their absence. "No artificial family," the report declared,
"can ever substitute for true family life"; it went on to lament the
growing trend toward enlarging public institutions.[49]

By contrast with this view, in the late 1890s not one of the en-
thusiasts who proposed massive institutionalization raised a question about its possible hazards, despite the fact that in general they
were deeply mistrustful of institutions. Johnson of Indiana offered
this comforting and rosy picture of his institution for the retarded. "As soon as one event of joy is over, we are planning for and
expecting the next," he told the "Children of the State" Conference. "So the years slip by, and the child-men and child-women
hardly notice the flight of time."[50]

The Illinois officials in the audience must have known that,
whether or not this sentimental vision accurately depicted the reality at the Indiana institution, it most certainly did not describe
conditions in their own state. They knew the facility at Lincoln
to be fearfully overcrowded, defeating all efforts at meaningful classification of patients (as they had come to be called by that time),
even in such obvious areas as the quarantine of sick and tubercu-
lar people from those in good health. Yet not one of the papers at
the conference discussed the deleterious aspects of large institutions or offered suggestions on how to avoid the dangers of mistreatment and abuse. As with delinquent girls, and for very much
the same reasons, the energy of reformers was all directed toward
removing retarded and epileptic people from society rather than
giving creative thought to their lives once they were securely "put
away."[51]

It is hard to escape the conclusion that, in many respects, philanthropists had simply given up on the people they did not regard as fit, frightened by the prospect of a degenerating race and
unable to imagine a place in their complex, fast-changing world
for those who could not manage for themselves. The ascendancy
of the scientific outlook had brought great improvement in the
case of the blind and deaf. The advent of the germ theory of disease and the advances made in studying and treating specific diseases gave hope that preventive measures, many of them quite simple, could greatly reduce the incidence of blindness. Surgical
advances brightened the prospects for helping both the blind and

deaf, while technology provided improved equipment to assist those who were stricken.

But medical science offered nothing encouraging for the treatment of the retarded, and Darwinian science, as it influenced the popular mind, worked greatly to their detriment. Their philanthropic spokesmen, abandoning education as a primary goal, spoke in terms that could at best be called ambivalent and offered solutions designed far more to protect society than to further their interests. Their natural advocates, their parents, indicted as the hapless transmitters of a flawed inheritance, were effectively closed out of their children's concerns by the creators of public policy. For no other group among the children of the state did the prospect of the twentieth century offer so little promise.

9

Optimism Reborn, 1900–1940

The Progressive Era was a time of determined intervention toward handicapped children, particularly the mentally handicapped. It was in dealing with this group of the state's children that intervention wore its most intrusive aspect, a continuation and fulfillment of the commitment to segregation that had begun in the second half of the nineteenth century.

In one respect the movement for the segregation of the mentally handicapped seems an aberration and a contradiction of the Progressive commitment to limit the institutionalization of children wherever possible. The First White House Conference on Children in 1909 clearly articulated that goal. The juvenile court, through probation, aimed to reduce the need for institutionalization of both delinquent and dependent children. Foster care, which—at least in theory—had become the preferred mode of caring for children outside their homes by the turn of the century, had the same objective.

Yet the segregation of the mentally handicapped reflected other powerful persuasions of the Progressive Era. The prestige of physicians had soared in the years after 1880, and the medical metaphor influenced Progressive thinking profoundly. The Progressive Era saw the development of modern hospitals, institutions where the sick were isolated from the rest of the community for treatment. Even an occurrence as natural as childbirth developed into a highly medical procedure in the twentieth century, reducing both mother and baby to the place of almost inconsequential actors while elevating the doctor to the critical role in the drama.

In addition to the example of the hospital, quarantine for contagious diseases was a familiar reality of the time and provided a persuasive medical model for segregating those who, it was believed, would infect the nation's "germ plasm" if they were not isolated from society.[1]

Beyond the comfortingly medical appearance of institutionalization, the segregation of the mentally handicapped took place
against a background of racial segregation that had been pronounced acceptable by the United States Supreme Court. In the
landmark 1896 case Plessy v. Ferguson the court declared that
"separate" was acceptable as long as it was "equal." The stress
on minority and individual rights that would galvanize a later generation was eclipsed in the minds of many Progressives by an urgent conviction that the good of the whole must not be jeopardized by an unhealthy individual. Illinois state official A. L. Bowen
expressed this conviction when he wrote about the twentieth century's professionalization of charity in 1917: "Charity is service,
no longer almsgiving; modern charity or service thinks first of all
of the public, of society, of the community; of what effect the sick
man has upon the community; more particularly what effect the
treatment of the sick man will have upon the community. The
victim, the sick man, is a mere incident."[2]

For many of those who considered the fate of handicapped children, the individual child was clearly "a mere incident" whose
well-being might be sacrificed to preserve the community. This
frankly stated commitment to social control meant that for handicapped children, and especially the mentally handicapped, the
Progressive Era was more a time of coercion than assistance, an
age that saw the development of a rhetoric and mentality that last-
ed in the public mind long after officials themselves were prepared
to replace it with a more benign and compassionate view.

The Impact of Science

Two scientific developments exacerbated the pessimistic attitude toward the mentally handicapped in the first quarter of the
twentieth century. One was the popularization of the works of the
Austrian monk Gregor Mendel, whose studies in heredity, as they
were interpreted by an already anxious audience, confirmed for
social theorists their worst fears about transmitting faulty human
material from one generation to another.[3]

The other development was the introduction of intelligence testing, a process that most social thinkers, committed as they were
to the belief that social sciences could be made as precise as physical science, tended to regard as infallible. In reality, the intelligence tests, which first appeared as a French import, the Binet test,
around 1910, were being revised and modified almost from the

beginning in an effort to achieve a more objective and accurate reading. And some experts, notably psychologist William Healy of the Juvenile Psychopathic Institute and the Juvenile Court, expressed considerable scholarly skepticism about them. There was necessarily an arbitrary quality about such tests, Healy pointed out, since they set normal and subnormal on a point scale, whereas in real life, people might cope socially despite limited measurable intelligence. Healy also pointed out that environmental factors— cultural and language differences, a lack of formal education, psychological turmoil—could affect the actual score that designated a child's intellectual competence. Healy was joined in his warnings by a certain amount of public and newspaper opinion that scoffed at educators' and charity workers' reverence for intelligence tests. But for most people involved in the state's care of its wards, the intelligence test was regarded as a formidable weapon in the arsenal of science, a precise measure that allowed them to verify what they had long suspected: that there were far more mentally defective people in their society than could be safely tolerated.[4]

The rigidity of most theorists and practitioners in interpreting the new intelligence tests came in part from their pre-existing belief that the number of mental defectives in society was a major problem. In the official literature of the state of Illinois, it was never suggested that this lowering of society's intellectual level might relate to the massive immigration so notable in the first fifteen years of the century; immigrant groups were far too mobilized to tolerate such a direct indictment. But the notion was certainly reflected in the arrogant attitude toward the tests themselves; the refusal to take into account cultural or economic differences was very much in keeping with the unabashed conviction that white "native" American society was notably superior to the culture of the newcomers.

Although the most optimistic Americans, for example the settlement house workers of Hull-House, argued that the incoming cultures could add beauty and vitality to the existing society, in general, American culture was perceived to be the pinnacle of human achievement. Black educator Booker T. Washington gave a vivid illustration of this comfortable consensus when he spoke to the Child in the City conference in Chicago in 1911. In addressing "The Claims of the Colored Child" Washington mildly reproached the conference, complaining that black Americans were judged "by a pretty stiff yardstick. If the Negro were living in the midst of a Latin civilization, his efforts to keep near those people

would not be so great as to keep near you. . . . Some of those fel-
lows in Southern Europe are nearer to our gait than you are." Instead, according to Washington, black Americans were living in
the midst of "the most aggressive, the most pushing, and the highest civilization the world has seen" and thus faced great obstacles
in their attempts at improvement.[5]

Yet as firmly as Americans asserted their society's place as the
high point of civilization, the happy result of aeons of evolution,
they perceived that superiority to be a fragile thing. Theories of
heredity convinced them that most defects, especially mental ones,
were passed on from generation to generation and grew in geomet-
ric proportion; intelligence tests seemed to confirm the bad news
and indicate that the corruption of their civilization was imminent. A feeble-minded woman, according to one writer, was twice
as likely to reproduce as a normal woman, and her children would
inevitably be defective also. The fear of race suicide was a constant theme in the social welfare literature of the time, writers
insisting that every defect that appeared in a child was introduced
into the common stock permanently. Their estimates of the number of retarded people were staggering.[6]

Dr. Healy, along with his colleague Dr. Augusta Bronner, urged
a conservative interpretation of the causes of mental impairment,
reminding their associates that "birth accident, brain disease, brain
cell poisoning, metabolic glandular disorders and even accidents"
could cause mental damage. "We have no proof whatsoever that
there has been any interference with the germ plasm in these cases
so that there will be an inheritance of mental weakness," Healy
insisted.

But such caution was very much a minority view. Speaking for
the majority were officials like Dr. Clara Hayes, a staff doctor at
the Peoria State Mental Hospital who asserted in 1915 that there
were 18,000 mental defectives at large in the State of Illinois,
"18,000 idiots and imbeciles who are a menace to society, a burden to the State and a blot on civilization." A law that would enforce the segregation of this army of the unfit in institutions
would, she argued, eliminate the problem in two or three generations and would accomplish "one of the most brilliant humanitarian achievements of the ages."[7]

The Call for Institutionalization on a Mass Scale

It was common for advocates of segregation to preen themselves
on their humanitarianism; but the benevolence was all reserved

for the "generations unborn" whom they were preserving from weakness and defects. There was very little discussion proportionately about the humane treatment of the mentally impaired once they were institutionalized. Fears of race contamination so dominated the rhetoric that the emphasis of reformers was overwhelmingly the prevention of procreation.

Eugenics, the so-called science of human breeding, was at its zenith in the first quarter of the twentieth century, advocating an extensive control of reproduction. The most basic means for this was total and permanent segregation in institutions; this applied both to the feeble-minded and people with epilepsy. Although sterilization and even castration (delicately termed testectomy and oophrectomy) were advocated at one point by the State Board of Charities and other officials dealing with the retarded, Illinois never legalized sterilization in its institutions, as neighboring Indiana did. The churches objected to sterilization, and many of those in the social welfare establishment did as well. Frederick Wines, the venerable Illinois social theorist who had headed the State Board of Charities in its early years, objected that sterilization was an unnecessary physical intrusion when a segregation policy was enforced and carefully maintained. He also worried that if sterilization were practiced on the unfit, it might unduly encourage those among the general population who wanted a means to indulge promiscuity without consequences. Wines's view continued to dominate in Illinois, so that although sterilization bills were proposed, none ever passed the legislature. Even after the United States Supreme Court upheld the constitutionality of sterilizing the unfit in 1927, the measure remained unpopular in Illinois.[8]

But a rejection of sterilization in no way indicated that officials in Illinois were not worried about the propagation of the unfit. Officials repeatedly emphasized the need for massive institutionalization, impelled both by a concern about the unfit reproducing and by fears about the crime and disorder they might inflict on society.

Families and State Officials

With the goal of permanent institutionalization in mind, officials worked very hard to separate mentally handicapped people from their families. The location of the state's only institution for the retarded was itself a deterrent to family involvement. Lincoln was in western Illinois, and to reach it from Chicago, travelers had to

catch the train at 3:00 A.M. The letterhead of the institution bore
the unfriendly injunction "No Visiting on Sundays," surely the most
likely visiting day for working people who had to travel a long distance. In the early years of the twentieth century the vacation period that an inmate could enjoy was reduced to two weeks, which
could not be extended legally. Once a formal commitment law was
passed, each inmate's vacation had to be granted by the board of
administrators and could not be for longer than two weeks. The officials at the institution were under orders to call in police if the
inmate had not returned after the vacation time had elapsed, but
they used their discretion in doing so, allowing a longer time at
home if the situation and the family were deemed worthy enough.
Without this special arrangement, the only option families had to
extend a visit was to keep their children out beyond the given date,
thus risking trouble with the law and losing their places in the institution. This rule was created because of the desperate crowding
in the institution, an attempt to guarantee that a spot would not
remain vacant while a child stayed for a prolonged visit with his
family. But it was also an attempt to limit visitation with parents
whom the authorities considered disreputable.[9]

In fact, officials had few good things to say about families. Either they were condemned as sentimental and overly protective
of their handicapped children or condemned as shameless exploit-
ers of them, and officials argued for the earliest possible separation from parents and placement in the Lincoln institution. In
answer to the question "Are they not better cared for in their
homes?" Dr. Hardt of the Lincoln Asylum replied, "Yes, if we
could be assured that the parents are mentally strong enough and
so situated financially that the whole effort would be brought forth
for this backward child." But, he continued, such was not generally the case. "The bleeding hearts of many mothers who have
defective children have no space left for argument or judgement."[10]

There was some recognition of the hardship families experienced in visiting Lincoln; proposals were made to build an institution near Chicago, an event according to Juvenile Protective
Association studies, that would have reconciled many Chicago
families to the hard necessity of institutionalizing a loved one. But
this proposed institution never materialized. Parental resistance
to placing mentally disabled children was dealt with instead by
the 1915 passage of a commitment law modeled on the juvenile
court and lunacy laws. This law allowed interested citizens to
bring a mentally retarded person to the attention of the court,

whether the family was willing to participate or not. The notion was that competent parents would not be bothered, but those who allowed their feeble-minded offspring to menace the neighborhood would forfeit their rights of parenthood. Officials frequently voiced their contention that most retarded people were the children of the lower classes; only very occasionally did anyone remember to acknowledge that the tragedy could affect even prosperous people. The assumption was that those few unfortunates born to middle-class parents would be properly controlled and cared for, but that the lower classes needed the firm hand of the state to prevent their children endangering both present and future generations.[11]

Part of the reason for driving such a determined wedge between parents and their children was this class perception, the implied criticism that most retarded children belonged to the feckless, if not unworthy, poor. In addition, professionalism had taken firm hold in the first years of the twentieth century, and the administrators and staffs of state institutions operated from the same arrogant premise as most specialists, convinced that they knew far more and should be trusted far more than mere laymen, even if those laymen were parents. There were those who raised civil liberties issues and defended parental rights in the Progressive Era, but the state officials dealing with the retarded were not among them. The chief administrators of the Illinois institution were generally doctors, and the medical model was the dominant mode of reality for them. Physicians, more than any other profession, had risen dramatically in prestige with the successful control of many diseases in the last years of the nineteenth century. They would brook no criticism from any portion of the population, least of all from parents whose flawed children were seen to be a product of their own damaged "germ plasm."

The Conditions of Institutional Life

Perhaps another reason that it was convenient to detach families from involvement in their retarded children's lives was that the Illinois institution at Lincoln really could not bear scrutiny. An incident in 1907 offered a painful example of this sorry reality. The incident centered around an accident to an epileptic patient, Frank Giroux. At the urging of their doctor, the Giroux family had just placed their son at Lincoln to grant relief to a mother worn out from the constant nursing he required. On December 24, only two weeks after Frank was placed, his father boarded the 3:00

A.M. train to Lincoln, bringing presents for his son and the other children at the institution with the amiable plan of brightening their Christmas. He found his son badly burned, an accident that had happened only the night before when Frank had fallen against an uncovered radiator in the throes of an epileptic seizure. Mr. Giroux was assured that his son was doing fine and encouraged to go home. He left, but his wife arrived the next day and finally took Frank home with her in early January. He was terribly burned, as photographs from the subsequent investigation attest, and according to his family's doctors, his care at the institution had been shockingly inadequate.[12]

As usual with child welfare scandals in Illinois, the family's tragedy was grist for the political mill. The Giroux family complained to their representative in the Illinois House of Representatives, who happened to be an enemy of both the governor and the new civil service law that had been instituted in 1905, a law that represented a significant departure from tradition in a state where patronage was deeply embedded in the political system. The House Investigating Committee clearly saw the incident as an opportunity to attack the institution's new superintendent (and through him the governor who had appointed him), as well as the civil service appointed doctors in the institution. Their questioning was designed to uncover far more than the obvious negligence of the attendant in charge of Frank's ward, who had been absent when the boy fell. In his rebuttal of the committee's findings, Governor Charles Deneen explicitly accused the investigatory committee of playing politics, of refusing to call certain witnesses and refusing to allow cross examination of all witnesses, together with other legal irregularities.

In the end, although a few thousand pages of committee reports and rebuttals had been churned out, the situation was not much clearer than when the investigation began. There was evidence given to show that the institution had acted disingenuously (the doctors and staff had certainly been less than candid with the Giroux family); conversely, the tactics of the legislators were hardly above reproach, and much of the evidence that they gathered was from dubious sources. Julia Lathrop, a long-time member of the State Board of Charities, tried mightily to make the point that any investigation of the Lincoln institution should not focus solely on the eleven-month tenure of the present superintendent but should rather go back to the condition of the institution in previous administrations. The institution had been in terrible shape for years,

she insisted, and it was unfair to pillory a man because he had
not righted such major problems in a mere eleven months. (Dr.
Hardt, the accused superintendent, had been responsible among
other things for abolishing the cruel physical punishments and
restraints formerly used at the institution.)[13]

Lathrop also urged the committee to consider the broader issue raised by the Giroux catastrophe, the question of how to train
and keep humane attendants for these vulnerable wards of the
state. Mincing no words, Lathrop told the unfriendly committee
that their attempt to blame the superintendent for the accident
missed the point.

> When he is gone the rest of the twenty four hours depends entirely
> on the intelligence, the devotion, the ability, the tact, and the good
> will of this human being who is fifteen and a half or sixteen or more
> hours on duty, and who is taxed almost beyond human endurance.
> I think the people of the state of Illinois ought to realize that the
> matter of accidents and disasters in asylums is purely a matter of
> dollars and cents, to be reckoned in the pay of attendants, and that
> no doctors, no staff, no Board of Charities, no other organization in
> the world can make good institutions so long as the attendant ser-
> vice is not brought up to a different standard.

The problem lay not in the current administrator, according to
Lathrop, but in the fact that public institutions were "a football
between the different political parties" and suffered from the General Assembly's reluctance to fund them adequately.[14]

Lathrop, although as committed as other social thinkers to institutionalization of the retarded and epileptic, differed from most
publicists in that she gave thought to the fate of inmates once they
had been admitted. She fought for better wages and hours for institutional staff, and she was responsible for an innovative program
at the Chicago School of Civics and Philanthropy that offered training courses to attendants in state hospitals. The introduction of
women as attendants in the men's wards, both in the state mental hospitals and at the Lincoln asylum for the retarded, was another solution Lathrop and others urged to upgrade the care of institutionalized people. Proponents of this innovation argued that
much brutality would be eliminated by replacing low level, dis-
contented men with women, whom they regarded as natural nurturers, much less likely than men to slide into the abusive prac-
tices that institutional settings seemed to invite.[15]

Perhaps such efforts ameliorated conditions at the Lincoln institution to some degree, but no great revolution in care could

happen as long as money was scarce, expectations for the quality of retarded people's lives were so low, and crowding and under-staffing continued.

The Involuntary Commitment Law and Its Consequences

Those who urged the segregation of the unfit as a premier social welfare cause anticipated the creation of at least five more institutions for the mentally unfit in Illinois, including an institution for feeble-minded women of childbearing age and an institution for defective delinquents. This expectation was never fulfilled. Reformers recognized the financial limitations on their plans in 1915, acknowledging that what institutional money there was had to go to the long-awaited institution and colony for epileptics located at Dixon, Illinois. Since there was no point in agitating for institutions that could simply not be funded, they decided to concentrate instead on the writing and passage of an involuntary commitment law that would remove the reliance on parents' cooperation as the only way to achieve the institutionalization of retarded children.[16]

Clearly there was a serious flaw in the decision to push for a commitment law. Since the only existing institution for the retarded was already overcrowded and there were no more institutions likely to be funded or built for some time, it was a recipe for disaster to pass a commitment law that was likely to increase greatly the population of the sole available institution. Yet, as obvious as this flaw might appear in retrospect, it was not obvious to the coalition that passed the law in 1915. They regarded their commitment law as a triumph and congratulated themselves that they had, among other things, removed some dangerous and troublesome people from society without doing them the injustice of sending them to prisons, where they would be badly treated and out of place.

The coalition's triumph was short-lived. Within a year, officials were protesting that the new commitment law was being used to dump all sorts of inappropriate people into the Lincoln asylum. Counties that wanted to avoid support of the poor or dependent children were able to get a diagnosis of feeble-mindedness from an obliging local doctor and sent these burdensome citizens to Lincoln, at state expense. The executive secretary of the Illinois Charities Commission, A. L. Bowen, described in detail a number of inappropriate placements in a 1916 report: one woman with five children whose husband had deserted her; a young Syrian man "unfamiliar with our language and customs" who was given six minutes in court and committed to what he was told was "a college"; a deaf-mute man, "a dipsomaniac but not feeble-minded," according to Bowen; four orphans returned from a private institution in St. Louis and hastily committed to Lincoln under the new law. Another problem that the institution was totally unequipped to deal with was the placement of "defective delinquents." The girls were apparently no trouble; they were mostly sex offenders and fairly tractable. But the boys and young men were a violent group who would have been sent to the state reformatory at Pontiac before the commitment law. Bowen noted in dismay:

> As I passed through the wards where these boys are housed, I made a note of their depredations. They have smashed glass by the wholesale, broken up beds and with the side rails battered down doors and ripped out panels. No lock or key had been proof against them. The fire extinguishers have been emptied and ruined. The plumbing and all pipes have been shot to pieces. They have organized riots and attacked attendants and employees. They are not only troublesome and unmanageable themselves, but their influence over the other boys has been vicious.

This onslaught of new and very difficult inmates naturally caused the quality of life at Lincoln to deteriorate, as Bowen so vividly described. Furthermore, the institution, filled to capacity before the commitment law, was now desperately overcrowded. By 1918, an institution with a capacity for sixteen hundred people was housing twenty-five hundred.[17]

Clearly, another institution for the retarded had to be opened, but the possibility of building anything new was all the more unlikely once the country had entered the First World War. Manpower and material were scarce, and inflation discouraged any ambitious plans that might have survived earlier political and legislative defeats. What finally resulted was that the Epileptic Hospital and Colony established in 1918 at Dixon, Illinois, was converted within a year into a second institution for the feeble-minded. It ostensibly housed less educable inmates, but in fact, the patients were a pretty mixed lot from the beginning, classification becoming less possible as time went on and the new institution experienced crowding problems of its own.[18]

Illinois officials took a determinedly cheerful tone toward the conversion of Dixon to an asylum for the retarded, but in reality it represented a major failure in their attempts to segregate those whom they had designated the unfit. There had been a widespread belief that the Dixon Colony would be warmly accepted by people with epilepsy and their families. The notion was that the control of epileptic seizures would be far better managed under the strict dietary and health regimen planned at this institution and that such a congregation of epileptic patients would allow medical studies to gain further knowledge of the illness. Furthermore, contended state officials, although epilepsy was a fearful and repellent condition to ordinary people, epileptic people felt a kinship and sympathy for one another and would experience far more kindness from one another in their separate world than they could possibly expect in the larger society. The colony was planned to incorporate every grade of epilepsy, from the profoundly mentally impaired to people with normal capacities. Of course, it was assumed that the separate world would be a strictly celibate one, a primary purpose of the institution being the control of this "hereditary taint" and the ultimate protection of the larger society from "racial poisoning."[19]

Much to the surprise of officials and reformers, removal to a separate colony did not win much approval among those afflicted with epilepsy in Illinois. The largest number of patients ever settled there was ninety-two, most of them very helpless custodial cases. Officials frankly acknowledged that the flaw was the voluntary aspect of commitment, but they were already desperately juggling the results of one commitment law, and they were prepared to make a virtue of necessity. Dixon offered a barely used, ready-made solution to the problem of overcrowding at Lincoln, and officials willingly surrendered their long-fought-for institution for epileptics to this new purpose.

In fact, the whole problem of epilepsy receded from the state literature with the close of the institution. People with epilepsy had been as badly used verbally as the retarded, officials emphasizing the strain they placed on families, the horrors of epileptic seizures, and the contaminating effects of the condition for future generations. But once the Dixon project failed, public attention was drawn away from them markedly. They ceased to be the objects of either opprobrium or compassion. Those who were institutionalized continued to be placed with the retarded (as they had been before the Dixon experiment) or sometimes placed in mental hospitals; those who could manage in society were no longer a subject of comment in the state literature. When they reappeared in the literature on the handicapped in later years, the tone of the discussion had become one of optimism and tolerance.[20]

The opening of the Dixon institution to retarded people eased the crowding crisis temporarily, but there was never a sense that there was really enough room to respond adequately to the state's retarded population. Especially in the years of the Great Depression of the 1930s, when the total inmate population of the state's institutions expanded dramatically, the waiting lists at Lincoln and Dixon grew in proportion.[21]

The Cook County Juvenile Detention Home, itself in dire straits, housed some of these waiting children, along with delinquent boys and girls awaiting placement in the equally overcrowded reformatories of the state. In the 1930s one change in policy that eased crowding and classification problems at Lincoln and Dixon was the establishment of the Illinois Security Hospital, which had as its purpose the housing of all criminally mentally ill patients. The "defective delinquent" men and boys who had caused such concern at Lincoln were sent to this new facility instead.[22]

It was not only crowding that troubled the institutions for the mentally retarded, however. The daily life of inmates, so different in reality from the fatuous and sentimental descriptions sometimes offered in the state literature, continued to be an exercise in mere endurance. In 1919, for example, the state inspectors remarked with distaste on the abysmal indoor recreation facilities at Lincoln: "About noon snow began to fall and the inmates were compelled to spend the afternoon indoors. We saw the catacomb rooms at their best or worst, as you are amind to call them. The wrong committed in compelling these children to spend their playtime in a basement is hardly describable." Another report noted with alarm that of the infants and small children committed to the institution, 30 percent died in less than eighteen months after commitment. In addition, Lincoln suffered from considerable administrative instability in the 1920s, owing to the deaths of two superintendents.[23]

In 1929, the institution, in concert with the Institute for Juvenile Research, attempted to inject some substantive education into the low level custodial treatment of this group of the state's wards. The institution launched a full-scale recreation program that very much resembled in spirit a contemporary experiment, the Chicago Area Project on delinquency prevention. Recreation director Bertha Schlotter and her staff shared the CAP goal of awakening the self respect of their subjects, encouraging them to take some control over their lives, to exercise decision making rather than holding out obedience as the only fit virtue for institutionalized people. Schlotter's report was carefully worded, but it was clear that in three years their programs had turned the institution upside down and had encountered considerable staff resistance. Before their arrival, she wrote, the girls would sit all day on a row of hard benches in a barren and ugly room; their sole occupation was picking plaster off the walls, which consequently were full of holes. The institution staff insisted that these young people were hopeless, that they could not learn to play and enjoy themselves, that they broke every toy they were given. The reality, Schlotter reported, was that these children saw toys so rarely that they did not know how to play with them. Traditionally the institution's token gesture to Christmas cheer was to buy an assortment of extremely cheap and ill-made toys, to pass them out on Christmas day and wait the hour or so until they were broken. Then the debris was swept up, Christmas declared to be over, and the bleakness of daily life resumed. The new recreational staff insisted on investing in good toys that were available to children every day as part of therapeutic play. Once the children had gotten used to the toys, they were able to take care of them on a par with ordinary children, according to Schlotter.[24]

The Changing Attitude toward the Handicapped

The interest in the quality of life for mentally retarded people that informed Schlotter's recreation program was a more commonly expressed concern by the 1930s certainly than it had been fifteen or twenty years earlier. Although in reality most institutional life continued to be very substandard, the rhetoric in regard to the mentally retarded and in fact the handicapped generally was beginning to change as early as 1920 and was notably less abusive and hysterical by the 1930s.[25]

One obvious cause for this change in tone was the fact that the crusade for institutionalization succeeded all too well; existing institutions suffered terribly from crowding. On another level, it became clear that the segregated "society within a society" that reformers had projected would never be a fiscal possibility. Such a thing was to some extent pipe dreaming even in 1914 and 1915, at the height of the eugenics scare. The inflation caused by the First World War and the catastrophe of the Great Depression guaranteed that a massive network of institutions would never be achieved.

In the 1920s, Illinois officials, following the lead of the New Jersey state school for the retarded, began to experiment with placing young women from Lincoln in free foster homes where they worked and earned money as domestics while still supervised by the institution. Such a plan contrasted sharply with the earlier insistence that foster home and individual home placement was out of the question for retarded young people. When institutions were filled to overflowing, the notion of out-placement for the most competent inmates took on a much more appealing aspect. The official literature talked for the first time, too, about dealing with the mentally retarded as "outpatients" and actually including the parents in training and support for their handicapped children.[26]

The First World War itself had changed thinking about the retarded in at least two ways. With a shortage of personnel, many patients from both the mental hospitals and the institutions for the retarded were pressed into service to keep the various asylums going, and officials argued that they proved themselves competent beyond any former expectations. In addition, the much-revered intelligence tests were administered to the country's soldiers, with the staggering result that 47.3 percent of the white soldiers and 89 percent of the black soldiers were found to have a mental age of twelve of younger.

There were two ways of reading this information, both of which encouraged optimism about the retarded. One analysis contended that the tests were badly flawed and should not be taken too seriously (a conclusion heartily seconded by a psychologist who had tested a group of Iowa farmers, not one of whom tested above the "moronic" level). A second way of reading the tests, the way offered by many psychologists, was that "feeble-mindedness . . . is of much greater frequency of occurrence than had been originally supposed." This news, somewhat ironically, comforted rather than alarmed psychologists, because they reasoned that since so many "hidden" retarded people were coping in society without obvious problems, the retarded person's capacity to manage socially was greater than professionals had thought and the need for massive institutionalization had been exaggerated.[27]

Just as science had brought the bad news to the pessimists of the late nineteenth and early twentieth centuries about the dangers of "mental defectives," now science offered an optimistic outlook regarding this most despised group of handicapped people. Not only did the intelligence tests offer cheerful "scientific" news. The continual study of the mentally handicapped, furthered certainly by their congregation in institutions, had produced information about the causes of mental retardation that contradicted the hereditary determinism of eugenics. The discovery that a thyroid imbalance caused cretinism, for example, offered hope that much retardation could be prevented, perhaps even cured. And a more elaborate understanding of genetics, of the difference between congenital and hereditary ailments, reduced the level of panic that had been the single greatest cause of earlier harsh attitudes. As early as 1919, a careful study of babies and young children who had accompanied their retarded mothers to the Lincoln institution challenged the notion that hereditary mental retardation was inevitable. The study found many children of normal intelligence, despite all the environmental disadvantages to which the children had been exposed. The mentally retarded, who had gone from the position of "worthy" to "unworthy" subjects of charity were vastly rehabilitated when it came to be appreciated that their tragic situation posed no real threat to the population at large or to future generations.[28]

The Care of Physically Handicapped Children in the Progressive Era

Another feature of the re-establishment of the mentally retarded as "worthy" recipients of public assistance was the gradual increase of public interest in physically handicapped children, especially after poliomyelitis plagues became a regular and terrifying feature of American life. Before an interest in crippled children became a notable part of the state literature, the attention to physically handicapped children in the state had waned somewhat. It was striking that, as increased concern and hostility to retarded people had grown, the problems of deaf and blind children in the early years of the twentieth century were eclipsed in the public consciousness. The annual reports of the institutions for the blind and deaf continued to be produced, as did the state inspectors' reports, but the energetic agitation on behalf of these children and their problems that had characterized the nineteenth century was replaced by a lackluster and fairly rote presentation of their needs and prospects. The ambitious superintendent Phillip Gillette of the School for the Deaf was replaced by his son, whose reports were competent but by no means imbued with the fervor that had characterized his pioneering father.

The greatest concentration of effort in the first years of the twentieth century was on the prevention of handicaps, especially blindness, rather than improving the quality of life for those already afflicted. Since the late nineteenth century, physicians had known that a drop of silver nitrate in an infant's eyes could prevent the ravages of infection and blindness that resulted when a woman infected with gonorrhea gave birth. This was a major breakthrough. One Illinois official estimated that almost 25 percent of the children at the Illinois School for the Blind suffered from this easily prevented form of blindness. The effort to pass and enforce public health laws obliging doctors, nurses, and midwifes to make use of the silver nitrate solution constituted a substantial aspect of work with the blind in the early twentieth century. In 1915 the Illinois legislature passed a law mandating that all nurses, doctors, and midwifes report cases of inflamed eyes in newborn infants. Efforts to contain the spread of the eye disease trachoma, which was especially prevalent in the southern regions of the state, also occupied medical and reforming attention.[29]

One achievement of which reformers were especially proud was the passage of a compulsory education law for blind and deaf children in 1917. This law, although intended to insure that blind and deaf children received the same right to education that ordinary children enjoyed, in fact was more coercive than standard compulsory education laws. In the city of Chicago, where there were special schools for blind and deaf children within the public school system, it did not occasion much disruption for most children. But for those in the city who could not find places in these special schools and for families in other areas of Illinois, it meant not that the state was assuming control of their children's lives for a certain number of hours each day but that in reality, most of the child's life would be spent separate from the family and at some considerable distance. That these separations occasioned hardship, officials acknowledged. They discussed one case, for example, where the child and her parents fought bitterly against separation. The official recounting the family's parting expressed sympathy but regarded the separation as a non-negotiable necessity. He added comfortably that in any case, the girl, being Mexican and blessed with a mercurial Latin temperament, cheered up very quickly once her parents were actually out of her presence.[30]

The undercurrent of coercion that appeared in the public literature regarding the blind and deaf in the first years of the century reflected the fear of tainted heredity that affected dealings with even these most "worthy" of handicapped children. The question

of hereditary blindness occupied much of the literature on the
blind, and the officials at the Jacksonville School assured the public
that they spared no efforts to keep boys and girls rigidly segregated so that the school would produce no love matches resulting in
another generation of blind children. The cruel industrial metaphor that so dominated the language of eugenicists, the concept
of defective and damaged goods, also affected attitudes toward the
blind and deaf, as shown in one official's earnest explanation that
blind children were best off in state institutions. "The special
needs of the blind child are too great to be adequately met in our
common schools," he wrote in 1910. "Their machinery is adjusted to the requirements of the normal child. To expect it to turn
out a finished article from defective material is unreasonable."[31]

Though some of the panic and meanspiritedness that society
directed at the mentally impaired spilled over onto the more "acceptable" groups of handicapped children, probably the most det-
rimental effect was a loss of force and energy in their behalf, a
subtle devaluing that inevitably occurred when the obsession with
race purity and perfection reached its height. But there was never
a point where the adult physically handicapped were urged to take
up residence in segregated colonies as people with epilepsy were.
In fact, in Illinois one great success for the blind in the Progressive Era was the passage of a blind pension, which addressed the
enduring difficulties of blind citizens in finding occupations that
could support them. The deaf, with less effective lobbyists and
society's comfortable conviction that they could always find manual work, were passed over in this legislation, as were all other
groups of physically handicapped people.[32]

The pension for the blind illustrates a striking thing about the
state's approach to the handicapped, the selective recognition of
those in need. A member of the Board of Public Welfare Commissioners summed up the state's erratic approach to all its children
in a 1918 report. "Illinois neglects a large group of its unfortunate
children," she contended. While blind, deaf, feeble-minded, and
delinquent children were considered state charges, "to the dependent, the crippled, the tuberculous, the Department of Public Welfare offers nothing." The care of these children was left to the
counties, and the counties were notorious for their lack of ardor
in their care of dependent people.[33]

But crippled children were beginning to impinge on the public
consciousness fifteen years into the new century. Probably the
greatest cause of this awareness was the poliomyelitis plagues that

began to ravage the population at regular intervals. The disease was terrifying because its cause was unknown. (One article in the state periodical the *Institution Quarterly* suggested that, like other, earlier plagues, it might be borne by rats.) The disease affected mainly children and young people, and—critical for public consciousness—was no respecter of persons. Infantile paralysis, as it was called, cut across class lines; the patrician Franklin Delano Roosevelt, future president of the United States, was among its victims. And because it struck as epidemics, polio greatly increased the visibility of crippled children and directed public attention to their needs.[34]

Crippled children, who had been absolutely ignored by the state in the nineteenth century, became the focal point of attention once they were recognized in the twentieth century. For one thing, surgical and prosthetic procedures could offer them real relief and in some cases could lead to a restoration of mobility. Also, crippled children seized the public imagination because, like blind children, they were easier to identify with than the deaf and the retarded for whom normal communication was limited. And because so many crippled children were handicapped through disease, they did not raise the specter of "hereditary taint" and "racial poison" that children born handicapped did. Their tragedy was more in keeping with the sense of affliction expressed by mid-nineteenth century literature than with the sense of defects common in late nineteenth- and early twentieth-century parlance.[35]

The introduction of the word "handicapped," in fact, signaled the change in attitude that came to affect children both mentally and physically impaired. To call a child "handicapped" stressed the sense of that child's burden and disadvantages, the inequalities that he or she inevitably faced, rather than emphasizing the defective or damaged quality of body or mind. The change of terms and the quality of analysis shifted the emphasis from the "defective's" impact on society to the quality of life for the individual child restricted by physical or mental limitations. Like the nineteenth-century term "afflicted," the term "handicapped" evoked compassion rather than revulsion and stressed the lack of culpability for the problem and the deserving quality of the person in need. In contrast to the earlier emphasis on the good of society over the needs of an individual, the 1930 White House Conference on Children prepared "The Handicapped Child's Bill of Rights," which emphasized the right of every child, no matter how physically or mentally limited, to the fullest possible development of his potential: "to be brought up and educated by those who understand the nature of the burden he has to bear and who consider it a privilege to help him bear it . . . to grow up in a world which does not set him apart . . . but which welcomes him, exactly as it welcomes every child, which offers him identical privileges and identical responsibilities."[36]

The White House Conference stress on inclusion was echoed in the 1931 report of the Illinois legislature's Child Welfare Committee, which urged support within the community for parents and schools, so that handicapped children could remain at home whenever possible. Nine years later, the discussions of handicapped children in the collection of essays *Children in a Depression Decade* sounded an upbeat note, citing efforts made nationwide in the 1930s to incorporate classes for handicapped children, even the mentally retarded, into the public school curriculum. According to one expert, there had been "a decided change from the institutional idea to the community supervision thought" for all but the most severely mentally impaired, with the possibility of further community living for the retarded in the future. The report also emphasized the strides that medical science had made in the understanding, prevention, and treatment of diseases and conditions that resulted in handicaps. The discovery of sulfa drugs, for example, and their use in treating scarlet fever and meningitis reduced the incident of both deafness and mental retardation among children.[37]

The growing involvement of the federal government in the health and welfare of children was embodied in the passage of the Social Security Act of 1935, which, in addition to Aid to Dependent Children, provided a grant to the blind and made funds available for assistance to crippled children, especially in rural regions and in other areas where their care had been previously neglected. Local communities were best equipped to run programs for children in need, according to the general social thought of the day, but the federal and state government should provide financial assistance as well as other support to enable local communities to offer effective services. "The safety of our democracy depends in large measure upon the welfare of our children," wrote veteran child welfare advocate Homer Folks in the report of the 1940 White House Conference. Both mentally and physically handicapped children were emphatically included in that definition.[38]

Above all, "work with handicapped children must be carried on in an atmosphere of optimism," according to the new thinking.

"Many of these children are potential assets to the community, and unless we treat them as such, we fail in a basic public duty." The literature discussing the care of handicapped children had done a 180 degree turn from the early days of the century. With its emphasis on optimism, a normal life for handicapped people in the community, and the right to equal treatment for this disadvantaged group, it contrasted sharply with the embattled vision of an earlier age when handicapped children were described as "the culls of society" and were seen and spoken of more as a waste management problem than as human beings with rights and potential.

But as usual in children's issues, the rhetoric was well in advance of the reality, as advocates for handicapped children ruefully acknowledged. Those who worked with the handicapped, especially in institutions, were still underpaid and overworked. Institutions were crowded and unimaginative and subject to all the problems that had made reformers suspicious of them from the mid-nineteenth century onward. Community services were limited even in cities and almost nonexistent in rural areas. The most influential professionals endorsed the declaration that a handicapped child was entitled "to a life on which his handicap casts no shadow," but with the shadow of world war looming once again, progress in child welfare was about to experience a serious disruption. Significant change would develop only in the postwar world.[39]

10

Progress for Handicapped Children, 1940–90

The scarcity of materials and personnel that resulted from the nation's involvement in the Second World War, coming as it did after the prolonged depression of the 1930s, affected services for handicapped children in many ways. Institutions and schools experienced manpower shortages. Medical attention to the armed services was a top priority, so that both physical and mental health needs were underserved in the civilian population. The Department of Public Welfare indefinitely postponed its plan to build an institution for the training of educable retarded delinquent adolescents, recognizing that the material, equipment, and builders simply were not available.[1]

But though World War II caused real hardship and scarcity for Illinois' handicapped children, it accelerated the optimistic and positive assessment of their needs and rights that had been developing through the 1930s. As with the First World War, the shortage of personnel put the physically and mentally handicapped into the position of doing work that might not have been available to them in peacetime. Advocates for the handicapped noted pointedly that in a society where workers were scarce, it was a wise economy for the state to nurture and appreciate each individual's contribution and to recognize that many handicapped people could offer far more than their fellow citizens were willing to admit. A considerable number of high functioning mentally retarded young men joined the armed forces, the spokesmen noted, the ultimate contribution in that war-pressed era.[2]

The value of handicapped people and their right to a normal and fulfilling life was even more profoundly underscored by the political nature of the war. Advocates for the handicapped lost no opportunity to contrast the democracies' emphasis on individual rights and protection of the vulnerable with the fascist countries' ruthless state dominance and determination to create a master race by the extermination of all those they deemed unfit. To a striking degree, those praising the American commitment to the handicapped romanticized the history of the movement in the United States. They depicted a steady line of progress and an unwavering faith and commitment to handicapped people that conveniently omitted the eugenic hysteria that had dominated both literature and policy in the first years of the twentieth century. As one speaker at an Illinois conference insisted, the impact of the eugenic view had been limited and had gained no currency among "'child minded' professional people."

So compelling was the contrast between the fascist dictatorships and democracy (particularly this edited version that obliterated the uncomfortably Hitlerian tenor of the earlier American outcry against the "unfit") that the director of the Illinois Commission for Handicapped Children confidently asserted, "Few members of a democracy would be unwilling to offer [services to the handicapped] from purely altruistic reasons." He went on to add that, fortunately, altruism and the community's interests coincided in the matter of assistance to handicapped children. Education and training of the handicapped was "a humanitarian program that pays dividends," in the words of another speaker, who stressed the happy marriage between altruism and self-interest that investment in the handicapped exemplified. Every handicapped person who became a contributor to society lightened the taxpayers' burden and added talent to the general weal.

The return of soldiers injured in body and mind by the war, coupled with an aging population that faced its own risk of handicaps and limitations, gave an immediacy and urgency to the issue that those in child welfare were quick to note. And professionals concerned with the care of the handicapped, like others involved in child welfare, believed that a decade after the inauguration of Franklin Roosevelt's New Deal, the nation had arrived at a "pro-state philosophy" that would permit maximum attention to the unfinished and neglected business of caring for those in need.[3]

Extraordinary advances in science and technology continued apace in these years, further fostering an optimistic climate. In regard to handicaps, by far the most heartening news was in the area of prevention of defects. The availability first of sulfa drugs in the late 1930s and of antibiotics after the Second World War, coupled with an improved standard of living and public health efforts such as immunization programs meant the possibility of controlling diseases that had once left their victims blind, deaf, or otherwise physically or mentally impaired. Such diseases as scarlet fever, rheumatic fever, tuberculosis, pneumonia, and venereal disease were now susceptible to effective treatment and could be controlled before massive damage had been done.

The Henry Horner Trachoma Clinics in Illinois were an example of the successful combination of public health efforts and new and effective drugs. Named after Depression era Governor Horner, who enthusiastically supported the effort, the mobile clinics reached especially into the southern rural regions of the state to combat the highly contagious disease, trachoma, which was responsible for so much blindness in the state. Education and emphasis on good hygiene was especially important with trachoma, which could be spread by the use of contaminated water and towels. But the advent of sulfa drugs and antibiotics gave physicians another weapon, a sure and relatively simple means of treating those already infected, so that by 1960 the Illinois report to the White House Conference on Children and Youth could proudly announce that not one new case of blindness from trachoma had been reported in the state since 1951.[4]

Technological advances also provided some spectacular successes. The development of hearing aids and the wider availability of eye glasses meant that a whole contingent of people who had had to deal with severe perceptual limitations in the past could lead a normal or close to normal life. (The fact that five children who merely needed glasses had been found learning braille in the state school for the blind in 1933 testifies not only to the poor screening of applicants but also to the reality that without the simple accouterment of eye glasses, these children were profoundly handicapped.) Small wonder, then, that those who spoke in behalf of the handicapped viewed the future with such optimism, despite occasional setbacks.[5]

But as early as the 1940s, those who worked with the handicapped recognized that even science had its dark side and could sometimes actually increase the number of handicapped children. The ironic concomitant of "miracle drugs," for example, was that many severely disabled children who would have quickly succumbed to infection earlier in the century now survived, profoundly handicapped. Over-zealous administration of anesthesia to women in childbirth resulted in birth defects from oxygen deprivation. And a new disease, retrolental fibroplasia, was a striking case of technology creating new problems. Between ten and twelve thousand infants were blinded before the medical community discovered in the early 1950s that the disease was caused by the excessive administration of oxygen to babies in incubators.[6]

The occasional negative references to the scientific marvels that filled the news were a portent of things to come, but in the 1940s and 1950s, science and medicine still held sway, and the intense awareness of the debit side of scientific progress that was to characterize a later age was absent. Overwhelmingly, the augers were auspicious.

The Limitations of State Assistance to Handicapped Children

For all the enthusiastic hopes about prevention, prospects for children already handicapped were sobering. Delivery of services to children in need because of physical or mental limitations was patchy at best. Chicago had always pioneered in schools for deaf, blind, and crippled children, but in most other areas of Illinois, special education facilities were virtually nonexistent. By the 1940s, it was a cliché of social welfare that all possible efforts should be made to keep handicapped children (with the oft-repeated exception of severely retarded children) at home, leading lives as normal as possible. But special education was the province of each local school board, and very few districts outside Chicago showed an interest in educating handicapped children. Although the state provided inducements for special education, paying supplementary amounts for the education of handicapped children, in 1940 only 220 school districts out of 11,995 took advantage of this money. In all, the money reached only 2,198 children, 70 percent of whom lived in Chicago. One circumstance that militated against better special education was the staggering number of school districts in the state, a problem that Illinois educators targeted in the postwar years. Such a plethora of districts isolated handicapped children, leaving only one or two in a district, a minority that had very little visibility or power. With many fewer districts, advocates for school district reform argued, there would be a more efficient pooling of resources for handicapped children and a greater likelihood that special education programs would be initiated.[7]

Rural children also suffered from a lack of medical treatment. In recognition of this nationwide health problem, Title V of the

1935 Social Security Act had designated funds specifically for work with crippled children in rural regions. This part of the Social Security Act increased the outreach to children in Illinois by creating a Division of Crippled Children,[8] but professionals found themselves frustrated in the early years of the program by the limited definition of "crippled." It included primarily orthopedically damaged children, while excluding some of the most needy physically handicapped, those with ailments like tuberculosis and heart disease, for whom treatment was just as urgent. This early bureaucratic limitation, which was remedied in the next few years by various amendments to the original law, reflected an enduring reality about the nature of handicapping ailments; some disabilities simply attracted more attention and received more resources than other, equally devastating diseases. The blind had long ranked as the elite of the handicapped world in terms of public attention and resources, while the mentally handicapped consistently received the least sympathetic regard. Following the polio epidemics of the early twentieth century, the interest in crippled children increased, and was greatly aided in the 1930s by the support of President Franklin Roosevelt, an inspiring example of the struggle to overcome polio's damaging effects. By the 1940s, orthopedically handicapped children had gone from obscurity to being the most touted of handicapped children, with significant support both from private philanthropy such as the March of Dimes and from the government.[9]

Even the grant provided by the state of Illinois to supplement the cost of educating handicapped children reflected the arbitrary quality of attention to various handicaps. In 1940 the state provided a school district $300.00 in supplemental assistance for a crippled child, $250.00 for a blind child, and $110.00 for a deaf child. This funding was equalized by the early 1940s; but when, in 1943, money became available for educable mentally handicapped children, the payment was set at about half the rate for physically handicapped children. Those concerned with the care of the mentally retarded pointed out repeatedly that mental handicaps composed the largest proportion of handicaps in Illinois, yet the monies allocated to the institutions for the retarded were always the least generous in the budget allotment. The 1945 Child Welfare Commission noted that the Lincoln institution had the lowest per capita allocation of all state institutions, a situation that had gone on for years. There were only eight teachers for 503 pupils, 64 pupils per teacher; and only 12 percent of the inmates were enrolled in classes at all. Together, Lincoln and Dixon had over 8,000 inmates in 1949, living together in conditions of dreadful overcrowding. Combined, the two institutions had never had more than six social workers to serve over 8,000 patients—a ratio of one worker for every 1400 inmates.[10]

Acknowledging the tendency to underfund the mentally handicapped, the Director of the Department of Public Welfare remarked baldly that "the mentally deficient child has no charm of manner," but added that the investment of state monies on their behalf was crucial "from the standpoint of giving the state the best possible salvage from the material God sends us to develop."[11]

His harsh metaphor reflected the reality of the era. Concern for handicapped children and the sponsorship by various private organizations had raised the awareness level and increased the public's sensitivity to many disabilities. Perhaps the best example of this growing tolerance was epilepsy, which had experienced an extraordinary reconstruction in the public mind since the early part of the century when even such compassionate social policy thinkers as Julia Lathrop had advocated total segregation of people with epilepsy, not only for their own sake but to spare the general populace the unpleasantness of the disease and from concerns about its hereditary effects. The advent of drugs that controlled epileptic seizures and the vigorous efforts of the Epilepsy Society, changed epilepsy from a disease described with loathing to one classified in a deliberately matter of fact manner with other physical handicaps, and a condition for which professionals urged the greatest normalization possible.[12]

But a ring of intolerance still surrounded the mentally handicapped, and this inner circle of exclusion and segregation was accepted and fostered by professionals who worked with the retarded. Some officials urged greater community support and inclusion for the educable mentally handicapped, expressing bafflement at public rejection of this disability. ("It is difficult to understand why there should be a stigma attached to having a low-powered brain," one professional complained, "when no stigma is attached to the visual or hearing mechanism. The child with an inadequate brain should no more be an object of derision than the child with inadequate eyes.") But other officials characterized the mentally retarded as "salvage" or "the 'seconds' of the human race." Insisting that "the child who is hopelessly retarded should be placed in a public institution or under private care before the mother leaves the hospital" was a common and unabashed view held by physicians, social workers, and educators who contended that "this should be done to protect the mental health of the parents and other members of the family." Those advocating greater tolerance for mentally handicapped people eroded their case by demanding tolerance only for a limited group of educable children and dismissing the rest as unsalvageable.

In practical terms, the decision that a child was too retarded to be kept at home was generally made by no one more expert than a family doctor. This meant that a number of children who might in fact be educable were institutionalized before there was an opportunity to determine mental capacity. Although children with Down's syndrome (or mongolism in 1940s terms) included a wide range of mental capabilities, these children were routinely classed among those who should go directly from the hospital nursery to institutions (a goal by no means easy to accomplish, since the waiting lists at the public institutions numbered into the thousands).[13]

There were other groups that went unrecognized and unserved as well. The multiply-handicapped (as they were labeled), while a small population in absolute terms, were almost entirely overlooked, especially if their disabilities were both physical and mental. And despite the fact that the Institute for Juvenile Research had been one of the earliest child study centers in the country to apply the diagnostic and treatment procedures of psychology to children, emotionally disturbed children and their parents had difficulty getting assistance in Illinois, particularly if they needed residential placement. Even less recognized were children diagnosed psychotic. Their fate was to be placed in the adult wards of mental hospitals, where their treatment was unlikely to be in any way geared to their special problems and circumstances. From 1938 to 1942, the Child Welfare Commission of the legislature noted, 317 children under sixteen had been committed to state mental hospitals, because there were virtually no other services available to them.[14]

Postwar Efforts to Improve the Care of Handicapped Children

In the postwar years, the state of Illinois attempted to deal with many of these problems, broadening the scope of state involvement and trying to reduce the arbitrary selection of those served. One of the most important agencies urging reform was the Illinois Commission for Handicapped Children, a commission charged to act as a coordinating body for the scattered resources available for handicapped children, as well as to research problem areas and suggest a plan of action for improvement. Another critical government agency was the Department of Special Education in the Office of Public Instruction, whose first director, Ray Graham, made a major impact on the state through his vigorous advocacy for special education. These two agencies urged consolidation of school districts and supported the training of special education teachers, as well as the vigorous recruitment of those few who were available. They were successful enough so that by 1946 Illinois State University, the designated teachers' college, had drawn up a curriculum for special education and was taking its first tentative steps toward offering a program.

Another urgent need targeted by these agencies was the creation of a Hospital School to serve orthopedically handicapped children who were too impaired to attend regular schools and were consequently falling behind seriously in their education. The Hospital School opened in Chicago in 1945. Other institutional successes were the opening of the Grace Abbott Children's Center for mentally ill children on the grounds of the Peoria State Hospital in 1951 and the expansion of clinics for crippled children. In 1942, there had been 58 centers to diagnose and treat crippled children in Illinois; by 1950, there were 247 clinics functioning.[15]

By the early 1950s, advocates for handicapped children could point proudly to their record, but they had also begun to worry that the special needs of handicapped children might be overlooked in the desperate effort to respond to the rapidly escalating birthrate that had begun shortly after the war and was to continue without abatement for a decade and more. Children's services everywhere, from schools to hospital nurseries, were stretched to the utmost, and the vice chairman of the Commission for Handicapped Children, addressing the Governor's Conference on Exceptional Children in 1951, exhorted those present not to let their successes be swept aside in the general scramble to respond to the burgeoning population of young children.[16]

The Growth of the Parents' Movement

His fears were unfounded. The rights and needs of handicapped children were to receive greater attention than ever before in the 1950s and 1960s, owing in large part to a hitherto unacknowledged source of energy and power, parents' groups.

There was probably no group of parents who had endured harsher criticism or more unsympathetic treatment from society at large than the parents of handicapped children. From the nineteenth century onward, professionals had alternately criticized them as too protective or not protective enough of their disabled children and had worked hard to replace parental involvement with state authority in some cases, while sedulously ignoring other types of handicapped children altogether. In the years when a crude hereditary theory dominated thinking, parents were not only blamed as incompetent caretakers of their children but often were indicted for causing and passing on the actual handicaps themselves. The parents of mentally retarded children had been the most severely criticized, characterized as vicious, mentally limited, poor, and appallingly prolific.

By the mid-twentieth century, the criticism of parents had taken an entirely different aspect. Gone was the class-ridden and frankly repressive tone of the early century, and in its place were the iron hand and velvet glove of "therapy." It was generally acknowledged that handicaps were an affliction that cut across class lines, and parents in the postwar years were not so much indicted as they were discounted, included as part of the handicap rather than being enlisted as knowledgeable and deeply concerned supporters of their disabled children. The conventional wisdom was that the presence of a handicapped child put such stress on a family that they would need professional counseling to learn to accept the child's limitations and work with them realistically. An example of this therapizing, as it worked in practice, was given by a United States Office of Education official, speaking to an Illinois conference in 1947. He read the letter of a mother who had written to the department seeking help for her child, who had cerebral palsy. "She is not a burden to us," wrote the mother, "in fact I feel proud to be a parent picked to raise a crippled child. Anyone can raise a perfect one. But when it comes to education, my hands are tied. I don't know where to start so if there is a program set up for this type of child I would like to know about it." The Office of Education official acknowledged the difficulty, remarking with condescension that "even a professional person would have difficulty in working out a suitable plan." He went on to suggest that this mother, in all likelihood, needed counseling to convince her to institutionalize her child. At no time did he applaud the mother's courage and commitment, nor acknowledge that her basic request for educational assistance was a need that was sadly ignored in American society.[17]

By the 1950s, parents' groups, especially parents of the most neglected group, the mentally retarded, had begun to organize, and their impact was immediate and powerful. The first group of parents of retarded children had been organized as far back as 1933 in Cleveland, but the movement gained its first real prominence in 1950 with the organization of local groups across the country and the national convention in Minneapolis of the National Association for Retarded Children. Professionals and state agencies acknowledged the sudden appearance of the parents' lobby with a variety of responses, ranging from hearty approval to unctuous and patronizing reminders to parents that progress took time and professionals, after all, knew best. Dr. Grover F. Powers, in an address to the American Academy of Pediatrics, noted that "parents themselves have come to the rescue of the professional workers and are helping their children and themselves mightily thereby." But writer Edith Stern, author of *The Handicapped Child*, told the 1950 Illinois Conference on Exceptional Children, "In the handicap situations, the parents are the ones that have the emotions, and the professionals are the ones that have the objectivity." She went on to add, elucidating the hostilities between professionals and parents, "The more devoted to the job the staff is, the more likely they are to shut out the parents; and the more devoted the parents are, the unhappier that they are that somebody else can do better with the child."[18]

Stern's condescending analysis, with its double-edged sympathy to parents, was already outdated rhetoric by the time of the 1950 Illinois conference, though it would have been perfectly acceptable a year earlier. The difference was that there were several parent-representatives at the 1950 conference, and their responses to professional platitudes and unconscious arrogance made the gathering a memorable one. One doctor, describing what he clearly felt to be compassionate behavior, explained his technique in dealing with parents of Down's syndrome children: "Usually we get a picture of it and show it to them, because they will believe it more. If you tell them that there is no stigma, that it wasn't their fault, then they feel better." It was critical, he insisted, to persuade the parents to leave their baby at the hospital, to convince them that the child would only cause "a lot of heartache in your home and in your neighborhood. It is going to be a stigma on the other children growing up."[19]

The doctor was uttering no more than conventional wisdom, but the conventional wisdom of professionals was under fire in 1950. In response to the doctor's description and query about the appropriateness of his course, Mr. Thorell, a parent from the Rockford Association for Retarded Children addressed the convention. In his speech, Thorell reflected two things that were crucial about the newly founded parents' movement: it was a movement that cut across class lines and could tap the confidence and expertise of people used to positions of leadership; and, mobilized at last, this long-suffering group of parents was unlikely to relinquish their involvement and return to an earlier, passive role in regard to their children's welfare. Thorell began by telling his audience that, although he was not a medical or social service professional, he was the vice president of a company that did a significant international trade and he was not particularly intimidated by so-called professional credentials. He went on to say, regarding the doctor's tidying of a family tragedy by institutionalizing the baby, "I couldn't help but compare that with the old Chinese custom of taking the unwanted child and dropping it over the wall." He spoke passionately for the right of mentally handicapped children "to live as full and complete a life as they can," to remain as much as possible within the normal boundaries of society. In response to a question asking what would become of his daughter when he died, he replied that she might have to be institutionalized some day, but that she would be a far more complete person than would have been possible had she been placed in an institution at birth.[20]

Not coincidentally were parents of retarded children at the vanguard of the parents' movement. Mr. Thorell told the conference that the support system for parents of mentally handicapped children had been so abysmally lacking that their family doctor had not even told them that their daughter had Down's syndrome (a condition with very clear symptoms that had been identified in the nineteenth century). His experience was not an uncommon one. A 1962 Children's Bureau report on "Mongoloid Children and Their Families" noted that of the fifty families studied, twenty-three, nearly half, were told initially that the baby was normal. In eight more cases, the doctors said nothing, leaving the parents to endure months of uncertainty and worry before a correct diagnosis was finally made. The parents in the study generally had charitable assessments to account for the doctors' lack of candor. The doctors, however, accounted for their dissembling either by insisting that it was "best for the parents to find out for themselves," or, more frankly, by admitting that they "could not bring [themselves] to tell the mother."[21]

Such a lack of support characterized the experience of parents with retarded children. In Illinois, at midcentury, when significant progress was being made for other handicapped groups, a bill to promote the educational rights of retarded children was rejected with ugly rhetoric depicting "these little monsters sitting alongside of your own normal child in the public schools." Parents of retarded children were told to institutionalize them; yet when they came to that difficult decision, they faced waiting lists of massive proportions and no public assistance to keep their children in the few private institutions that existed while they waited for admittance to Lincoln or Dixon. And while Edith Stern, cheery author of *The Handicapped Child,* assured the parents of retarded children that institutions for the mentally retarded were kindly and humanely run, the state of Illinois numbered 10,396 people in its two institutions for the retarded by 1954, and not the most euphemistic of bureaucrats attempted to describe the care as better than minimal.[22]

Parents' groups set up educational programs of their own for their retarded children, in churches, settlement houses and other community centers, paying for the cost of education themselves and contributing as much as possible in volunteer time. As their numbers grew, so did their determination and their conviction that their children were being cheated out of a guaranteed right. As advocates for the group pointed out, the constitution of the state guaranteed the right of education to all children, not exempting the handicapped, and the parents' groups became progressively more persistent in their demands that their children share in the prosperity and possibilities of the age.[23]

Nor were parents of retarded children the only parents embittered by their treatment, as a 1951 study of state services showed. The Commission for Handicapped Children conducted a survey of unmet needs, directed especially at families whose children were rejected for care at the new Hospital School. What they learned was sobering, and it was a solemn and intensely self-critical staff that presented its findings to the annual Exceptional Children's Conference. Far from the comforting ideal of professionals who "knew best," the survey spoke of professionals on all levels who were insensitive to families' anguish. Some promised too much initially, and then simply disappeared when they were unable to deliver on their promises. Equally devastating, others conveyed to the parents the notion, in the words of one social worker, that "there is nothing that can be done, just resign yourselves to a hopeless future."[24]

Those analyzing the negative responses of families in the survey denounced the myth of professional objectivity and spoke instead of social workers and medical people who rode the same emotional roller coaster of fear and hope as parents but were able to disguise their withdrawal from involvement as "objectivity." These speakers, considerably in advance of the general rebellion against professionalism that would come in the 1960s and 1970s, urged upon their audience the task of some vigorous soul searching and rethinking of the long-held authoritarian relationship between professionals and parents of handicapped children. The child "comes to us as a whole child with his whole family and his whole problem," social worker Elizabeth Meek told the convention. "His family may have resources within themselves and ideas about what use they wish to make about their situation and if we disregard those feelings and disregard those resources, we must not be surprised if another study a few years from now shows again that some families want no part of our fine programs, if they think coldly of us as being 'the state.'"[25]

State and Federal Involvement in the 1960s

The image of the state as juggernaut, mindlessly crushing family hopes and feelings, was especially distressing for a generation of social service professionals with a "pro-state" philosophy. But in fact, the state, while it could prove indifferent and withholding to families desperately trying to cope with the multiple problems caused by the presence of a handicapped child, was to provide the crucial force necessary to bring handicapped children into the mainstream of society, a goal both their parents and professionals were beginning to advocate in the 1950s.

Once more, presidential influence affected the struggle in a very specific way. In the early 1960s, President John F. Kennedy, whose sister was mentally retarded and whose family was active in the movement to improve conditions for the retarded, played a key role in raising national awareness about retarded people. Kennedy appointed a "President's Panel on Mental Retardation."

The need for the study was great. Two years earlier Gunnar Dybwad, executive director of National Association for Retarded Children, had called for parents' groups to concentrate not only on humanizing the daily lives of institutions but to pressure legislators to invest in research, noting that he could not name a single comprehensive, controlled study concerning residential care of the mentally retarded. Now, with a friend in the White House and a presidential panel actually concentrating on a problem that had for years been locked in society's attic, the plight of the retarded received some much needed public attention. The panel's final report recommended

1. research into the causes of retardation and the care of those already handicapped
2. improved social and educational services and active recruitment of professionals for the field of special education through fellowships and grants;
3. a new legal and social concept of the retarded, including protection of their civil rights;
4. emphasis on preventative health measures, including improved infant and maternal health care;
5. programs of education and information to increase public awareness of the problem of mental retardation;
6. community-centered, comprehensive programs for the retarded.[26]

These suggestions were by no means especially innovative. The President's Panel urged for the retarded much of what had been advocated earlier for other groups of handicapped people; but the retarded had never received the attention or services accorded to other groups with special needs. And, the committee urged, by emphasizing the study of the retarded, "information of a generic nature" that would benefit other, less neglected groups, was likely to result.[27]

The 1960s was a time of transition in special education. The decade saw significant gains in raising public awareness about the needs of retarded children, along with some financial and legislative support. But modest federal and state gains did not make a major impact on the daily lives of many children. In 1963, President Kennedy proposed that a program of prevention, community services, and research should be inaugurated, and Congress did amend the Social Security Act in that year to include project research and planning grants for mental retardation. By 1967, the federal government was spending over 400 million dollars a year on programs benefiting the mentally retarded, while more than twice that amount was spent by state and local governments and private citizens together. Such efforts had led to "extraordinary growth in the services which the mentally retarded and their families may call upon," according to President Johnson's Committee on Mental Retardation. Nevertheless, the major part of the work was yet to be accomplished. "Half the nation's 25,000 school districts offer no classes for pupils having special learning problems and needs," according to the President's Committee. "Three-quarters of the nation's 201,000 institutionalized mentally retarded live in buildings 50 years old or more. . . . The 81,000 full-time staff in public facilities for the mentally retarded must be almost doubled to reach *minimum adequacy.*"[28]

Though the situation for retarded people was the worst, the availability of special education for any handicapped children was still extremely limited in the early to mid 1960s. In terms of real services, the need was desperate. Only about 25 percent of children in the United Stated needing special education because of a physical or mental handicap were actually attending any public or private school in 1965. The need for special education teachers and services was acute, but the federal Elementary and Secondary Education Act of 1965 (ESEA), while it did not exclude handicapped children, had no special programs designated to help them.[29]

However, by the mid 1960s, groups representing handicapped children were beginning to forge themselves into an effective coalition. The effectiveness of advocating the right to education of *all* handicapped children, rather than fragmenting their power and influence by concentrating on particular disabilities, was becoming clearer to those lobbying for the handicapped. In 1966, they pressed for and won an amendment to the ESEA, Title VI , which authorized 50 million dollars in fiscal 1967 and 150 million dollars in fiscal 1968 to assist states to develop and expand programs for the education of handicapped children. Title VI was a limited victory, in that the legislation did not incorporate any of the radical departures such as "least restrictive environment" or "mainstreaming" that characterized later laws concerning handicapped children. Nor did it speak of education as a right of all children. It simply made money available to states if they chose to take advantage of it. But it was a first success for a new coalition. And, of major importance, the new law established a Bureau of Education for the Handicapped in the Federal Office of Education, an agency that would prove critical in advocating further change. In 1970, the Education of the Handicapped law replaced Title VI of ESEA, broadening the authority of the Office of Education to encourage research and training in "specific learning disabilities," a recently recognized category of handicapped children. The new law also increased appropriations for programs generally.[30]

At the same time that significant activity was taking place at the federal level, a critical special education law passed the Illinois legislature. In 1965, the General Assembly passed the first law mandating education for the handicapped in the state, to be implemented by July 1, 1969. The law was not a complete "Bill of Rights for Handicapped Children," as the federal law passed a decade later would be called. For one thing, it allowed a differential in the ages of mandatory education: three to twenty-one for physically handicapped children and multiply-handicapped children; five to twenty-one for mentally handicapped, "maladjusted," and speech-impaired children. Further, it left an escape clause in the provisions for severely mentally retarded children and emotionally disturbed children, stating that "any such child shall be regarded as eligible for special education facilities only as long as benefit to him from the program can be determined to exist." It did not articulate the necessity for "the least restrictive environment," calling instead on school boards and planners to make maximum use of state facilities run by the Department of Children and Family Services and the Department of Mental Health (that is, the institutions for the blind, deaf, retarded, mentally ill, and the Hospital School). But the law did clearly enjoin the newly established Special Education Advisory Committees to report to the Superintendent of Public Instruction "a comprehensive plan whereby all handicapped children resident in the county may receive a good common school education." Such a plan meant the recruitment of specialized professionals for both elementary and high schools and the creation of programs to respond to handicapped children. The local school districts were to bear the cost, together with a state reimbursement granted according to a set formula. The sanction against any county that failed to implement plans or keep up with yearly reports would be a loss of state funding to their schools.[31]

Anti-Institutional Thinking and Its Impact

The 1965 Illinois Special Education Law, despite its limitations, was a major victory for special education advocates, offering genuine opportunities for children who might have been institutionalized earlier because there were no resources for them at home. This was not only in keeping with the recommendations of President Kennedy's panel but also a reflection of the powerful anti-institutional persuasion expressed by theorists and practitioners

of social welfare in the 1960s. In all areas of social welfare, thinkers stressed the malevolent effects of institutions on the human
personality, a destructiveness affecting inmates and staff alike.
Proposing much the same arguments that had been made against
child care institutions in an earlier era, critics of institutions for
the mentally ill and mentally retarded pointed to the dehuman-
ization that went on in the atmosphere of a "total asylum," in the
phrase of one of the best known critics of the phenomenon, Erving Goffman. Goffman and others argued that, far from offering
any rehabilitative features, institutions stripped inmates of all individuality; rewarded docility rather than initiative, experimenta-
tion, and growth; and made the smooth operation of a rigid routine the cardinal virtue for both inmates and staff. Because
institutions generally had overworked, undertrained, and underpaid staffs, with few systemic controls to balance the power gap
between inmates and employees, the possibility for both neglect
and outright abuse was ever-present.[32]

Illinois citizens faced a painful illustration of the hazards of institutional life for children when, in the early 1970s, as part of a
series of court actions against state agencies, the Juvenile Office
of the Legal Aid Society of Chicago exposed several shocking cases. The office brought suit on behalf of children lost in the bureaucratic shuffle and improperly placed in mental institutions for
lack of other facilities; who had been kept for weeks in solitary
confinement ("quiet rooms"); or who had been restrained spread-
eagled on their beds for seventy-seven hours at a time for a variety of infractions.[33]

Conditions had changed very little since the days when Julia
Lathrop had sternly told the 1907 committee investigating abuses at Lincoln that good care was a matter of dollars and cents. But
the analysis espoused by theorists in the 1960s and 1970s differed
sharply from that of Lathrop and her era, in that social thinkers
no longer accepted the notion that there were some people who
needed to be segregated from society. Whereas Lathrop argued for
training and high quality staff to humanize institutions, 1960s
thinkers contended that institutions by their very nature were
destructive and that social welfare as a whole had to think in terms
of returning people to the community, to their families if at all
possible, or to a modified familial setting as an alternative. This
anti-institutional thinking challenged every aspect of social welfare, from prisons and reform schools to such apparently benign
institutions as general hospitals, where patients and patient ad-

vocates began to argue for the patient's right to be informed and consulted about medical decisions and procedures. The impact was particularly strong in the area of mental health, reflected in the annual reports of the Illinois Department of Mental Health, where stress on "normalization" began to appear by the early 1960s. And because both Illinois institutions for the retarded remained desperately overcrowded and understaffed, with long waiting lists, the notion of deinstitutionalizing the more capable patients or relocating them to community facilities had practical as well as philosophical appeal.

There was emphasis on normalization for those who remained in institutions as well, with parents' groups playing a far more active role than would have been imaginable a generation earlier. Some patients began to receive training in grooming and other living skills, while others were resettled in experimental halfway houses, preparatory to a return to the community. Just as the inmates of Lincoln and Dixon were introduced to the community, the community was being introduced to them, encouraged to participate in patients' lives through volunteer work and to learn about the reality of mental disabilities by means of educational programs of all sorts.

Despite these marks of progress, the report from Dixon in 1964 noted that by American Association of Mental Deficiency standards, overcrowding at Dixon was still 66 percent, with a growing number of severely retarded patients. "The institution traditionally has provided only custodial care of minimal quality for the severely retarded," remarked the superintendent. "It is now being challenged to extend significant training to these persons, and it is finding many old attitudes and programs not valid."[34]

In 1970, The Department of Mental Health noted a rapid decrease in patient population for the first time in the history of Lincoln and Dixon, in part because the state had added four more facilities for retarded people, but also because "the trend within the Department of Mental Health today is to encourage families to keep a retarded member at home unless his or her presence creates insurmountable difficulties—or unless an institution can do more for the retarded person than the home."[35]

The 1970s were to further accelerate this trend toward deinstitutionalization. On a national level, a number of court cases showed that the new attitudes toward institutions were becoming part of legal as well as social welfare thinking. The United States District Court in Alabama found in a 1972 suit brought against Partlow State School and Hospital, for example, that the only justifiable grounds for involuntary hospitalization of the mentally retarded was for treatment, not mere custodial care, or "warehousing," in the judge's unequivocal phrase. He wrote: "Because the only constitutional justification for civilly committing a mental retardate, therefore, is habilitation, it follows ineluctably that once committed such a person is possessed of an inviolable constitutional right to habilitation." This decision set standards of what such habilitation entailed. It required not only the elimination of the appalling conditions that occasioned the suit in the first place but decreed that each inmate had a right to training, education, and the opportunity "to develop and realize his fullest potential. The institution shall implement the principle of normalization so that each resident may live as normally as possible." Even more significant was the injunction that no mentally retarded person could be admitted to the institution if there were programs and services available in the community that could "afford adequate habilitation." Only if it was determined that the institution was genuinely the least restrictive environment could a mentally retarded person be admitted, and as an inmate, he or she had a right to something as closely approximating normal living conditions as possible.[36]

This decision, which made humanizing institutions a legal requirement rather than merely desirable policy, was handed down in April 1972. In May of the same year, advocates for the education of handicapped children enjoyed another judicial success, this time in the United States District Court in Pennsylvania. The court found in favor of the Pennsylvania Association for Retarded Children, which had brought suit against the state of Pennsylvania for depriving retarded children of their right to education both through policy and statute. A three-judge court ruled unanimously that the equal protection clause of the Fourteenth Amendment entitled retarded children (and by extension all handicapped children) ages six to twenty-one to a free and public education appropriate to their learning capacities. Other similar decisions in state and federal courts unmistakably indicated that handicapped children and their advocates were no longer seeking benevolence but were framing the argument in contemporary terms. Drawing on the idiom of the civil rights movement that had so shaped the character of the age, they found that they, like the earlier movement, had a strong and important ally in the courts.[37]

The Education for All Handicapped Children Act

As important as judicial support was, the critical event for handicapped children happened not in the courts but in the United States Congress in 1975. This was Public Law 94-142, "The Education for All Handicapped Children Law," strengthened by Section 504 of the Rehabilitation Act of 1973. P.L. 94-142 developed out of an ongoing effort on the part of parents, legislators and special education advocates that had resulted in increasing state and federal legislative attention to the handicapped in the early 1970s, at the same time that the federal courts were articulating a right to special education. P.L. 94-142 was by far the most comprehensive legislation to be achieved. It required full public education "at no cost" to handicapped children ages three to twenty-one, regardless of the seriousness of their handicaps. It was notable among federal laws concerning education, because it was mandatory rather than permissive. If a state wanted to participate in the funding provided, every school system in the state had to abide by the regulations set forth in the law. Section 504 held that "no otherwise qualified handicapped individual . . . shall solely by reason of his/her handicap, be excluded from participation in, be denied the benefits of, or be subject to discrimination under any program or activity receiving federal financial assistance." In effect, any state that received federal funding for its schools must offer free public education to handicapped children, on penalty of losing its federal funding. The law was also notable for its explicit requirement that a child must be educated in the least restrictive environment possible, with an individualized education program that set out short- and long-term goals. The law spelled out parents' rights to full involvement in the child's program, including notification and prior approval of any changes in the education plan, the right to confidentiality, and the right to due process if the parents and the school district disagreed.

The law addressed two opposite concerns of parents in its scrupulous monitoring of the school's actions from the point of the first evaluation of the child. On the one hand, some children, especially poor and minority students, faced the possibility that they might be placed in special education classes because of discrimination, either in a testing process that did not allow for cultural differences or in more direct discrimination, as a desire to rid a classroom of a student deemed troublesome. At exactly the opposite extreme were children who were clearly handicapped, who needed special programs that school districts might be reluctant to offer. P.L. 94-142 gave parents the leverage to challenge doubtful decisions in both types of cases.[38]

It was clear from the writing of the law, from the care taken to institute due process and appeals procedures, that the authors of the legislation expected its implementation to include considerable combat between parents and school districts. Such provisions proved to be justified in practice. Unlike some states, Illinois already had a fairly strong special education law, but P.L. 94-142 included provisions that put considerably greater demands on school districts. The sections of the Illinois law allowing fewer years of education for mentally handicapped children had already been removed by the time P.L. 94-142 became operative, but Illinois law still allowed the schools to exclude maladjusted or retarded children if it was determined that the schools could offer no program that would benefit them. Further, Illinois law allowed placement of handicapped children in private special education facilities if a school district could not offer them specialized services, with the parents paying the difference between the state allotment (maximum $2500 a year) and the actual cost of tuition and transportation.

By contrast, the federal law flatly required that all children, regardless of the severity of their handicaps, had a right to a free, public education, and an education that took place in the least restrictive environment, as much in a normal school setting as possible. Nor did Illinois law allow for the stringent protection of parental rights that the federal law enforced. A 1974 report on special education in Illinois declared that "parents, often ignored in the past as sources of diagnostic information, are now working partners—or should be." There was no such pious invocation in the federal law. Parents were indisputably a crucial part of the situation, not only in diagnosing but in planning every step of the child's individualized learning program; and if they were not included, they had avenues of redress.[39]

Those avenues were traveled early and often. From the beginning P.L. 94-142 was a much litigated piece of legislation, with school districts, parents, and advocacy groups seeking to determine in concrete terms what the provisions of the law meant in practice. That there was intransigence on the part of school districts, many parents would ruefully acknowledge. P.L. 94-142 was not an end but a beginning, a law that gave their children a theoretical right to education if they were prepared to fight for it.[40]

On the other hand, the school districts had a number of complaints about the new law as well. Not the least of these was the fact that the federal government, despite its vigorous action in setting the terms of the law, provided only a small percentage of the cost. The federal funding level of P.L. 94-142 was scheduled to reach 40 percent of the National Average Per Pupil Expenditure by FY 1982, but the actual funding fell far short. In 1981, it had only reached one-third of the proposed funding. By 1991 funding was at 9 percent of the National Average Per Pupil Expenditure, compared to the optimal 40 percent designated in the law, with some experts arguing that, adjusted for inflation, the figure was more accurately 6.7 percent. Federal law mandated increased special education offerings, but state and local school districts bore the financial burden of these programs.[41]

In addition to financial issues, educators were often frustrated by the tremendous increase in paperwork that came with the preparation of individual education plans, scrupulous notification and communication with parents, and verification of other aspects of the law to federal monitors. As with most federal programs, there were complaints that the implementation of accountability created a flood of paperwork that—far from producing better education—simply took teachers away from teaching and left them swamped with forms, meetings, and other activities that were sops to a mindless bureaucracy. As one teacher wrote poignantly, "On the IEP [Individual Education Program] my name goes on the line after 'Local Education Agency Representative.' I used to be called a teacher, but I don't teach much any more. Last year I was out of class the equivalent of 30 to 40 whole days because of conferences, testing, phone calls, securing confidential records, and the like." His complaint was not against P.L. 94-142, which he acknowledged as necessary, but against the half-heartedness of its implementation, which forced "the combat soldier" (the special education teacher) to make up for deficient funding and resources by doing more than they had been called upon to do already.

Yet some educators spoke positively of the law's procedures, approving of the provisions that involved parents in their children's educations and contending that short- and long-range planning encouraged teachers to focus on a broader perspective than mere day-to-day teaching.[42]

The 1980s: The Conservative Reaction

P.L. 94-142, which was mandated to reach full implementation by 1980, came of age in hard times for vulnerable people. The "Reagan Revolution" that dominated the first years of the 1980s was committed to cutting back federal involvement and federal funding, particularly in areas of social welfare. One of the Reagan administration's first targets was P.L. 94-142. The administration proposed plans to amend P.L. 94-142 drastically, not only cutting back funding but also aiming to remove the critical aspect of the law that enforced parental participation, as well as restricting the eligibility for special programs to the severely handicapped, cutting back on support services and eliminating the crucial recourse to due process. The response from advocate groups for the handicapped was prompt, concerted, and vociferous. "Join us, we get things done," Illinois' Coordinating Council for Handicapped Children promised in a flier urging parents and concerned citizens to "Stop the burial of P.L. 94-142." And so it proved. A nationwide chorus of protest was sounded by such coalitions, and their lobbying power was so effective that a surprised, if not chastened, Reagan administration backed off hastily.[43]

But the attempt to gut the law let the handicapped coalitions know unmistakably that the security of having a friend in the White House and at the Department of Education was over. Like other groups involved in securing civil rights for minorities, they would be fighting a holding action, not striding forward in the new decade.

One of the major problems faced by parents and advocates of the handicapped was that P. L. 94-142 stopped at age twenty-one. After that point, there were some resources and provisions for the handicapped, but these provisions were not the carefully articulated and monitored requirements of the Education for All Handicapped Children Law. Public Law 94-142 had been won in part through the argument that handicapped children were claiming their right: a free, public education like that given to other children in the United States. But beyond age twenty-one, the old presumption that each individual would be able to manage independently applied, and the power of the federal mandate ended. Certainly there were strong advocates for and among the adult handicapped, but social thinkers worried especially about the situation of aging parents caring for adult handicapped children who were still as dependent as young children, yet chronologically of age and no longer eligible for the intensive attention and assistance received in their school years. With few respite programs or supports, these parents, despite all the reforms of recent years, faced much the same isolation in dealing with their handicapped children that people had endured forty years earlier.[44]

Certainly provisions for the most vulnerable among handicapped adults gave cause for anxiety. Early in the Reagan administration, there was an attempt to purge the rolls of the Supplemental Security Income Program (SSI), which had been created by Congress in 1972 to replace the earlier conglomerate of social programs (Aid to the Blind, Old Age Assistance, and Aid to the Totally and Permanently Disabled) that had been added to federal social welfare legislation over the years.[45]

It was a program critical to all kinds of handicapped people: the mentally ill, mentally retarded and others disabled to the point where work was not an option. SSI experienced the full onslaught of Reagan administration dictates and Reagan administration zeal. A 1980 law had ordered periodic reviews of SSI recipients, and the Reagan administration used these reviews to purge the rolls. From March of 1981 until June of 1983, 266,000 people were cut from federal disability rolls. As was the case with P.L. 94-142, advocacy groups, politicians, and the courts all protested vehemently. Democrat Pete Start of California said that the SSI program was being run with the "heart of a Doberman pinscher and the mind of a piranha." Courts began to order the reinstatement of those dropped from the rolls. By June of 1983, so much pressure had been placed on the Department of Health and Human Services that the regulations regarding SSI reviews were rewritten to exempt a large contingent of the mentally ill, mentally retarded and seriously physically impaired from reviews. Ultimately, many of those who had been removed from SSI were reinstated. But the two-year policy left no doubt that the handicapped could not look to the executive branch for support as long as an administration hostile to social welfare protections held power.[46]

And the lack of zeal toward the disabled, especially the mentally disabled, was by no means restricted to the federal government. By the mid 1970s, the presence of homeless people, many of them former mental patients, led to accusations that the deinstitutionalization so vigorously fought for in the 1960s had degenerated into the dumping of the mentally handicapped on the streets, where they coped for themselves as best they could. When Illinois officials had discussed the new movement away from institutionalization and toward community care in the early 1960s, one of them had written, "Though far more expensive than providing custodial care, enactment of local-state-federal partnerships assure Illinois citizens of competent and available assistance when mental disorder occurs." But the movement for deinstitutionalization, which had posited strong, effective, and constant community supports for the

mentally handicapped, had proven to be a useful creed for those simply interested in cutting budgets. Deinstitutionalization became
dumping when the critical aspect of community mental health supports was missing, and in Illinois and across the country, this came
to be the case, particularly when the federal government proved an
unwilling partner in the local-state-federal partnership envisioned
in the 1960s. The Governor's Task Force on the Future of Mental
Health in Illinois declared in early 1987, "Deinstitutionalization,
as an overall policy for the Department [of Mental Health and Developmental Disabilities] in the sixties and seventies, had unintended consequences that we dare not repeat and must correct. It is clear
that institutional care for some mentally disabled persons will be a
continuing necessity."[47]

Yet institutions were in dire straits also. The task force's review
of institutional conditions, as well as a report by the League of
Women Voters, spoke of a system that was underfunded, with inadequate staffing and all the enduring problems of neglect and
abuse that had led people to a belief in deinstitutionalization in
the first place. According to the task force report, state funding
for institutions, taking federal medicaid payments and inflation
into account, had actually decreased since 1987, with disastrous
results for patient care. A series of *Chicago Tribune* reports in 1986
revealed that a 1985 Mental Health Department internal memo
(obtained through the Freedom of Information Act) had detailed
abuse in mental health facilities, ranging from the withholding of
food to misuse of and overuse of "timeout" (the placing of a patient in an isolated room for a period of time) to outright abuse
that resulted in broken arms and ribs. Grimmest of all was the
report's contention that patients were beaten or sexually assaulted while in restraints. In May of 1985, a twenty-five-year-old mentally retarded man had died of asphyxiation when tied to a toilet
at the Howe Development Center in Tinley Park. So shocking was
the Mental Health in-house report that some state officials actually considered assigning state troopers to the state's mental health
facilities to see if that might insure patients' safety. The plan was
abandoned as too costly.[48]

Even after these scandals broke and after the unequivocal warnings voiced by the Governor's task force and the League of Wom-
en Voters, the state's mental health budget, along with its education and social service budgets continued to be cut. The League
of Women Voters statistic that Illinois ranked ninth in the nation
in income level and thirty-eighth in mental health expenditures

was apparently not sufficiently compelling to legislators, who steadfastly refused to pass a substantive income tax increase. It was especially embittering to advocates for social services that in 1988 the same General Assembly that could not manage to raise taxes for social services and education did rally at the eleventh hour to find the funding for a new baseball stadium to keep the White Sox in Chicago.[49]

Conclusion

Despite the disturbing evidence of people badly served both in the community and in institutions, it was certainly true that much progress had been made in behalf of handicapped people. Science and technology continued to aid in both prevention of handicaps and a growing capacity to reduce the handicapping effects of a whole range of conditions through improved surgical techniques and prosthetic devices. One of the most dramatic preventive triumphs was the development of a vaccine for polio in the 1950s. Another notable development was the introduction of a simple test that could be routinized in every hospital nursery to check for phenylketonuria. The PKU test screened for a metabolic disorder which, though controllable by diet and medical therapy, could cause mental retardation if untreated. Increased knowledge of the effect of drugs on fetal development encouraged more conservative use of medications for pregnant women during gestation and delivery. And the rebellion against a medical superclass that characterized the 1960s–1980s meant that expectant parents often monitored the mother's diet, medication, and delivery more militantly than the health professionals involved.[50]

The situation was not entirely positive, however. At the same time that the general public was showing more concern for prenatal conditions that might result in handicapping conditions for children, the rate of childbirth was going up among populations at greater risk to have handicapped children. At one end of the spectrum women over thirty-five were having first children, a reflection of changing work and social patterns. At the other end of the spectrum, teenaged pregnancy, with its attendant risks, was a growing concern in the late twentieth century. So, too, were drug and alcohol related births.

Particularly frustrating for those concerned about prevention of childhood handicaps and infant mortality were the skewed priorities exemplified in the care of infants born premature or with life threatening conditions. Medical technology had advanced so far from the days of the first leaky hospital incubators that medical people were often able to save infants who, in an earlier era, would have certainly died, either because of conditions that interfered with basic life functions or because they had not developed to a point of viability outside the womb. Saving the babies, however, did not guarantee that all their capacities could be developed or restored. And often, after massive intervention, a child might be left alive but profoundly disabled, both mentally and physically. The new techniques and capabilities raised painful ethical dilemmas about the cost—economic, psychological, and social—as well as posing difficult questions about the state's relationship to parents in deciding when to intervene and when to refuse medical intervention. Particularly frustrating was the ironic reality that hundreds of thousands of dollars of medical care would be directed to the premature infant of a woman who had had no prenatal care whatever. Since the days of President Kennedy's first panel on mental retardation, public health experts had linked better prenatal care to a reduction in the birthrate of handicapped children. Yet the heroic efforts were all directed to the care of newborns at risk, while efforts to provide the far more effective measures of prenatal care languished for lack of money and support.[51]

Modernity unquestionably had its hazards, as the negative aspects of both technological advances and deinstitutionalization demonstrated. But for handicapped children, unlike dependent or delinquent children, there was genuine progress to be seen from the beginning of the century to its conclusion—in the medical capacity to care for disabled children; in the development of special education and greater access to it; and in the quality of their daily lives.

Government, which at the turn of the century had been more coercive toward handicapped children than toward any other children of the state, seemed by the end of the century to have achieved its most balanced relationship toward disabled children and their families. In general, state intervention was sought and welcomed by the handicapped and their advocates. The level of concern about state intrusion that characterized the discussion of policy toward status offenders and dependent children did not dominate public policy considerations concerning children with disabilities. On the whole, government, especially the federal government, was regarded as an ally.

Two examples of government support for the handicapped as the century moved to its conclusion were the 1990 United States Supreme Court Zebley decision and the 1990 Americans With Disabilities Act. In Zebley the Supreme Court overturned SSI rules for evaluating disabilities in children, finding that such rules were stricter than the standard for evaluating adults. Striking down the Social Security Administration's regulations allowed many disabled children who had previously been closed off from SSI to apply for this support.[52]

Even more far reaching was the Americans With Disabilities Act, regarded as landmark civil rights legislation akin to the 1964 Civil Rights Law that had effected so much change for minorities and women. The Americans With Disabilities Act, which applied to employment, public accommodations, state and local government services, and telecommunications supplemented the support already given handicapped children through P.L. 94-142 and addressed to some extent the gap that was left for the disabled and their families once the critical age of twenty-one was reached. Both in terms of access to services and employment, the act was more comprehensive than any law yet passed in behalf of the adult handicapped, and its impact was expected to be significant.[53]

The growing public consciousness of the rights of the handicapped and their increasing visibility in the larger world was a critical change that had occurred in the last half of the twentieth century. Certainly no one could argue that there was a surfeit of generosity in the community at large. Nothing was going to be granted to the disabled, children or adults, without determined effort. The numerous lawsuits connected with P.L. 94-142 testified to that, while the struggle to establish community centers for the mentally handicapped in residential communities demonstrated that many of the old prejudices and fears of the mentally handicapped were still powerful. But a crucial thing had happened for disabled children when parents' groups had formed at midcentury and had transcended the essentially fragmenting nature of concern for particular disabilities to think in broader terms about a lobbying effort for all handicapped children. Disabled children, unlike other groups of the state's children, had a highly mobilized force of their most natural advocates, their parents, fighting for their rights. And once mobilized—as their fierce response to the Reagan administration attacks on their programs made clear—it was unlikely that they would let their hard-won empowerment be diminished by the discouragements and defeats of an unfriendly age.

Conclusion

Of all the children of the state, handicapped children have enjoyed the steadiest improvement in their prospects in the course of the twentieth century. This is especially striking because handicapped children, particularly the mentally handicapped, had experienced the parental state at its most coercive during the eugenics scare that paralleled the Progressive Era. While Progressive policies for dependent and delinquent children had focused on redeeming their childhoods and their futures through a variety of interventionist programs, reformers' main concern with the mentally handicapped and epileptic children was to isolate them early and completely from the rest of society to curb the threat of contamination.

Three developments reversed this unpromising outlook for handicapped children. First, the extraordinary advances in science and medicine led to the control and prevention of many handicaps, as their cause became better understood. Further, technological advances could help to mitigate some of the devastating effects of physical handicaps through such means as prosthetic devices and reconstructive surgery.

Second, at about midcentury, the parents of handicapped children began to assert their right to a role in their children's lives, receiving strong support from social thinkers who attacked at its very essence the Progressive proposal permanently to hospitalize the unfit. The new philosophy, actually a full circle swing back to the view of reformers who had established the first special schools in the years before the Civil War, shared with an earlier age the belief that the goal of special education was to establish the disabled as functioning members of the larger society. The modern advocates differed only in the contention that initial institutionalization was not an appropriate means, that education should take place at home and on a local level whenever possible.

Third, and closely tied to the new parental militance, was the critical fact that disabilities cut across class lines. Handicapped children were thus not only spared the taint of "unworthiness" that inevitably affected policy toward the children of the poor. They also found natural advocates in politicians, business people, and educators, who had a special commitment and understanding of the issue because they were speaking out of their own experience and for their own children and relatives.

This highly mobilized and increasingly sophisticated group of advocates was joined by a strong parallel movement on the part of the adult disabled. Together these groups continued to exert an extraordinarily successful pressure on government and society long after the fervor of 1960s reforms had died down in other areas. The working relationship forged with the state, while by no means without flaws, was in reality a balance of the Progressive belief in intervention and support of the state's children, coupled with the mid-twentieth century's commitment to individual rights and a wariness about the power of the state. In programs for handicapped children, advocates looked to the state as a partner, but they fashioned deliberate checks on excess intervention and carefully incorporated a parental voice in the laws that mandated education rights for their children.

The progress for handicapped children is heartening, but it provides no blueprint for work with dependent and delinquent children. The elements of change so critical to improved circumstances for handicapped children simply do not pertain to the other, more reform-resistant categories of the state's children. Technology and science have not improved their situation in any significant way. The lack of coping parents is the very definition of dependency, and for most delinquent children, the role of the parent as advocate is greatly circumscribed. And overwhelmingly, dependent and delinquent children are the children of the poor, not because middle-class children do not get into trouble but because there are often alternative resources (such as in-patient psychiatric programs) where they are placed.

The problem remains for dependent and delinquent children: where are they to find advocates who will speak for them as passionately and personally as those who speak for handicapped children? Who will strike the balance achieved by advocates for the handicapped, controlling the juggernaut aspect of the state while harnessing its power?

The Progressive vision of government as parent was naive,

sometimes unconscionably so. In regard to the juvenile court, reformers in a state as corrupt and uncivic as Illinois should have
seen clearly that reliance on the basic goodness of judges was a
slender hope. It should have been obvious that mass institutionalization and involuntary commitment laws for the mentally handicapped would result in making already terrible institutions worse.

The most thoughtful Progressives hoped to mitigate the effects
of broad intervention by assuring that the flexibility they were
committed to was in the hands of wise people—by instituting civil
service reforms; by looking to women, whom they believed to be
natural nurturers, to work with the state's wards; by a growing
emphasis on professionalization, which, by definition, implied an
advocacy for one's clients that went beyond mere amateur sentiment and well beyond mere venal considerations.

By the late twentieth century, it was clear that the Progressive
vision of a parental state was a delusion, both because of funding
problems and because the bureaucratic nature of the state had become an all too familiar reality not anticipated by the Progressives.
Reformers critical of a destructively interventionist state sought
programs and policies that reasserted the rights and protections
of individuals and looked to people in the community, not the
state itself, to be the advocates for the state's children.

The rejection of "government as usual" came, though from different philosophies, from both the left and the right of the political spectrum. It was part of a much broader intellectual shift, a
kind of privatization and rejection of the state that, by the last
decade of the twentieth century, could be witnessed not only in
domestic affairs but internationally, as the European map redrawn
after World War I fractured into many small nations, each fighting
for independence. One goal for the new countries was freedom
from coercive centralization. The world of children's policy shared
this rejection of coercive state action, but, as in European politics,
rejection of centralization could lead to a fragmentation so severe
as to cause chaos.

In fact, by the 1990s, the sense of chaos was so strong in children's services that some people began to suggest a sharp pendulum swing back to an intervention more coercive than anything
proposed by the Progressives. This was especially clear in the treatment of delinquents, where the ever-expanding list of transfers to
the adult court demonstrated a commitment to a "get tough" attitude that predated the juvenile court by many years. Similarly,
in dealing with dependent children, the call to "bring back the

orphanage" gained momentum as the child welfare and foster care system strained under the burden of a greatly increased and difficult case load. The sense, as usual for Americans, was that they wanted a quick fix solution to problems that were years in the making.

Such a pendulum swing threatened not only more recent reforms, but the accumulated wisdom of the twentieth century. The Progressives displayed a certain *hubris* in their pervading sense of modernism, convinced that nothing old-fashioned could possibly be of use to them. At its worst, this could foster the mentality that the interests of the state overrode the interests of the individual. It led to an insensitivity to civil liberties in the name of "helping." It led finally to a new reform movement that rejected its basic principles.

But the later reform movement, anti-state as the Progressives had been pro-state, had its own set of problems. Though radical in origin, it played to deeply rooted conservative, individualistic tendencies in the American character. Americans are an anomalous people, in that they revere youth and loath dependency. The child welfare reforms of the 1960s and beyond, which had as their chief function the limitation of the state, did not provide an alternative solution to the state as parent and advocate. They sought primarily to get children out of "the system," showing a naïveté as great as the Progressives' in relying on altruistic individuals within the community to shape and guide children in need or trouble, with only token support from the larger society.

It is easy to point out the flaws of any reform movement. What is just as important is a careful assessment of what reformers did right. From midcentury on, reformers in social welfare and children's policy were not only challenging the role of the state. They were also asserting the critical rights of the individual, the right to due process, the right to a real family, the right as a family to be treated with dignity. The reforms of the 1960s and beyond asserted civil liberties considerations for children and their parents that had never been acknowledged in the country's history. They recognized the need for normality, the right of the state's children to live as much like other children as possible. This was their great insight, and it should not be lost.

Similarly, Progressive America provided an insight that was critical, a recognition that, if we as a nation are to deliver on the promise of democracy, and if we are to survive as a democratic nation, we must do more for our children than abandon them to the randomness of individual circumstances. Certainly it is clear that the personal advocate, parent or relative, fights hardest and most sincerely for children. But what about those children who do not have advocates? The child welfare Progressives to their great credit, attempted to even the odds for all children, to provide some level of consistency in their care and education that would overcome the disabilities of family and environment. The Progressives asserted that all children are the children of the state, an unpalatable notion for most late twentieth-century Americans. But the concept—the belief that the well-being of every child redounds to the health of the state and is thus society's legitimate and inescapable concern—is as correct at the end of the twentieth century as it was at its beginning.

In the late twentieth century, the country faces a crisis in child welfare as severe as that at the beginning of the century, with many similarities to the earlier era. But we have one significant advantage over Progressive reformers. We have the advantage of a century of history to learn from, both the mistakes and the successes of our forbears. If we are to avoid the mistakes caused by uninformed arrogance—a quality that characterized both earlier reform movements—we need to do better than react out of frustration and despair, proposing quick fix solutions that will in reality fix nothing. We must try for a solution that does not ignore the past, either its mistakes or its insights, but incorporates its lessons into our policies.

Notes

Introduction

1. *Chicago Tribune*, Apr. 21, 1991, Sec. 3, p. 2.
2. *Revised Laws of Illinois*, 1827, pp. 364–66; *Revised Laws of Illinois*, 1829, pp. 150–53. See Edith Abbott and Sophonisba Breckinridge, *Truancy and Non-Attendance in the Chicago Schools* (Chicago, 1917), for a discussion of the school lands and their sale.
3. State of Illinois, 45th General Assembly, House of Representatives, Special Investigating Committee, *Report of the Special Committee to Investigate State Institutions* (Chicago, 1908), p. 14.
4. Proverbs 22:15.
5. Florence Kelley, *Some Ethical Gains through Legislation* (New York, 1905), pp. 45–46.
6. Kelley, *Ethical Gains*, pp. 10–11.
7. The Progressives argued that, because times had changed, women should vote; child labor should be restricted; an income tax was necessary; there should be municipal ownership of utilities; new professions should develop—to name just a few of their concerns. Progressive thinkers like John Dewey and William James showed a continuing awareness of the country's changed circumstances. And virtually all the works of Jane Addams express her consciousness of change and modernity. See Morton White, *Social Thought in America: The Revolt Against Formalism* (New York, 1949).
8. *Proceedings of the Governor's Conference on Exceptional Children* (Chicago, 1942), p. 30.
9. I am especially indebted to William Chafe, *The Unfinished Journey: America since World War II*, 2d ed. (New York, 1991), for a broad view of "the liberal consensus" and its rejection.
10. Anthony Platt, *The Child Savers: The Invention of Delinquency* (Chicago, 1969), chaps. 4, 5, p. 185.
11. David Rothman, *Conscience and Convenience: The Asylum and Its Alternatives in Progressive America* (Boston, 1980); Michael B. Katz, *In the Shadow of the Poorhouse: A Social History of Welfare in America* (New York, 1986), p. 145; Willard Gaylin, Ira Glasser, Steven Marcus, and David Rothman, *Doing Good: The Limits of Benevolence* (New York,

1981), p. 81. See the bibliographical essay for a more developed list of historians who dealt with the issue of social control.

12. Illinois Department of Mental Health, *Annual Report, 1966–1967* (Springfield, 1967), pp. 7–8.

13. See especially Charles Murray, *Losing Ground: American Social Policy, 1950–1980* (New York, 1986).

14. Children's Defense Fund, *CDF Reports*, Feb./Mar. 1990, pp. 1, 13–14.

15. See especially Lizbeth Schorr and Daniel Schorr, *Within Our Reach: Breaking the Cycle of Disadvantage and Despair* (New York, 1989), for a discussion of positive intervention. For a conservative vision of intervention, see Karl Zinsmeister, "Growing Up Scared," *Atlantic* (June 1990): 49–66.

Chapter 1: Miminal Offerings, 1818–99

1. *Report of the Department of Public Welfare Children's Committee* (Springfield, Ill., 1921), p. 67.

2. From *The Laws of the Indiana Territory, 1801–1809*, edited with an introduction by Francis S. Philbrick, collections of the Illinois State Historical Library, Volume 21, Law Series, Vol. 2, Springfield, 1930, cited in Naomi Harwood, "The History of the Care of Dependent Children in Cook County to 1899" (Field Study, School of Social Service Administration, University of Chicago, 1941), p. 18.

3. Ibid, pp. 18–19.

4. Ibid., p. 18.

5. Thomas Cowls v. Ann Cowls, 8 Ill. 435 (1846).

6. *Revised Laws of Illinois*, 1826–27, pp. 309–10.

In practice, however, some counties still placed paupers with those who would provide care for the least amount of money long into the nineteenth century, as the State Board of Charities noted. The 1827 law merely stopped the humiliating process of public auction. See, for example, State Board of Commissioners of Public Charities, *First Biennial Report*, 1870, p. 138.

7. See Steven Mintz and Susan Kellogg, *Domestic Revolutions: A Social History of American Family Life* (New York, 1989), chap. 3 for a discussion of nineteenth-century attitudes toward children.

8. *6th Census of the United States*, 1840, pp. 84–87; *9th Census of the United States*, 1870, vol. 1; *Population Statistics*, Table II, State of Illinois, 110; *12th Census of the United States*, 1900, vol. I: *Population Statistics*, Part I, Table 8, 443; City of Chicago, *Charter and Ordinances*, 1856, p. 339.

9. See Charles Rosenberg, *The Cholera Years* (Chicago, 1962), for further discussion of the cholera plagues and their impact. See Mintz and Kellogg, *Domestic Revolutions*, chap. 5 for a general discussion of urbanization.

10. Julia Lathrop, "The Cook County Charities" in *Hull-House Maps*

and Papers: A Presentation of Nationalities and Wages in a Congested District of Chicago (1895; reprint, New York, 1970), p. 144.

11. James Brown, *The History of Public Assistance in Chicago* (Chicago, 1941), parts 1, 2.

12. *Laws of Illinois*, 1854, p. 24; *Revised Statutes of Illinois*, 1874, p. 147. (The law was revised on Feb. 25, 1874, to take effect July 1, 1874, but it is not listed in the session laws for that year, only in the *Revised Statutes*.)

13. Quoted in Harwood, "Dependent Children," p. 44.

14. Lathrop, "Cook County Charities," p. 148.

15. Ibid., p. 149; Sophonisba Breckinridge, *The Illinois Poor Law and Its Administration* (Chicago, 1939), p. 89.

16. Lathrop, "The Cook County Charities," pp. 148–49; Brown, *Public Assistance in Chicago*, chaps. 3, 8; Harwood, "Dependent Children," pp. 94–97.

17. State Board of Charities, *First Biennial Report*, 1870, p. 3; Harwood, "Dependent Children," p. 89.

18. State Board of Charities, *Sixth Biennial Report*, 1880, p. 289; Breckinridge, *Illinois Poor Law*, pp. 91–92.

19. Harwood, "Dependent Children," pp. 143–48.

20. *Laws of Illinois*, 1895, p. 177; *Laws of Illinois*, 1919, p. 697; Breckinridge, *Illinois Poor Law*, pp. 38–42, p. 93; Homer Folks, *The Care of Destitute, Neglected and Delinquent Children* (New York, 1900), pp. 48–51.

Michigan, Massachusetts, New York, Wisconsin, Pennsylvania, Connecticut, Rhode Island, Maryland, New Hampshire, Indiana, New Jersey, and Ohio all had laws outlawing the presence of children in almshouses by the turn of the century.

21. Folks, *Care of Destitute Children*, p. 95.

22. *Fifth Biennial Report of the Trustees, etc., of the Illinois Soldiers' Orphans' Home*, 1879, quoted in Harwood, "Dependent Children," p. 100.

23. Harwood, "Dependent Children," pp. 99–100.

24. Alice Channing, "The Illinois Soldiers' Orphans' Home" (Master's thesis, University of Chicago, 1926), pp. 10, 17, 22–24.

25. Ibid., pp. 24–27, 64–66.

26. Ibid., pp. 10–13.

27. Robert Mennel, *Thorns and Thistles: Juvenile Delinquents in the United States, 1825–1940*, 1825–1940 (Hanover, N.H., 1973), p. 30; E. C. Wines and Theodore M. Dwight, *Report on The Prisons and Reformatories of the United States and Canada* (Albany, 1867), p. 67.

28. Harwood, "Dependent Children," chaps. 2, 5.

29. Ibid., pp. 127–33; *Laws of Illinois*, 1887, p. 102.

Jacob Riis noted in his 1893 study of New York tenements, *How the Other Half Lives*, that the Sisters of Charity had a policy of asking the mothers who brought their babies to the Foundling Asylum if they would stay and nurse their own babies and one other until the infants were strong enough to manage on cow's milk. Four hundred and sixty mothers agreed to the proposition in 1892, according to Riis (p. 146, Dover edition, 1970).

30. U.S. Bureau of the Census, *Twelfth Census of the United States, 1900, Population Statistics*, Vol. 1 (Washington, D.C., 1901), 1:16; Oscar Dudley, "Saving the Children: Sixteen Years' Work among the Dependent Youth of Chicago" in *History of Child Saving in the United States at the Twentieth National Conference of Charities and Correction in Chicago, 1893* (Boston, 1893), pp. 102–7. Dudley was possibly drawing on the example of the spectacular 1874 "Little Mary Ellen" case in which the New York SPCA had intervened in behalf of an abused child. The newspapers in the New York case had made much of the sickening irony that New York SPCA had a society to protect animals but no similar organization for the protection of children. See Robert Bremner et al., eds., *Children and Youth in America: A Documentary History*, 3 vols. (Cambridge, 1971–74), 2:185.

31. Padrones were Italian labor bosses who recruited workers to come to America. They bought the services of poor Italian children from their parents for a set number of years and used the children as beggars and street musicians. They were noted for their brutality to the children who lived in virtual slavery, and both the Italian and United States government attempted to suppress this traffic in what was virtually child slavery. See Bremner et al., *Children and Youth*, 2:197–201.

32. Dudley, "Saving the Children," p. 106.

33. Harwood, "Dependent Children," pp. 74–80, 186.

34. *Laws of Illinois*, 1879, pp. 309–13; *Laws of Illinois*, 1883, pp. 133–36. Arlien Johnson, *Public Policy and Private Charities: A Study of Legislation in the United States and of Administration in Illinois* (Chicago, 1931), pp. 91–100; Harwood, "Dependent Children," pp. 169–80; Dudley, "Saving the Children," pp. 107–15.

35. In the Matter of the Petition of Alexander Ferrier, 103 Ill. 367 (1882) raised the issue of civil liberties, while County of McLean v. Laura B. Humphreys, 104 Ill. 378 (1882) and County of Cook v. The Chicago Industrial School for Girls, 125 Ill. 540 (1888) were challenges to Catholic industrial schools that were receiving state funds. In the McLean County case, the Supreme Court upheld the subsidy system, but in the Chicago Industrial School case, the court found against the school, chiefly because it was only a legal contrivance, not an actual school.

36. Folks, *Care of Destitute Children*, p. 63.

37. Ibid., p. 129.

38. Ibid., chaps. 5–8; *Laws of Illinois*, 1899, pp. 131–37.

39. See David Rothman, *The Discovery of the Asylum: Social Order and Disorder in the New Republic* (Boston, 1971).

40. Ibid., pp. 258–60. An example of a sensational attack against institutionalization in general and against the New York House of Refuge in particular is Elijah Devoe, *The Refuge System; or, Prison Discipline Applied to Juvenile Delinquents* (New York, 1848). Devoe presents an

astute look at the development of the institutional personality, although his pamphlet could hardly be called a measured or judicious tract.

41. Charles Loring Brace, *The Dangerous Classes of New York and Twenty Years Work among Them*, (New York, 1872), chaps. 19, 20. For an extensive discussion of Braces's activities, see: Miriam Langsam, *Children West: A History of the Placing-Out System of the New York Children's Aid Society, 1853–1890* (Madison, Wis., 1964).

42. Henry Thurston, *The Dependent Child: A Story of Changing Aims and Methods in the Care of Dependent Children* (New York, 1930), pp. 128–36; *Laws of Illinois*, 1899, pp. 131–37.

43. Ibid., p. 136; Folks, *Care of Destitute Children*, p. 131.

44. The First White House Conference on Children in 1909 held the preservation of the family to be a primary objective of the state.

Chapter 2: Extending the Boundaries of Care, 1899–1950

1. "Proceedings of the Illinois Conference on Charities" in Illinois Board of State Commissioners of Public Charities, *Sixteenth Biennial Report*, 1899, pp. 279, 281; Timothy D. Hurley, "Origin of the Juvenile Court Law" in *The Child, the Clinic and the Court* (New York, 1927), pp. 322–30.

2. "An Act to Regulate the Treatment and Control of Dependent, Neglected and Delinquent Children" in *Laws of Illinois*, 1899, pp. 131–37.

3. Timothy Hurley, *Origin of the Juvenile Court* (Chicago, 1907), p. 79.

4. Helen Jeter, *The Chicago Juvenile Court* (Children's Bureau Publication #104: Washington, D.C., 1922), p. 21; *Laws of Illinois*, 1905, pp. 152–53.

5. Hurley, *Juvenile Court*, pp. 79–80. For a discussion of Progressive principles and the Progressive mentality, see, for example, David Noble, *The Progressive Mind, 1890–1917* (Chicago, 1970) and Robert M. Crunden, *Ministers of Reform: The Progressives' Achievement in American Civilization, 1889–1920* (New York, 1982). I am especially indebted to John W. Chambers, *The Tyranny of Change in the Progressive Era, 1900–1917* (New York, 1980) for the insight that a belief in intervention is a characteristic that holds true for Progressives of many different types. Also important for the background of the section was Susan Tiffin, *In Whose Best Interest? Child Welfare Reform in the Progressive Era* (Westport, Conn., 1982).

6. Edgar Guest quoted in Mary Cable, *The Little Darlings* (New York, 1972), p. 168; Merrit Pinckney, "Public Pensions to Widows: Experiences and Observations Which Lead Me to Favor Such a Law" in *Selected Articles on Mothers' Pensions*, comp. Edna N. Bullock (White Plains, N.Y., 1915), p. 152.

7. Louis deKoven Bowen, *Growing Up with a City* (New York, 1926), p. 115.

8. See Joseph Hawes, *Children in Urban Society: Juvenile Delinquency in Nineteenth Century America* (New York, 1971), pp. 223–62, for a discussion of Judge Ben Lindsey, who most typified the role of judge as paternal figure.

9. Tiffin, *In Whose Best Interests*, p. 221; Julian W. Mack, "The Chancery Procedure in the Juvenile Court" in *The Child, the Clinic, and the Court*, pp. 314–15.

10. Mack, "Chancery Procedure," p. 313.

11. Jeter, *Chicago Juvenile Court*, p. 85; Johnson, *Public Policy and Private Charities*, p. 91; *Report of the Department of Public Welfare, Children's Committee* (Springfield, Ill., 1920), p. 43; *Laws of Illinois*, 1923, p. 181.

12. Sophonisba Breckinridge and Edith Abbott, *The Delinquent Child in the Home: A Study of the Delinquent Wards of the Juvenile Courts of Chicago* (New York, 1912), p. 12; Bertha Corman, "Study of 446 Delinquent Girls with Institutional Experience" (Master's thesis, University of Chicago, 1923), pp. 31, 38. See also, Department of Visitation of Children Placed in Family Homes, *Fifth Annual Report*, 1910 (Springfield, Ill., 1911), pp. 12–13.

13. *Report of the Department of Public Welfare Children's Committee* (Springfield, Ill., 1921), pp. 38–39; *Report of the Committee on Child Welfare Legislation*, 1931 (Springfield, Ill., 1931), pp. 23, 198.

14. Sandra Stehno, "Foster Care for Dependent Black Children in Chicago, 1899–1934" (Ph.D. diss., University of Chicago, 1985), pp. 186–87; Louise de Koven Bowen, "The Colored People of Chicago: Where Their Opportunity is Choked—Where Open," *Survey* 31 (Nov. 11, 1913): 117–20, cited in Stehno, "Foster Care for Dependent Black Children," p. 57; Corman, "A Study of 446 Delinquent Girls with Institutional Experience," p. 11; *Report of the Child Welfare Committee to the 65th General Assembly, 1947* (Springfield, Ill., 1947), pp. 53, 89.

15. Charlotte Ashby Crawley, "Dependent Negro Children in Chicago in 1926" (Master's thesis, University of Chicago, 1927), pp. 83–85; Stehno, "Foster Care for Dependent Black Children," chaps. 1–3.

16. *Report of the Children's Committee, 1920*, pp. 132–33.

17. For a thorough discussion of the agencies that assisted black children, see Stehno, "Foster Care for Dependent Black Children."

18. Grace E. Benjamin, "The Constitutionality and Jurisdiction of the Juvenile Court of Cook County" (Ph.D. diss., University of Chicago, 1932), pp. 33–37, 45; *Laws of Illinois*, 1879, p. 309; *Laws of Illinois*, 1883, p. 168; Jeter, *Chicago Juvenile Court*, pp. 92, 94–95.

19. Jeter, *Chicago Juvenile Court*, pp. 28–29. A 1912 Illinois Supreme Court decision, Witter v. Cook County Commissioners, 256 Ill. 616 (1912), found the civil service requirement for probation officers to be a violation of the separation of powers between the executive and judicial branches of government and ruled that the court had the exclusive right to select its staff. The probation staff did have to take a court-administered examination, but the biggest drawback of the judicial appointment

system, according to Jeter, was that there was no effective procedure for the removal of incompetent probation officers once they were established in the job.

20. John Kahlert, *Child Dependency in Illinois* (Springfield, Ill., 1940), pp. 23, 32.

21. For examples of the assertion that the juvenile court was not set up for effective execution of administrative functions, see Julia Lathrop, "The Background of the Juvenile Court in Illinois" in *The Child, the Clinic and the Court*, pp. 296–97; Jeter, *The Chicago Juvenile Court*, p. 107; *The White House Conference on Children in a Democracy, 1939–40, Final Report* (Washington, D.C., 1940), p. 271. Breckinridge's remarks come from Sophonisba Breckinridge, "Government's Role in Child Welfare" in *Children in a Depression Decade*, edited by James H. S. Bossard (Philadelphia, 1940), pp. 47–48.

22. *Laws of Illinois*, 1905, p. 88; State Board of Commissioners of Public Charities, *20th Biennial Report*, 1906–8, p. 231.

23. Elizabeth Milchrist, *State Administration of Child Welfare in Illinois* (Chicago, 1937), pp. 24–31.

24. Tiffin, *In Whose Best Interests*, p. 209; Arthur A. Guild, *Baby Farms in Chicago: An Investigation Made for the Juvenile Protective Association* (n.p., 1917), pp 7–25. "An Ordinance Requiring the Licensing of Homes Regulating the Establishment and Maintenance Thereof" in Guild, *Baby Farms*, appendix; *Laws of Illinois*, 1919, pp. 248–50. For a discussion of the incidence of venereal disease in children, see Karen J. Taylor, "Venereal Disease in Nineteenth Century Children," *Journal of Psychohistory* 12 (Spring, 1983): 431–36.

25. *Report of the Children's Committee, 1920*, pp. 5, 45; *Child Welfare Committee, 1931*, p. 65.

26. Milchrist, *State Administration*, pp. 89–90, 100, 104.

27. *Report of the Children's Committee, 1920*, pp. 60, 67, 87; Milchrist, *State Administration*, pp. 35, 54, 70, 83.

28. Kahlert, *Child Dependency*, pp. 11, 31; Breckinridge, "Government's Role in Child Welfare," pp. 47–48.

29. *Laws of Illinois*, 1933, pp. 203–6; Kahlert, *Child Dependency*, pp. 11, 16–17, 91.

30. *Report of the Illinois Child Welfare Functions Commission to the Members of the 64th General Assembly* (Springfield, 1945), pp. 5–7.

31. Ibid., pp. 6–7.

32. *Report of the Child Welfare Commission to the Members of the 66th General Assembly, Feb. 14, 1949* (Springfield, 1949), pp. 3–5.

33. Mark H. Leff, "Consensus for Reform: The Mothers' Pension Movement in the Progressive Era" in *Compassion and Responsibility: Readings in the History of Social Welfare Policy in the United States*, ed. Steven Diner and Frank Bruel (Chicago, 1980), pp. 246–47; *Proceedings of the Conference on the Care of Dependent Children, 1909* in Robert Bremner et al., *Children and Youth*, 2:357–69.

34. W. Morland Graham, "Mothers' Pensions and Their Failure in Illinois" in *Institution Quarterly* 7 (Sept. 1916): 7–8; *Laws of Illinois*, 1911, pp. 126–27. For a discussion of working mothers, see Helen Russell Wright, *Children of Wage-Earning Mothers: A Study of a Select Group in Chicago* (Children's Bureau Publication #102: Washington, D.C., 1922), pp. 121–26.

35. *Laws of Illinois*, 1913, pp. 127–30.

36. Tiffin, *In Whose Best Interests?*, pp. 121–26; C. C. Carstens, "Public Pensions to Widows with Children," in Bullock, *Mothers' Pensions*, pp. 159–75.

37. Annette Marie Garrett, "The Administration of the Aid to Mothers' Law in Illinois, 1917–1925" (Master's thesis, University of Chicago, 1925), pp. 16, 22–24.

38. "Wildfire Spread of Widows' Pensions" in *Everybody's Magazine*, June 1915, quoted in Bullock, *Mothers' Pensions*, p. 87; *Laws of Illinois*, 1915, p. 243; *Laws of Illinois*, 1917, p. 220; *Laws of Illinois*, 1923, p. 169.

39. Kahlert, *Child Dependency*, p. 17; Milchrist, *State Administration*, p. 61; "Mothers' Aid in the United States" in *Dependent and Neglected Children: Report of the Committee on the Socially Handicapped, White House Conference on Child Health and Protection, 1930* (New York, 1933), pp. 219–20, 221; Arthur Miles, *Federal Aid and Public Assistance in Illinois* (Chicago, 1941), pp. 214–15; Edith Abbott and Sophonisba Breckinridge, *The Administration of the Aid to Mothers' Law in Illinois* (Children's Bureau Publication #82: Washington, D.C., 1921), pp. 130–58.

40. Edwin E. Witte, *The Development of the Social Security Act* (Madison, 1963), quoted in Bremner et al., *Children and Youth*, 3:529–30; Breckinridge, "Government's Role in Child Welfare," p. 47; *U.S. Statutes at Large*, 49:627–29. For a discussion of the inclusion of Aid to Dependent Children into the Social Security Act, see Lela Costin *Two Sisters for Social Justice: A Biography of Grace and Edith Abbott* (Urbana, 1983) and Robyn Muncy, *Creating a Female Dominion in American Reform, 1890–1935* (New York, 1991).

41. Miles, *Federal Aid in Illinois*, p. 219.

42. Ernest K. Lindley quoted in Mary Irene Atkinson, "Child Welfare Work in Rural Communities" in *Children in a Depression Decade*, p. 215.

43. Wallace W. Clark, *An Appraisal of ADC in Illinois* (n.p., 1943), pp. 1, 4, 11.

44. Sophonisba Breckinridge, Preface to Miles, *Federal Aid in Illinois*, p. vii; Edith Abbott, "The Hull House of Jane Addams" *Social Service Review* 26 (Sept. 1952): 337–38; Muncy, *Creating a Female Dominion in Reform*, pp. 153–54; Costin, *Two Sisters for Social Justice*, pp. 205–26.

Chapter 3: Coherence and Crisis, 1950–90

1. Mintz and Kellogg, *Domestic Revolutions*, p. 179; *Newsweek*, Nov. 19, 1973, cover page.

2. Illinois passed its first effective adoption law in 1945. The law did

not have the strict provisions set forth by the U.S. Children's Bureau, but it did require a home study and a probationary period before the adoption became final. *Laws of Illinois*, 1945, pp. 10–18; John Kahlert, *Child Dependency in Illinois* (Springfield, Ill., 1940), p. 93; Governor's Committee on the White House Conference, 1950, *Children and Youth in Illinois* (Springfield, 1951), pp. 20, 31–32; Malcolm Bush, *Families in Distress: Public, Private, and Civic Responses* (Berkeley, Calif., 1988), pp. 29–36. For a discussion of social work's swing to the right and concentration on the middle class in the 1950s, see John H. Ehrenreich, *The Altruistic Imagination: A History of Social Work and Social Policy in the United States* (Ithaca, N.Y., 1985), chap. 5.

3. Illinois Commission on Children, *Report of a Committee for a Comprehensive Family and Child Welfare Program in Illinois* (Springfield, 1962), p. 5.

For earlier discussions of the fragmented nature of child welfare, see Governor's Committee for the Midcentury White House Conference on Children, *Children and Youth in Illinois*, p. 29; Committee to Study Public State-Wide Services in Illinois, *Public State-Wide Services for Children in Illinois: A Report of the Study of Eighteen Health, Welfare and Educational Agencies* (Springfield, 1955), pp. 55–57; Illinois Committee for the Golden Anniversary White House Conference on Children and Youth, 1960, *Children and Youth in Illinois* (Springfield, 1960), p. 20.

4. Ruth Werner, *Public Financing of Voluntary Agency Foster Care* (New York, 1961), pp. 78–79; Sandra Stehno, "Foster Care for Dependent Black Children in Chicago, 1899–1934" (Ph.D. diss., University of Chicago, 1985), pp. 258–61; Marion Abenhaus, Former Director of the Chicago Child Care Society, quoted in Bush, *Families in Distress*, p. 40.

5. Committee for the White House Conference, 1960, *Children and Youth*, p. 7; Stehno, "Foster Care for Dependent Black Children," pp. 268–69; Bush, *Families in Distress*, pp. 39–43; *Laws of Illinois*, 1963, pp. 1061–73.

Michael Katz, *In The Shadow of the Poor House: A Social History of Welfare in America* (New York, 1986), p. 263, notes that the notion of the private sector as pacesetter was an assumption nationwide.

6. Edward Weaver, Former Director of the Department of Children and Family Services, quoted in Bush, *Families in Distress*, p. 44. See *Families in Distress* for a discussion of the relationship of the state agency and the voluntary sector.

7. Robert Bremner et al., eds., *Children and Youth in America: A Documentary History*, 3 vols. (Cambridge, 1971–74), 3:520. For a discussion of the development of AFDC, see Bremner, *Children and Youth*, 3:538–609. See also Katz, *In the Shadow of the Poorhouse*, chap. 9.

8. *U.S. Statutes at Large*, 87:12. (The law indexing Social Security to inflation was P.L. 93–66.)

9. Bremner et al., *Children and Youth*, 3:520–21.

10. King v. Smith, 392 U.S. 309 (1968), quoted in Bremner et al., *Children and Youth*, 3:589–90.

11. *Addenda to Facts, Fallacies and Future: A Study of the Aid to Dependent Children Program of Cook County, Illinois* (New York, 1960), p. 7; Kathryn Goodwin, *ADC: Problem and Promise* (n.p., 1959), pp. 7–10.

12. Lester M. Salamon, *Welfare: The Elusive Consensus* (New York, 1978), pp. 91–98; Katz, *In the Shadow of the Poorhouse*, p. 269.

13. Constant dollar figures comparing AFDC families in 1975 and 1980: Table #688 "CPI for Selected Items and Groups: 1960–1975,"U.S. Bureau of the Census. *Statistical Abstract of the United States: 1975* (Washington, D.C., 1975), p. 422; Table #808 "CPI for Selected Items and Groups: 1970–1980." U.S. Bureau of the Census. *Statistical Abstract of the United States, 1980* (Washington, D.C., 1980), p. 487; Mark Testa & Edward Lawlor, *The State of the Child, 1985* (Chicago, 1986), Table #22, p. 42; Center on Budget and Policy Priorities, "AFDC Benefits in Illinois: Inadequate To Cover Basic Living Costs, Low By Comparison To Other States" (Washington, D.C., 1990), pp. 1, 6, 7, photocopied; Center for Budget and Policy Priorities, "Statement by Robert Greenstein, Director" (Washington, 1990), p. 1, photocopied. (These materials were obtained from the Illinois Public Welfare Coalition.)

14. *U.S. Statutes at Large,* 102:2343–2428.

15. "Family Support Act of 1988: Summary of Major Provisions and Impact on Illinois," unattributed. Photocopy from the Illinois Public Welfare Coalition, Chicago, (n.d.).

16. Malcolm Bush, Executive Vice President, Illinois Action for Children, Interview, Oct. 18, 1988.

In fact, there was an almost immediate disagreement between AFDC clients and their lawyers and the federal Health and Human Services Department charged with implementing the Family Assistance Act concerning the child care provisions of the law. Parents in California filed suit to enforce access to child care support. See *Youth Law News* 12 (Mar.–Apr. 1991): 10.

17. The 1962 amendments to the Social Security Act made children who had been receiving AFDC payment in their own homes eligible for AFDC if they were removed from their homes through judicial proceedings. In fact, the stipend was higher for a child in out-of-home care than for a child who remained in his family. One of the points of the 1980 Adoption Assistance Act, in insisting on frequent reviews of children's case plans, was to make sure that children did not remain in care because there was a financial inducement to leave them there. See Robert Mnookin, *Child, Family, and State: Problems and Materials on Children and the Law* (Boston, 1978), pp. 521–24. Jane Knitzer, Mary Lee Allen and Brenda McGowan, *Children without Homes: An Examination of Public Responsibility* (Washington, D.C., 1978) makes a major point of the concern that children were kept in care for financial reasons. See especially pp. 658–62.

18. See Supreme Court Justice William Brennan's statement on the connection between poverty and substitute care in Smith v. Organization

of Foster Families for Equality and Reform, 431 U.S. 816, 97 S. Ct., 2094, 53 L. Ed. 2d 14 (1977), cited in Mnookin, *Child, Family and State*, p. 535. (This is an abbreviated version of the case with notes.)

19. See for example, John Kahlert, *Child Dependency in Illinois* (Springfield, Ill., 1940), which is the most comprehensive look at Illinois children in substitute care in that era.

20. Samuel X. Radbill, "A History of Child Abuse and Infanticide," in *The Battered Child*, ed. C. Henry Kempe and Ray E. Helfer (Chicago, 1969), p. 15.

21. *Laws of Illinois*, 1965, pp. 235–36.

22. Interview with Marilyn Clarke, A.C.S.W., Foster Care Specialist, Oct. 29, 1985. Clarke was connected with the celebrated Lindquist case that got so much publicity in the state in 1972.

23. *Laws of Illinois*, 1975, pp. 146–50. See also Department of Children and Family Services, *The New Abused and Neglected Child Reporting Act: A Comparative Analysis with the Repealed Abused Child Act* (Departmental pamphlet, place and date not given).

24. *Laws of Illinois*, 1980, pp. 1686–89.

25. For an expression of legislative concern, see Illinois Legislative Investigating Commission, *The Child Victim: A Report to the General Assembly*, (Chicago, 1983). For an example of the critics' suspicions of legislators' motives, see TRB, "Greasy Kid Stuff," *New Republic* (May 13, 1985): 4, 42; Douglas J. Besharov, "Right versus Rights: The Dilemma of Child Protection," *Public Welfare* (Spring, 1985), p. 20. Besharov notes (p. 23) that the 1981 National Study of the Incidence and Severity of Child Abuse and Neglect found that 50 percent of substantiated reports concerned comparatively minor problems. Besharov continued this discussion in *The Vulnerable Social Worker: Liability for Serving Children and Families*, (NASW) (Silver Spring, M.d., 1985) and *Recognizing Child Abuse: A Guide for the Concerned* (New York, 1990).

26. Besharov, "Right Versus Rights," p. 23.

27. Ibid., p. 20.

28. Ibid., pp. 24–25.

29. Bush, *Families in Distress*, p. 50; Patrick Murphy is quoted in Richard Wexler, "Invasion of the Child Savers," *The Progressive* (Sept. 1985): 20; See also Jean Bethke Elshtain, "Invasion of the Child Savers: How We Succumb to Hype and Hysteria," *Progressive* (May, 1985): 23–24. Wexler has enlarged his discussion in *Wounded Innocents: The Real Victims of the War Against Child Abuse* (Buffalo, N.Y., 1990).

30. William M. Trumbull, "Proposed New Juvenile Court Act for Illinois," *Illinois Bar Journal* (Mar. 1965): 616–18; *Laws of Illinois*, 1965, pp. 259–60.

31. In Re Nyce, 131 Ill App 2d 481 (1971); In Re Brooks, 63 Ill App 3d 328, 379 N.E. 2d 872, 20 Ill Dec. 39 (1978), cited in Catherine Ryan and Diane J. Romza, "Recent Developments in Illinois Regarding Child Abuse and Neglect" (Paper, 1982), p. 14.

32. Stanley v. Illinois, 405 U.S. 645 (1971). Section 704–3 and 704–4 of the Juvenile Court Act provide for the notification of parents.

33. Memo to Charles Johnson et al., from Margaret Kennedy, Director, DCFS concerning Burgos Decree Compliance, May 18, 1978; Memo from Jack M. Donahue, Chicago Regional Operations, DCFS, to Service Providers concerning the Burgos Decision, July 10, 1978.

34. Santoskey v. Kramer, 455 U.S. 745 (1982).

35. The concept of "psychological parents" was first stated in Joseph Goldstein, Anna Freud, and Albert J. Solnit, *Beyond the Best Interests of the Child* (New York, 1973).

36. Smith, in *Child, Family and State*, pp. 536, 550–51.

37. Ibid., pp. 529–37.

38. See, for example, "Foster Parents Give up on DCFS," *Chicago Tribune*, Feb. 3, 1991, p. 1.

39. Department of Children and Family Services, "Foster Family Home License Compliance Record," pp. 1–13; Justice Brennan quoted in Mnookin, *Child, Family and State*, p. 535.

40. Smith, in *Child, Family and State*, p. 535.

41. From Dec. 1984–June 1985 and occasionally thereafter, I acted as a court watcher in the Cook County dependency court at 1100 S. Hamilton in Chicago. Some of the particulars of the court process are drawn from that experience.

42. On the issue of foster care and its problems, see, for example, Helen D. Stone, ed., *Foster Care in Question: A National Reassessment by Twenty-One Experts* (New York, 1970); Alvin L. Schorr, ed., *Children and Decent People* (New York, 1974); Mnookin, *Child, Family, and State*, pp. 447–594.

43. Vivian Hargrave, Joan Shireman, Peter Conor, *Where Love and Need Are One: A Demonstration of the Use of Subsidy to Facilitate the Adoption of Black Children in Need of Permanent Homes* (n.p., 1975), pp. 7, 8, 35, 72; Interview with Vivian Hargrave, Department of Children and Family Services, Feb. 18, 1986.

44. *U.S. Statutes at Large*, 94:500.

45. Children's Defense Fund, "Summary of Child Welfare Provisions in H.R. 3434 "The Adoption Assistance and Child Welfare Act of 1980" (mimeographed pamphlet, 1980), pp. 1–8.

46. Clarke Interview, Oct. 29, 1985.

47. Malcolm Bush and Harold Goldman, "The Psychological Parenting and Permanency Principles in Child Welfare: A Reappraisal and Critique," *American Journal of Orthopsychiatry*, 52 (Apr. 1982): 225–26; Clarke Interview, Oct. 29, 1985.

48. *Laws of Illinois*, 1972, pp. 750–51; *Laws of Illinois*, 1973, 2:3043–46; *Laws of Illinois*, 1982, pp. 2381–96.

There were only forty-two group homes in Illinois as of June 1985, with 367 beds open for DCFS placements. Department of Children and Family Services, Office of Financial Management, unpublished statistics. Calculations compiled by Mary Ann Hartnett.

An example of the declining availability of care for teenagers that I observed when I worked at NORC in the mid 1980s was the closing of Chapin Hall. This institution had provided residential care for children since 1862, when it had opened as the Chicago Nursery and Half Orphan Asylum. Anxious about the increasingly difficult nature of their clients, Chapin Hall's board of directors voted a total change of mission and policy, closing the institution and all direct services to children. Chapin Hall's money was redirected to a "think-tank" on children's issues at the University of Chicago.

49. Patrick Murphy, *Our Kindly Parent—The State: The Juvenile Justice System and How It Works* (New York, 1974), pp. 139–49; Clarke Interview, Oct. 29, 1985.

50. Bush, *Families in Distress*, pp. 48, 52; Harold Goldman, "Governor James R. Thompson's Special Task Force on Troubled Adolescents: A Study of Youth Service Reform in Illinois" (Ph.D. diss., University of Chicago, 1982), pp. 97–102. For Jerome Miller's point of view, particularly his opinion of Chicago's press, see Jerome Miller, "The Appeal: The Sins of the Press are Visited Upon the Oppressed," *Chicago Journalism Review* (Oct., 1974): 7–14.

51. Bush, *Families in Distress*, pp. 48–49; Better Government Association, *The State and Children in Need: A White Paper Prepared by the Child Advocacy Project of the Better Government Association* (Dec. 1979); American Humane Association, Children's Division, *Evaluation and Consulation, Cook County CPS Program, Illinois Department of Children and Family Services* (Chicago, 1978).

52. One fifth is a widely quoted percentage. I am drawing from Congressional Research Service, Congressional Budget Office, *Children in Poverty: Prepared for the Use of the House of Representatives Ways and Means Committee* (Washington, D.C., 1985), p. 33, which actually gives a figure of 22 percent; *Chicago Tribune*, Feb. 1, 1991, p. 1, quoting from the Center for the Study of Social Policy's 1991 *Kids Count Data Book*; Rule 706 Panel of Experts (regarding the lawsuit B.H. et al. v. Johnson), Final Consolidated Report (Chicago, 1991), p. 5. Photocopy courtesy of American Civil Liberties Union of Illinois.

53. For my assertion that the presiding judge's decision in dependency court was regarded as absolute, I am drawing from my own courtwatching experience, during which I had numerous conversations concerning this issue.

54. Diane Redleaf, "Quality of Representation Improves for Chicago Foster Children" in *Youth Law News* (May–June, 1988): 10–13; Patrick Murphy, "Commentary: Justice System No Deterrent to Child Abuse," *Chicago Sun Times*, Oct. 19, 1990, p. 37. In this article, Murphy gives three examples of cases that his office successfully appealed to a higher court.

55. *Chicago Tribune*, Apr. 18, 1991, p. 1.

56. Bob Greene, "Sarah Wins: 'Justice at Last,'" *Chicago Tribune*, Apr. 21, 1991, Sec. 5, p. 1; *Chicago Tribune*, Apr. 18, 1991, p. 1; *Chicago Sun Times*, Oct. 19, 1990, p. 37; *Chicago Tribune*, Apr. 21, 1991, Sec. 1, p. 1.

57. Rule 706 Panel of Experts, *Consolidated Report*, p. 2.

58. Rule 706 Panel of Experts, *Report,* pp. 3–4, 6–22; American Civil Liberties Union of Illinois Press Release, " Court Releases Experts' Report Detailing State's Mistreatment of Foster Children," Jan. 1991, p. 3. Photocopy courtesy of ACLU.

59. ACLU, "Press Release: Experts' Report," p. 5; *Chicago Tribune,* July 17, 1991, p. 1.

60. B.H. v. Suter [formerly Johnson], Case #88 C 5599, Consent Decree in U.S. District Court for the Northern District of Illinois, Eastern Division, Dec. 20, 1991. (My copy courtesy of the ACLU of Illinois.)

61. Telephone interview with Valerie Philip, Public Information Director, ACLU of Illinois, Jan. 9. 1992; telephone interview with Paul Cuadros, ACLU staff member, Jan. 27, 1992. Telephone interview with Janet Peters, Department of Children and Family Services, Jan. 15, 1992.

62. B.H. Consent Decree, p. 66; *Chicago Tribune,* Jan. 22, 1992, p. 11.

63. Joyce Ladner, "Bring Back the Orphanages" *Networker* (Jan.–Feb., 1990): p. 49 (Reprinted from the *Washington Post*); *Chicago Tribune,* Apr. 24, 1992, Sec. 1, p. 18; Interview with Malcolm Bush, Vice President, Voices for Illinois Children, Mar. 7, 1990. Bush, while not necessarily an advocate of institutions, predicted their reappearance as the number of special needs children grew.

Chapter 4: Defining Delinquency, 1818–99

1. Andrew A. Bruce, "One Hundred Years of Criminalized Development in Illinois," *Journal of the American Institute of Criminal Law and Criminology* 24 (May 1933–Apr. 1934): 21–22; *Laws of Illinois,* 1819, p. 216.

2. The Criminal Code of 1819 declared in a "reception statute" in Section 1 that the common law of Britain prevailed unless specifically repealed by legislation.

3. *Revised Laws of Illinois,* 1827, p. 124; Leslie A. Cranston, *Early Criminal Codes of Illinois and their Relation to the Common Law of England* (DuQuoin, Ill., 1930), pp. 17–18, 25.

The age of consent in Maine, Massachusetts, Connecticut, New Jersey, Maryland, and Virginia was ten in 1826; Vermont set it at age eleven. Cited in the *4th Annual Report of the Boston Prison Discipline Society,* p. 266.

4. *Laws of Illinois,* 1831, p. 113; E. C. Wines and Theodore Dwight, *Report on the Prisons and Reformatories of the United States and Canada* (Albany, N.Y., 1867), p. 67.

5. *Private Laws of Illinois,* 1851, p. 148.

There are a number of secondary sources that discuss the early reform schools as well, for example: Robert Pickett, *House of Refuge: Origins of Juvenile Reform in New York State, 1815–1857* (New York, 1969); Robert Mennel, *Thorns and Thistles: Juvenile Delinquents in the United States, 1825–1940* (Hanover, N.H., 1973); Joseph Hawes, *Children in Ur-*

ban Society: Juvenile Delinquency in Nineteenth Century America (New York, 1971); *1st Annual Report of the Chicago Reform School [AR CRS],* pp. 7–8; *2 AR CRS,* p. 14. For a discussion of Chicago's rapid growth, see Bessie Louise Pierce, *A History of Chicago,* vol. 2: *From Town to City, 1848–1871* (New York, 1940), pp. 3–34.

6. The New York House of Refuge, the Boston House of Reformation, and the Philadelphia House of Refuge all chose men with progressive notions of education as their first superintendents. In particular, Superintendent E. M. P. Wells of the Boston House of Reformation was experimental in his approach and deeply committed to an honor system of governing his institution. These early managers did not last long, however. Their progressive style came into conflict with management boards who replaced them with stricter superintendents. See Joan Gittens, "For Usefulness and Heaven: The Juvenile Reform Movement in the Ante-Bellum Period" (Ph.D. diss., University of Michigan, 1977), chaps. 3, 4.

7. *1 AR CRS,* pp. 14, 18; *2 AR CRS,* pp. 14–22; *3 AR CRS,* pp. 30–31; *6 AR CRS,* p. 10; *Rules and Regulations of the Chicago Reform School* (Chicago, 1870), p. 3.

8. Wines, *Report on the Prisons,* pp. 413, 423; *2 AR CRS,* p. 14; *4 AR CRS,* pp. 15–16.

9. *5 AR CRS,* pp. 7–9.

10. In the first annual report, for example, children were committed for reasons varying from street rioting and mail robbery to want of proper parental care. They ranged in age from six years to seventeen. *1 AR CRS,* p. 8.

11. *Rules of CRS,* pp. 2–3; *2 AR CRS,* pp. 14–20; *3 AR CRS,* pp. 21–24.

12. Chicago Reform School, *Manual of Devotion and Hymns for the Chicago Reform School* (Chicago, 1866), pp. 3, 5, 14, 67.

13. J. McMullen, D.D., Roman Catholic Bishop of Chicago, *Observations on the System of Moral and Religious Education Adopted in the Chicago Reform School, Addressed to the Honorable President and Board of Guardians* (Chicago, 1859), pp. 4–5, 8–10.

14. *4 AR CRS,* p. 18; *Rules of CRS,* pp. 4–5; *1 AR CRS,* p. 7; *4 AR CRS,* p. 10; *6 AR CRS,* p. 12.

15. *AR CRS,* p. 11; *6 AR CRS,* p. 10; *Laws of Illinois,* 1867, 3:31–32; *11 AR CRS,* p. 38; Wines, *Report on the Prisons,* p. 423; *14 AR CRS,* p. 23. See also the discussion of the laws concerning the Chicago Reform School in the O'Connell decision, cited below, pp. 280–83.

16. People ex. rel. O'Connell v. Turner 55 Ill. 280 (1870).

17. Ex Parte Crouse (Pennsylvania, 1838) had set the precedent for the reform schools' right to remove children from negligent parents. See Mennell, *Thorns and Thistles,* pp. 13–14, 125–27, for a discussion of nineteenth-century courts and the assertion of the *parens patriae* power of the state.

18. *15 AR CRS,* pp. 23–25, 26.

19. *16 AR CRS*, pp. 5–6, 32–33.

20. *Laws of Illinois*, 1879, pp. 309–13; In the Matter of the Petition of Alexander Ferrier, 103 Ill. 367 (1882).

21. *Laws of Illinois*, 1883, pp. 133–36. For a more complete discussion of the development of industrial schools, see part I, chaps. 1 and 2 of this book.

22. E. C. Wines, *The State of the Prisons and Child-Saving Institutions in the Civilized World* (Cambridge, Mass., 1880), p. 173; *Laws of Illinois*, 1867, pp. 38–44; *Laws of Illinois*, 1873, pp. 145–47; *Laws of Illinois*, 1891, pp. 128–32. For a discussion of the problems of the older reform schools, see, for example, Mennell, *Thorns and Thistles*, chap. 1.

23. *2nd Biennial Report of the Illinois Home for Juvenile Female Offenders*, pp. 7–11; *5th Biennial Report of the State Training School for Girls at Geneva*, Ill., p. 8; *8 AR CRS*, p. vi; *12 AR CRS*, p. 25.

24. *Geneva, 2nd Biennial Report*, pp. 10, 14; Charles Loring Brace, *The Dangerous Classes of New York and Twenty Years Work among Them* (New York, 1872), p. 116. See Gittens, "For Usefulness and Heaven," chap. 5, for a discussion of nineteenth-century attitudes towards delinquent girls. See also Barbara Meil Hobson, *Uneasy Virtue: The Politics of Prostitution and the American Reform Tradition* (New York, 1987); Estelle Freedman, *Their Sisters' Keepers: Women's Prison Reform in America, 1830–1930* (Ann Arbor, Mich.), 1981.

25. Timothy Hurley, *The Origin of the Illinois Juvenile Court Law* (Chicago, 1907), pp. 20, 69; Timothy Hurley, "The Origin of the Illinois Juvenile Court Law" in *The Child, the Clinic and the Court* (New York, 1925), p. 321; Joseph Hawes, *Children in Urban Society*, pp. 166–67.

26. *Laws of Illinois*, 1891, pp. 128–32; *Laws of Illinois*, 1893, pp. 23–31.

Chapter 5: Establishing the Juvenile Court, 1899–1925

1. For a description of the theory of the juvenile court, see *The Child, the Clinic and the Court* (New York, 1927), which is a collection of papers presented at the twenty-fifth anniversary conference of the Cook County Juvenile Court. A number of these papers discuss the origin of the court, attitudes toward parents, poverty, etc.

2. Society for the Prevention of Pauperism in the City of New York, *1st Annual Report*, p. 21. Robert Buroker, "From Voluntary Association to Welfare State: Social Welfare Reform in Illinois, 1890–1920 (Ph.D. diss., University of Chicago, 1973), contrasts the views of the "scientific philanthropists" of an earlier generation with the views of settlement reformers Jane Addams and Julia Lathrop, both of whom were instrumental in the founding of the Illinois Juvenile Court. While concerns about fostering dependency and the "unworthiness" of the poor had by no means disappeared in the Progressive Era, reformers connected with the settlement movement, especially Hull-House, openly and consistently challenged

such views. See John Ehrenreich, *The Altruistic Imagination* (Ithaca, N.Y., 1985). See also Jane Addams, "The Subtle Problems of Charity," *Atlantic Monthly* 83 (Feb., 1899): 163–78.

3. Timothy Hurley, *Origin of the Illinois Juvenile Court Law* (Chicago, 1907), pp. 18–19.

4. Ibid., pp. 18–26.

5. Bernard Flexner, "A Decade of the Juvenile Court" in *Proceedings of the National Conference of Charities and Corrections* (later called the National Conference of Social Work), 37 (Fort Wayne, Ind., 1910): 106–7; *Laws of Illinois*, 1899, pp. 131–37. The report of the Hotchkiss Committee, which studied the juvenile court in 1911, suggested that the jury provision be removed from the Illinois law, since it was only used to commit children to industrial schools and was strictly perfunctory. See *Report of the Committee Appointed Under Resolution of the Board of Commissioners of Cook County, Aug. 8, 1911* (Chicago, 1912), p. 16.

6. *Laws of Illinois*, 1907, p. 75; Ellen Ryerson, *The Best Laid Plans: America's Juvenile Court Experiment* (New York, 1978), p. 75.

7. Hurley, *Origin of the Juvenile Court Law*, pp. 39–44, 9.

8. *Chicago Tribune*, July 29, 1911, p. 1.

9. Julia Lathrop, Introduction to Sophonisba Breckinridge and Edith Abbott, *The Delinquent Child in the Home: A Study of the Delinquent Wards of the Juvenile Courts of Chicago* (New York, 1912), p. 9.

10. Louise De Koven Bowen, *Growing Up with a City* (New York, 1926), pp. 116–17. For a fuller description of the civil service struggle, see Robert Mennel, *Thorns and Thistles: Juvenile Delinquents in the United States, 1825–1940* (Hanover, N.H., 1973), pp. 140–42, and Elizabeth Parker, "Personnel and Organization of the Probation Department of the Juvenile Court of Cook County, 1899–1933" (Master's thesis, University of Chicago, 1934), pp. 1–65.

11. *Chicago Tribune*, July 30, 1911, p. 7. The Hearst challenge did not appear in either of the Chicago Hearst papers, the *Chicago American* or the *Herald Examiner*, which reported the controversy in a quite decorous fashion.

12. Hotchkiss Committee, *Report*, pp. 30–42.

13. Witter v. Cook County Commissioners 256 Ill. 616 (1912); Helen Jeter, *The Chicago Juvenile Court* (Children's Bureau Publication #104: Washington, D.C., 1922), pp. 28–29.

14. Lindsay v. Lindsay, 257 Ill. 328 (1913); Hotchkiss Committee, *Report*, p. 16.

15. Breckinridge and Abbott, *Delinquent Child*, p. 40.

16. Bowen, *Growing Up with a City*, pp. 109–11.

17. Louise De Koven Bowen, "The Early Days of the Juvenile Court," in *The Child, the Clinic, and the Court*, p. 309.

18. *Report of the Department of Public Welfare Children's Committee* (Springfield, 1921), pp. 15–33.

19. Julian Mack, "Legal Issues Involved in the Establishment of the Juvenile Court," Appendix 1 of *Delinquent Child*, p. 194.

20. *Laws of Illinois*, 1899, p. 194; *Laws of Illinois*, 1905, p. 152.

21. Breckinridge and Abbott, *Delinquent Child*, p. 12; Bertha Corman, "Study of 446 Delinquent Girls with Institutional Experience" (Master's thesis, University of Chicago, 1923), pp. 31, 38. See Dependency section, chap. 2, for a discussion of sexually abused children.

22. Merritt Pinckney, "The Delinquent Girl and the Juvenile Court," in *The Child in the City* (Chicago, 1912), p. 350.

23. Henry Thurston, "Ten Years of the Juvenile Court of Chicago," *Survey*, 23 (Oct. 1909–Mar. 1910): 658; Breckinridge and Abbott, *Delinquent Child*, pp. 38–39.

24. Breckinridge and Abbott, *Delinquent Child*, pp. 39–41.

25. Ibid., p. 27; Pinckney, "The Delinquent Girl," p. 349.

26. Lathrop, Introduction to *Delinquent Child*, p. 8; Illinois State Training School for Girls at Geneva, *9th Biennial Report*, p. 13; Geneva, *11th Biennial Report*, p. 7.

27. Geneva, *9th Biennial Report*, p. 6–8.

28. See, for example, State Board of Charities, *20th Biennial Report*, 1908, pp. 567–70. An earlier speech by Amigh is reprinted in the *Institution Quarterly* (Mar. 1912): 185–86, though by the time the speech was published, Amigh had been removed from office.

29. *Institution Quarterly* (Aug., 1910): 55–56; Sandra Harmon, "Altgeld the Suffragist" in *Chicago History* (Summer 1987): 24.

30. Geneva, *11th Biennial Report*, p. 7.

31. Geneva, *9th Biennial Report*, p. 6; *Children's Committee*, 1920, p. 32.

32. Hurley, *Origin of Juvenile Court*, p. 50.

33. Mennel, *Thorns and Thistles*, pp. 161–67.

34. Lathrop, Introduction to *Delinquent Child*, p. 8; Julian Mack, "The Chancery Procedure in the Juvenile Court," in *Child, Clinic, Court*, p. 318.

35. For a description of children held in adult jails, see Edith Abbott, *The One Hundred and One County Jails of Illinois and Why They Ought to Be Abolished* (n.p., 1916).

36. Bowen, "Early Days of the Juvenile Court," in *Child, Clinic, Court*, pp. 308–9. For a discussion of reform in the 1920s, see Clarke Chambers, *Seedtime of Reform: American Social Service and Social Action, 1918–1933* (Westport, Conn., 1980).

37. Julia Lathrop, "Background of the Juvenile Court in Illinois," in *Child, Clinic, Court*, p. 295.

38. Miriam Van Waters, "The Juvenile Court from the Child's Viewpoint," pp. 224, 235–36; Frederick Cabot, "The Detention of Children as a Part of Treatment," p. 251; Mack, "Chancery Procedure," p. 317, all of the above in *Child, Clinic, Court*.

39. Van Waters, "Child's Viewpoint," p. 222.

Chapter 6: Harsh Measures, 1925–49

1. Quoted in Ellen Ryerson, *The Best-Laid Plans: America's Juvenile Court Experiment* (New York, 1978), p. 93; The Department of Public Welfare, *Report of the Co-ordination Committee* (n.p., 1943), p. 23.

2. The Co-ordination Committee of the Department of Public Welfare noted in its analysis that the idea of inherited criminality was experiencing something of a revival, led by Harvard professor Ernest Hooten, whose works included *Crime and the Man, Twilight of Man,* and *Men, Apes and Morons.* But most scholars, according to the committee, found his work to be suspect.

3. For a thorough summary of the scholarship of the 1930s on delinquency, see the *Report of the Co-ordination Committee.*

4. For a discussion of the role of psychology in criminology and social work, see Ryerson, *Best-Laid Plans,* chap. 5. See also Roy Lubove, *The Professional Altruist: The Emergence of Social Work as a Career, 1880–1930* (New York, 1980), and John Ehrenreich, *The Altruistic Imagination: A History of Social Work and Social Policy in the United States* (Ithaca, N.Y., 1985).

5. Ryerson, *Best-Laid Plans,* p. 116; Quoted in Ryerson, p. 117.

6. Quoted in Lubove, *Professional Altruist,* p. 89.

7. Quoted in Ehrenreich, *Altruistic Imagination,* p. 67.

8. A History, *Report and Recommendations Submitted by the Committee Appointed by the Legislature to Study the Illinois St. Charles School for Boys and the Whole Subject of Juvenile Delinquency* (Springfield, 1939), p. 12. (Hereafter called Gunning Commission Hearings.)

9. For a fuller discussion of the sociological assessment of delinquency and the Chicago Area Project see Ryerson, *Best-Laid Plans,* chap. 6; for other discussions of CAP, see Robert Mennel, *Thorns and Thistles: Juvenile Delinquents in the United States, 1825–1940* (Hanover, N.H., 1973), chap. 6, and Steven Schlossman et al, *Delinquency Prevention in South Chicago: A Fifty-Year Assessment of the Chicago Area Project* (Santa Monica, Calif., 1984).

10. *Report of the Co-ordination Committee,* pp. 26–31.

11. Julian Mack, "Legal Problems Involved in the Establishment of the Juvenile Court" in *The Delinquent Child and the Home,* ed. Sophonisba Breckinridge and Edith Abbot (New York, 1912), p. 189; "Testimony of Judge Merritt Pinckney before the Cook County Civil Service Commission, Nov. 22, 23, 1911" in *Delinquent Child,* pp. 203–4.

12. Helen Jeter, *The Chicago Juvenile Court* (U.S. Children's Bureau Publication #104: Washington, D.C., 1922), p. 14.

13. People v. Fitzgerald 322 Ill. 54 (1926).

14. Benedict S. Alper, "Forty Years of the Juvenile Court," *American Sociological Review* 6 (1941): 230.

15. People v. Lattimore 362 Ill. 206 (1935); People ex rel. Malec v. Lewis 362 Ill 229 (1935); *Chicago Tribune,* Dec. 21, 1935, p.3.

16. Alper, "Juvenile Court," p. 230. For summaries of the jurisdictional issues of the court in the 1930s, see Fred Gross, *Detention and Criminal Prosecution of Children of Juvenile Court Age in Cook County, 1938–1942* (Chicago, 1942), chap. 2 and William Mavor Trumball, "Boys and Girls of Juvenile Court Age Held in Cook County Jail, 1936 and 1937" (Master's thesis, University of Chicago, 1936), chap. 1.

17. Alper, "Juvenile Court," p. 230; Gross, *Detention of Children*, pp. 162–63; Juvenile Court of Cook County, Illinois, *Fiftieth Anniversary Report* (Chicago, 1949), p. 24.

18. *Report of the Committee on Child Welfare Legislation, 1931* (Springfield, 1931), pp. 200, 202, 207.

19. *Annual Message of the Board of Commissioners of Cook County* (Chicago, 1937), p. 102.

20. Gross, *Detention of Children*, pp. 50–52.

21. *Gunning Commission Hearings*, 1939, pp. 70–71.

22. Ibid., p. 44.

23. Ibid., pp. 45, 55–58.

24. Interview with Sam Handler, A.C.S.W., psychiatric social worker at St. Charles and Sheridan from 1941 to 1944, May 15, 1986; Illinois Board of Public Welfare Commissioners, *Study and Reorganization of Illinois State Training School for Boys, 1941* (n.p., 1942), p. 30.

25. *Laws of Illinois*, 1943, pp. 294–95; *Laws of Illinois*, 1939, p. 325.

26. *Reorganization of State Training School*, pp. 10, 13–24.

27. Ibid., p. 14; Handler interview.

28. *Reorganization of State Training School*, pp. 10, 13–24.

29. Emma O. Lundberg, *Unto the Least of These: Social Services for Children* (New York, 1947), p. 318.

30. Albert J. Reiss, *A Survey of Probation Needs and Services in Illinois during 1946* (n.p., n.d.); *Report of the Child Welfare Commission of Illinois*, 1947 (n.p., n.d.), pp. 66–73, pp. 119–22; *Annual Message of the Board of Commissioners of Cook County*, 1939, p. 123. The new syphilis treatment was Marpharsen, a weaker form of the standard arsenic treatment. The new treatment could be dripped over an eight hour period into a patient's bloodstream. Earlier arsenic treatments had been so toxic that they had to be administered over an eighteen month period. Now early stage syphilis could be treated effectively in five days. See *Time Magazine*, Apr. 22, 1940, p. 75.

31. *Report of the Child Welfare Commission of Illinois*, 1949 (n.p., 1949), p. 5; *Laws of Illinois*, 1949, pp. 392–93.

32. *Child Welfare Commission*, 1949, pp. 9, 15.

33. Ellen Key, *Century of the Child* (New York, 1913).

Chapter 7: Rejecting the Parental State, 1950–90

1. *Laws of Illinois*, 1952, pp. 847–49; Governor's Survey Committee, *Report on the Illinois Youth Commission* (n.p., 1962), pp. 1–9.

2. Letter to Governor Otto Kerner from the Governor's Survey Committee, preface, *Report on IYC;* "Illinois' Treatment Approach to Juvenile Delinquency," in *Public Aid in Illinois* (Apr. 1969), p. 9; "Work Paper on Correctional Services" in *Community Mobilization for Youth: Work Papers for the First Report Meeting,* sponsored by the Mayor's Advisory Committee on Youth Welfare and the Welfare Council of Metropolitan Chicago (n.p., 1957), sec. 13, pp. 4–5, 27, 56.

3. *Chicago Tribune,* Feb. 21, 1961, part 1, p. 3; Governor's Committee, *Report on IYC,* p. 7.

4. Governor's Committee, *Report on IYC,* pp. 201–2, 217–18.

5. Ibid., pp. 78, 248, 138, 188–89, 129, 112; *Laws of Illinois,* 1961, p. 487.

6. Governor's Committee, *Report on IYC,* pp. 124, 185.

7. Ibid, part 3.

8. *Laws of Illinois,* 1969, p. 996.

9. *Laws of Illinois,* 1949, p. 375; National Council on Crime and Delinquency, *The Cook County Family (Juvenile) Court and Arthur J. Audy Home: An Appraisal and Recommendations* (n.p., 1963), pp. 23–32.

10. Ibid., p. 30.

11. Ibid., pp. 179, 168, 82.

12. Ibid., pp. 190, 163.

13. League of Women Voters of Cook County, *Cook County Detention* (Chicago, 1976), p. 2.

14. National Council on Crime and Delinquency, *Report of the Cook County Family Court,* pp. 179–82, 157.

15. Paul W. Alexander, "Constitutional Rights in the Juvenile Court," in *Justice for the Child: The Juvenile Court in Transition,* ed. Margaret K. Rosenheim (New York, 1962), pp. 82, 88; Alex Elson, "Juvenile Courts and Due Process" in *Justice for the Child,* pp. 98–99.

16. Sanford Fox, "Juvenile Justice Reform," *Stanford Law Review* 22 (June 1970): 1187–1239; Anthony Platt, *The Child Savers: The Invention of Delinquency* (Chicago, 1969), chaps. 4, 5.

17. National Council on Crime and Delinquency, *Report on Cook County Family Court,* p. 190.

18. In re Gault 387 U.S. 1, 87 S. Ct. 1428, 18 L. Ed. 2d 527 (1967).

19. Ibid.

20. McKeiver v. Pennsylvania 403 U.S. 528, 91 S. Ct. 1976, 29 L. Ed. 2d 647 (1971). For reactions to Gault, see, for example, George Davidson, "The Juvenile's Gideon" in *Illinois Bar Journal* (Feb., 1968): 488–503 and *Pursuing Justice for the Child,* ed. Margaret Rosenheim (Chicago, 1976), part 1.

21. League of Women Voters, *Analysis of the Juvenile Court Act* (Chicago, 1966), p. 1; *Laws of Illinois,* 1965, 2:2585–2611.

22. *Laws of Illinois,* 1977, 2:2387–90; *Laws of Illinois,* 1973, 2:1821–24; *Laws of Illinois,* 1972, 1:750–58; William Trumball, "Proposed New Juvenile Court Act in Illinois," *Illinois Bar Journal* (Mar. 1965): 610–12.

23. For a comprehensive look at the issue of status offenders, see National Council on Crime and Delinquency, *Status Offenders and the Juvenile Justice System: An Anthology,* ed. Richard Allinson (Hackensack, N.J., 1978).

24. Trumball, "New Juvenile Court Legislation," p. 612; *U.S. Statutes at Large,* 88:1110.

25. See, for example, *In the Matter of Walker,* in Robert Mnookin, *Child, Family, and State: Problems and Materials on Children and the Law* (Boston, 1978), pp. 715–22.

26. Patrick Murphy, *Our Kindly Parent—the State,* pp. 16–31, 67–68; *Laws of Illinois,* 1972, 1:750–51; *Laws of Illinois,* 1979, 2:2016–30.

27. David Reed et al., *Promises, Promises . . . : Does the Juvenile Court Deliver for Status Offenders? The Record in Cook County, Illinois* (Chicago, 1981), p. 186.

28. Reed, *Promises, Promises,* pp. 3–4.

29. *Laws of Illinois,* 1982, 2:2381–96. My source for the critique of the MRAI legislation is the staff of the Citizens Committee for the Cook County Juvenile Court, which, as early as 1989, had raised the question of whether the MRAI legislation was being used effectively. Their own informal studies of the Cook County Detention Center served to confirm their suspicions that young people who were merely status offenders were being held on delinquency petitions. I interviewed Citizens Committee Director Marlene Stern on March 10, 1990, and interviewed both Stern and Assistant Director Denise Kane on February 27, 1992.

30. Statistics quoted in "Illinois' Treatment Approach to Delinquency," pp. 10–12.

31. See, for example, National Council on Crime and Delinquency, *Rethinking Juvenile Justice: Implications for Illinois Statistical Trends* (n.p., 1984).

32. *Annual Report of the Cook County Juvenile Court, 1979–1980* p. 19; *Laws of Illinois,* 1979, 2:4223–25.

33. *Laws of Illinois,* 1982, 2:2414–32.

34. *Annual Report of the Cook County Juvenile Court, 1981–1982,* p. 16.

35. David Lambert, "National Trends Indicate Growing Hostility Toward Young People," and Barry Siegel, "Death Penalty Debate: How to Treat Youngsters Who Murder" (reprinted from *The Los Angeles Times,* 1985), *Youth Law News,* 7 (Jan./Feb. 1986): 1–3, 4–8.

36. National Advisory Committee for Juvenile Justice and Delinquency Prevention, Foreward to *Serious Juvenile Crime: A Redirected Federal Effort* (Washington, D.C., 1984); Advisory Committee, *Serious Juvenile Crime,* p.8.

37. "Embarrassing Questions for a Reagan Nominee," *Newsweek,* May 2, 1983, p. 37.

38. Advisory Committee, *Serious Juvenile Crime,* p.15.

39. See *Youth Law News* (July/Aug. 1989): 1–4 for a discussion of the

consolidated cases, Stanford v. Kentucky and Wilkins v. Missouri. *Youth Law News* (July/Aug. 1988): 7–10 discusses Thompson v. Oklahoma, a 1988 case that held the execution of minors fifteen years or younger to be cruel and unusual punishment and therefore unconstitutional.

40. Independent Voters of Illinois, *1985 Legislative Ratings, Illinois Senate.*

Chapter 8: From Hope to Fear, 1838–99

1. Writing the history of disabled children posed some challenges in the use of language. I have tried to be unobtrusive in the use of terminology, as well as sensitive to the implications of the language that I used.

The terminology has changed continuously over the past two centuries, often reflecting political and social realities. For example, reformers and teachers of the mid-nineteenth century used the word "afflicted" to describe disabled children. By the late nineteenth century, when a concern for the purity of the racial stock pervaded social thinking, the term "defective" came into use. The introduction of the term "handicapped" in the 1930s represented a deliberate rejection of earlier harsh language in favor of a term that evoked a compassionate acknowledgments of limitations.

I have used the words "handicapped" and "disabled" interchangeably throughout the manuscript as the most direct and neutral words available. I have used "retarded" and "mentally handicapped" with the same intention. I have aimed to used language that does not sound anachronistic when speaking of nineteenth- and early twentieth-century issues. Thus I have not, for example, used the term "developmental disabilities," because of its modern sound and connotations. When necessary, I have used the language of the time, such as the word "feebleminded," if the context called for it.

2. *Laws of Illinois*, 1833, pp. 180–81; *Laws of Illinois*, 1839, p. 138.

3. Phillip Gillette, "History of the Illinois Institution for the Education of the Deaf and Dumb" in *26th Biennial Report of the Illinois Institution for the Deaf and Dumb*, 1892, pp. 77–85. (Hereafter *BR =Biennial Report.*)

4. Ibid., pp. 85–96.

5. "Centennial History of Charitable Legislation in the State of Illinois" in *4th BR of the Board of State Commissioners of Public Charities, 1876*, pp. 129–33.

6. *Laws of Illinois*, 1838, pp. 162–64.

7. *Laws of Illinois*, 1815, p. 39.

8. *Report of the Committee on the Expediency of Appointing Commissioners to Inquire into the Condition of Idiots*, House Document #72 (Boston, 1847), p. 17. Quoted in Peter L. Tyor and Leland Bell, *Caring for the Retarded in America: A History* (Westport, Conn., 1984), p. 12. For a broader description of the antebellum reforming mind, see, for exam-

ple, John L. Thomas, "Romantic Reform in America, 1815–1865" in *Ante-Bellum Reform*, ed. David Brion Davis (New York, 1967), pp. 153–76; John Higham, *From Boundlessness to Consolidation* (Ann Arbor, Mich., 1969); Alice Felt Tyler, *Freedom's Ferment: Phases of American Social History from the Colonial Period to the Outbreak of the Civil War* (New York, 1944); and David Rothman, *The Discovery of the Asylum: Social Order and Disorder in the New Republic* (Boston, 1971).

9. Samuel G. Howe, *The Education of Laura Bridgman*, ed. Julia Ward Howe (Boston, 189?), pp. 1–30, 162–63.

10. Julia Reichmann Scott, "A Study of the State Care of the Blind in Illinois" (Master's thesis, University of Chicago, 1928), p. 7.

11. *34th Annual Report, Institution for the Education of the Deaf and Dumb*, 1874, pp. 8, 15–17 (Hereafter *AR*= Annual Report); Gillette, "History of the Illinois Institution for the Deaf," p. 77; *10th BR Institution for the Education of the Blind, 1867–68*, pp. 5–8; *12th BR, Institution for the Education of the Blind*, 1800, pp. 11–12.

12. Gillette, "History," pp. 91–92.

13. *10th BR, Institution for the Blind*, pp. 8–9, 20; *Proceedings of the 10th Convention of the American Instructors of the Deaf and Dumb, Held at Jacksonville, Illinois* (Springfield, Ill., 1882), pp. 16, 28.

14. *23rd BR, Institution for the Deaf*, 1886, p. 22.

15. *24th BR, Institution for the Deaf*, 1888, p. 68.

16. *10th BR, Institution for the Blind*, 1870, pp. 17–19, 24–25; *12th BR, Institution for the Blind*, 1874, p. 6; *15th BR, Institution for the Blind*, 1880, p. 12; *21st BR, Institution for the Deaf*, 1882, pp. 23–24; *22nd BR, Institution for the Deaf*, 1884, p. 9; *23rd BR, Institution for the Deaf*, 1886, p. 7; Gillette, "History," p. 97.

17. *12th BR, Institution for the Blind*, 1872, p. 6; *26th BR, Institution for the Blind*, 1900, p. 11; *21st BR, Institution for the Deaf*, 1882, p. 23.

18. *14th BR, Illinois State Board of Charities*, 1896, p. 77.

19. *10th BR, Institution for the Blind*, 1868, p. 15; Gillette, "History," pp. 71, 91; *24th BR, Institution for the Blind*, 1888, p. 70.

20. *12th BR, Institution for the Blind*, 1874, p. 5.

21. *1st AR of the Experimental School for Idiots and Feeble-minded Children*, 1866, p. 16.

22. Ibid., pp. 6–8.

23. Ibid., pp. 6, 11; *2nd AR, Experimental School for Feeble-minded Children*, 1866, p. 16.

24. See the first two annual reports for the reservations expressed by officials regarding support for their school.

25. *2nd BR, State Board of Charities*, 1872, p. 26; *25th BR, Institution for the Blind*, 1898, p. 21; *26th BR, Institution for the Blind*, 1900, p. 21.

26. *34th AR, Institution for the Deaf*, 1875, p. 56; *25th BR, Institution for the Deaf*, 1890, p. 18; *2nd BR, State Board of Charities*, 1872, pp. 99–100.

27. *2nd BR, State Board of Charities*, 1872, pp. 99–100.

28. *10th BR, Institution for the Blind*, 1868, pp. 20, 23, 24–25; *13th BR, Institution for the Blind*, 1874, p. 9; *17th BR, Institution for the Blind*, 1892, pp. 11–15; *25th BR, Institution for the Blind*, 1898, p. 12; *2nd BR, State Board of Charities*, 1872, pp. 25, 28; *9th BR, State Board of Charities*, 1886, p. 72.

29. *34th AR, Institution for the Deaf*, 1875, pp. 16–53, 55–56; *21st BR, Institution for the Deaf*, 1882, p. 10; *22nd BR, Institution for the Deaf*, 1884, pp. 17–19, 22–23; *2nd BR State Board of Charities*, 1872, pp. 39–40, 104–5; *4th BR, State Board of Charities*, 1876, p. 103; *7th BR, State Board of Charities*, 1882, p. 88–89; *8th BR, State Board of Charities*, 1884, pp. 153–58.

30. *1st AR, State Experimental School for the Feeble-minded*, 1866, p. 24.

31. *7th BR, State Institution for the Feeble-minded*, 1878, p. 12; *8th BR, State Institution for the Feeble-minded*, 1880, pp. 7, 12, 20.

32. Tyor and Bell, *Caring for the Retarded*, chap. 3.

33. *1st BR, State Board of Charities*, 1870, p. 128; *6th BR, State Board of Charities*, 1880, pp. 215, 243; *9th BR, State Board of Charities*, 1886, p. 132; *10th BR State Board of Charities*, 1888, pp. 8, 111.

34. Tyor and Bell, *Caring for the Retarded*, p. 13; *2nd BR, State Board of Charities*, 1872, pp. 24–25; *15th BR, State Board of Charities*, 1898, pp. 63, 293–94, 299; *14th BR, Institution for the Feeble-minded*, 1892, pp. 8, 17–18; *16th BR, Institution for the Feeble-minded*, 1896, p. 21; *8th BR, Institution for the Feeble-minded*, 1880, p. 23.

35. See Tyor and Bell, *Caring for the Retarded*, chaps. 1–5.

36. See John Higham, *Strangers in the Land: Patterns of American Nativism, 1860–1925* (New York, 1963), for an extensive discussion of the impact of immigration on nativist thinking. Carl Degler, *In Search of Human Nature: The Decline and Revival of Darwinism in American Thought* (New York, 1991) gives a comprehensive discussion of Darwinism and its impact.

37. *1st BR, State Board of Charities*, 1870, p. 19; *2nd BR, State Board of Charities*, 1872, p. 19.

38. *16th BR, State Institution for the Feeble-minded*, 1896, p. 10.

39. *15th BR, State Board of Charities*, 1898, p. 297.

40. For a fuller description of Dugdale's work, see Tyor and Bell, *Caring for the Retarded*, pp. 54–58.

41. *25th BR, Institution for the Deaf*, 1890, pp. 16–19; *8th BR, State Board of Charities*, 1884, pp. 150–58.

42. *15th BR, State Board of Charities*, 1898, pp. 297–98.

43. John 9:1–3.

44. *14th BR, State Institution for the Feeble-Minded*, 1892, p. 8.

45. *15th BR, State Board of Charities*, 1898, p. 304.

46. Ibid., p. 72.

47. *15th BR, State Board of Charities*, 1898, pp. 64–65.

48. Ibid., pp. 67, 64–65.
49. *2nd BR, State Board of Charities,* 1872, p. 30.
50. *15th BR, State Board of Charities,* 1898, p. 299.
51. Elizabeth Davis, "State Care of the Feeble-Minded in Illinois" (Master's thesis, University of Chicago, 1926), chaps. 1, 2.

Chapter 9: Optimism Reborn, 1900–1940

1. Paul Starr, *The Social Transformation of American Medicine: The Rise of a Sovereign Profession and the Making of a Vast Industry* (New York, 1982), chaps. 4, 5; Susan Sessions Rugh, "Being Born in Chicago" *Chicago History* (Winter 1986–1987): 4–21.

2. *Institution Quarterly* (hereafter *IQ*) 1 (Mar. 1917): 195.

3. See the *Institution Quarterly* (Aug. 1910): 29–36 for examples of the fascination with heredity. See also John Higham, *Strangers in the Land: Patterns of Nativism, 1860–1925* (New York, 1963), pp. 150–55.

4. *IQ* 6 (Mar. 1915): 184; *IQ* 7 (Sept. 1916): 101. See volumes 1–10 for a running commentary on the new intelligence tests. See also Peter Tyor and Leland Bell, *Caring for the Retarded in America: A History* (West Port, Conn., 1984), chap. 5, for a discussion of the national impact of intelligence tests.

5. See Higham, *Strangers in the Land,* pp. 151–53; Booker T. Washington, "The Claims of the Colored Child" in *The Child in the City* (Chicago, 1912), pp. 233–34.

6. For expressions of the fear of race suicide, see for example, *IQ* 1 (Aug. 1910): 37; *IQ* 5 (June 1914): 64; *IQ* 6 (June 1915): 98–101. This anxiety was so pervasive that the term "race suicide" or its equivalent surfaced in almost every discussion of the feeble-minded. See also *IQ* 7 (June 1916): 176 and *IQ* 7 (Dec. 1916): 20 on the prolific nature of feeble-minded women.

7. *IQ* 6 (Mar. 1915): 184–85; John S. Ransom, *A Study of Mentally Defective Children in Chicago* (Chicago, 1915), p. 42; *IQ* 6 (June 1915): 100–101.

Given the physical conditions of life at the time, it seems possible in retrospect that with urbanization there may have been an increase in retardation. Considering the adulterated quality of food and drugs, the widespread presence of venereal disease and other infectious diseases, a generally contaminated environment and nutritional inadequacies, possibly there were more children born mentally impaired than in an earlier time. But the issue is clouded by the lack of differentiation between environmental and genetic damage. Most people who worried about the mental health of the community interpreted notions of heredity so broadly that they virtually obscured any sense of birth defects. One essayist writing in the *Institution Quarterly* gave an example of this thinking when she spoke of a syphilitic father's tragic legacy to his children: one was epileptic, one had a cleft palate, and a third was institutionalized in the very mental hospital in which his father had died. She was convinced that all of this was hereditary in nature. *IQ* 9 (Dec. 1918): 292.

8. *12th Annual Convention, Illinois Conference of Charities and Corrections* (ICCC) p. 642; *IQ* (Aug. 1910): 36–37; *IQ* 7 (June 1916): 178. On the United States Supreme Court decision Carrie Buck v. J.H. Bell, May 2, 1927, see Harry H. Laughlin, *The Legal Status of Eugenic Sterilization* (Chicago, 1930), pp. 7–52. On other states' attitudes toward sterilization, see Leland and Bell, *Caring for the Retarded*, chaps. 4, 5.

9. State of Illinois, 45th General Assembly, House of Representatives, Special Investigating Committee, *Report of the Special Committee to Investigate State Institutions* (Chicago, 1908), p. 14; Ransom, *Mentally Defective Children in Chicago*, pp. 32–33; *IQ* 6 (Sept. 1915): 8–16.

10. *12th Annual Convention, ICCC*, p. 557; Ransom, *Mentally Defective Children in Chicago*, pp. 29–35; *12th Annual Convention ICCC*, p. 641.

11. Ransom, *Mentally Defective Children in Chicago*, pp. 32, 62; *IQ* 6 (June 1915): 50–51; *Laws of Illinois*, 1915, p. 245; *IQ* 7 (June 1916): 175–80; *IQ* 7 (June 1916): 172; *IQ* 15 (Sept. 1924): 95.

12. *Report of the Special Investigating Committee*, pp. 4–7.

13. *Report of the Special Investigating Committee*, pp. 5, 929–31; "Governor Charles Deneen's Message to the 45th General Assembly, May 23, 1908" in *21 BR, State Board of Charities*, 1910, pp. 75–141.

14. *Report of the Special Investigating Committee*, pp. 5, 171, 175; Jane Addams, *My Friend, Julia Lathrop* (New York, 1935), chap. 7.

15. *20 BR State Board of Charities*, 1906–8, pp. 57, 187; *IQ* 9 (March 1918): 25; Richard Cabot, M.D., "Humanizing the Hospitals" in *The Child in the City*, p. 43.

16. *IQ* 5 (June 1914): 9, 65; Ransom, "Mentally Defective Children in Chicago," p. 62; *IQ* 6 (June, 1915): 96–101; *IQ* 6 (Sept. 1915): 17; *IQ* 6 (June 1915): 50.

17. *IQ* 7 (June 1916): 93–95; *IQ* 9 (June 1918): 25.

18. *IQ* 7 (Dec. 1916): 66–69; *IQ* 8 (Mar. 1917): 57; *Laws of Illinois*, 1912, chap. 23, sec. 178; *IQ* 6 (Mar. 1915): 40–41; *IQ* 9 (June 1918): 33; *IQ* 10 (Mar. 1919): 7, 6.

19. Hugh T. Patrick, M.D., "The Need of an Institution for the Treatment of Epileptic Children" in *Child in the City*, pp. 213–33; *IQ* 5 (Dec. 1914): 85; *IQ* 7 (Dec. 1916): 21; *IQ* 14 (Dec. 1923): 178–79.

20. *IQ* 10 (Sept. 1919): 81; *IQ* 10 (Mar. 1919): 61; *Annual Report of the Department of Public Welfare*, 1929, pp. 24, 191.

21. The total inmate population of the state went from 29,375 in 1929 to 34,086 in Oct., 1932; from 1932 to 1935, it increased by 4,953. *AR DPW, 1931–35*, p. 11.

22. *Annual Message of the Board of Cook County Commissioners*, 1938, pp. 92–93; *Annual Message*, p. 99; Fred Gross, *Detention and Criminal Prosecution of Children of Juvenile Court Age in Cook County, 1938–1942* (Chicago, 1942), pp. 50–52; *AR DPW*, 1935, pp. 13–14.

23. *IQ* 10 (Mar. 1919): 60; *IQ* 14 (Mar. 1923): 1; *IQ* 16 (June 1925): 13; *IQ* 7 (Dec. 1917): 97.

24. *AR DPW*, 1931–35, pp. 132–43; Bertha Schlotter and Margaret Svendson, *An Experiment in Recreation with the Mentally Retarded* (Chicago, 1932), pp. 1–3.

25. For the changing mentality in the 1920s, see, for example, *IQ* 15 (June 1924): 73–75; *IQ* 17 (Sept. 1919): 120; *IQ* 9 (Dec. 1918): 127.

26. *IQ* 16 (Mar. 1919): 14–17; *IQ* 10 (Sept. 1919): 120; *IQ* 9 (Dec. 1918): 127.

27. *IQ* 10 (Sept. 1919): 78–80; Leland and Bell, *Caring for the Retarded*, p. 121; Jemru J. Goddard, *Human Efficiency and Levels of Intelligence* (Princeton, 1920) quoted in Leland and Bell, *Caring for the Retarded*, p. 121; *IQ* 15 (June 1924): 73–75.

28. *IQ* 10 (Sept. 1919): 52–58; *IQ* 7 (June 1916): 176; White House Conference on Child Health and Protection, *Addresses and Abstracts of Committee Reports* (New York, 1931), pp. 310–15; *AR DPW*, 1931–35, p. 144.

29. F. Park Lewis, M.D., "The Prevention of Blindness" in *The Child in the City*, pp. 55–79; *IQ* 7 (June 1916): 69; *IQ* 6 (June 1915): 65; *Laws of Illinois*, 1915, p. 366; *IQ* 7 (June 1916): 73–74; *Laws of Illinois*, 1917, p. 734.

30. *IQ* 8 (Mar. 1917): 105; *IQ* 14 (June, 1923): 100–101.

31. Lewis,"Prevention of Blindness," pp. 68–69; *IQ* 10 (Sept. 1919): 85–86; *IQ* 1 (Sept. 1910): 95.

32. *Laws of Illinois*, 1915, p. 256.

33. *IQ* 9 (Dec. 1918): 224.

34. *IQ* 7 (Dec. 1916): 25–27; *IQ* 10 (March 1919): 77.

35. See *Report of the Child Welfare Committee*, 1931, pp. 34–38 and the White House Conference, 1930, *Addresses*, pp. 299–301 for expressions of concern about crippled children. "The crippled occupy the attention of more volunteer and professional agencies than any other type of child service," according to the 1930 White House Conference report (p. 299). The 1940 White House Conference report was cheered enough by progress in work with physically handicapped children to call the improvement "gratifying." White House Conference on Children in a Democracy, 1940, *Final Report* (Washington, 1940), p. 276.

36. *IQ* 8 (Mar. 1917): 195; White House Conference, 1930, *Addresses*, pp. 291–92.

37. *Report of the Child Welfare Committee*, 1931, p. 37; William J. Ellis, "The Handicapped Child" in *Children in a Depression Decade*, ed. James H. Bossard (Philadelphia, 1940), pp. 138–45.

38. White House Conference, 1940, *Final Report*, Foreword, xv.

39. "Handicapped Child," p. 138; *IQ* 9 (Mar. 1918): 61; White House Conference, 1930, *Addresses*, p. 292.

Chapter 10: Progress for Handicapped Children, 1940–90

1. Illinois Commission for Handicapped Children [hereafter called ICHC], *The Commission Reports to the People of Illinois, June, 1941–*

June, 1946 (Springfield?, 1946), p. 11; ICHC, *Proceedings of the Governor's Conference on Exceptional Children*, 1942, pp. 13, 15, 23. [Hereafter cited as *Governor's Conference* with date.]

2. ICHC, *Commission Reports to the People*, pp.5–7; *Governor's Conference, 1942*, p. 5; *Governor's Conference, 1943*, pp. 18–19; *Governor's Conference*, 1946, p. 24.

3. *Governor's Conference*, 1942, p. 37; *Governor's Conference*, 1943, pp. 17–19; *Governor's Conference*, 1946, pp. 22–23; *Governor's Conference*, 1948, pp. 18–19; *Governor's Conference*, 1949, p. 19; ICHC, *Commission Reports to the People*, p. 6; *Governor's Conference*, 1943, p. 43; *Governor's Conference*, 1942, p. 30.

4. *Governor's Conference*, 1948, pp. 15–17, 31; *Governor's Conference*, 1951, pp. 22–23, 43; *Report of the Illinois Child Welfare Functions Commission to the 64th General Assembly* (Springfield, 1945), p. 2; Illinois Committee for the 1960 White House Conference on Children and Youth, *Children and Youth in Illinois* (n.p., 1960), p. 33.

5. *Report of the Child Welfare Commission, 1945* , pp. 34–36, 40, 40 n.

6. *Governor's Conference*, 1948, pp. 23, 31–32; Frances A. Koestler, *The Unseen Minority: A Social History of Blindness in America* (New York, 1976), pp. 414–17.

7. Lawrence Linck, *Some Unmet Needs of Physically Handicapped Children in Illinois* (n.p., 1940), pp. 10–11; *Governor's Conference*, 1943, p. 41.

8. The state of Illinois had rejected the Sheppard-Towner Act of the 1920s, which had provided federal money for children's health during that decade.

9. *Governor's Conference*, 1942, pp. 25–26, 27; *U.S. Statutes at Large*, part 1, 49:629–34.

10. *Governor's Conference*, 1942, pp. 25–26; Linck, *Some Unmet Needs*, p. 10; *Governor's Conference*, 1943, p. 10; ICHC, *Commission Reports to the People*, p. 15; *Child Welfare Commission*, 1945, p. 75; *Report of the Child Welfare Commission to the 66th General Assembly* (n.p., 1949), pp. 24–25.

11. *Governor's Conference*, 1942, p. 32.

12. *Governor's Conference*, 1946, p. 8; *Governor's Conference*, 1950, p. 56; *Governor's Conference*, 1953, p. 12; Linck, *Some Unmet Needs*, p. 12; Edith Stern, *The Handicapped Child: A Guide for Parents* (New York, 1950), pp. 52–72.

13. *Governor's Conference*, 1946, p. 10; *Governor's Conference*, 1949, p. 29; *Governor's Conference*, 1942, p. 40.

14. *Governor's Conference*, 1951, p. 13; *Illinois Committee for 1960 White House Conference, Children and Youth*, p. 33; ICHC, *Facilities for the Education and Institutional Care of Mentally Handicapped Children in Illinois* (Chicago, 1942), pp. 1–8; *Child Welfare Commission*, 1945, p. 21; *Child Welfare Commission*, 1949, pp. 6–8, 25–27.

15. ICHC, *Commission Reports to the People*, p. 13; *Governor's Conference*, 1946, pp. 7, 9; Charles Jay, *The Sesquicentennial: One Hundred*

and Fifty Years of Illinois Education (Springfield, 1968), p. 23; *Public Statewide Services for Children in Illinois: A Report of the Study of Eighteen Health, Welfare and Educational Agencies* (n.p., 1955), pp. 1–25; *Governor's Conference, 1951*, p. 17.

16. Governor's Committee for Illinois on the Midcentury White House Conference for Children and Youth, *Children and Youth in Illinois* (Springfield, 1951), p. 84; *Governor's Conference, 1951*, p. 17.

17. *Governor's Conference, 1949*, p. 29; *Governor's Conference, 1947*, pp. 14–15.

18. Robert Bremner et al., eds., *Children and Youth in America: A Documentary History*, 3 vols. (Cambridge, 1970–74), 3:1523; *Governor's Conference, 1950*, pp. 31–32.

19. *Governor's Conference, 1950*, pp. 50–51.

20. Ibid., pp. 51–55.

21. Elizabeth R. Kramm, "Families of Mongoloid Children" in *Publications of the United States Children's Bureau* (Publication #401: Washington, 1963), pp. 6–7.

22. *Governor's Conference, 1951*, p. 89; Stern, *The Handicapped Child*, p. 134; ICHC, *Biennial Report of ICHC, 1959–1961* (n.p., 1961), p. 6; Illinois Committee, 1960, *Children and Youth*, p. 37; *Public State-Wide Services for Children*, p. 17.

23. *Group Projects for Handicapped Children: Selected Papers Presented at the Eleventh Governor's Conference on Exceptional Children* (n.p., 1956), pp. 1–3; *Governor's Conference, 1950*, p. 5; *Governor's Conference, 1951*, pp. 33, 60, 83–85.

24. *Governor's Conference, 1952*, p. 47.

25. Ibid., p. 55.

26. Bremner, *Children and Youth*, 3:1535, 1543–44.

27. Ibid., pp. 1544–45.

28. Ibid., pp. 1544–45, 1556.

29. Erwin L. Levine and Elizabeth Wexler, *P L 94–142: An Act of Congress* (New York, 1981), pp. 20–24.

30. Ibid., pp. 33–37.

31. *Laws of Illinois*, 1965, pp. 1948–58.

32. Erving Goffman, *Asylums: Essays on the Social Situation of Mental Patients and Other Inmates*, New York, 1961. For extensive discussions of institutionalization, see, for example: Wolf Wolfensberger, *Normalization: The Principle of Normalization in Human Services* (Toronto, 1972); Pauline Morris, *Put Away: A Sociological Study of Institutions for the Mentally Retarded* (London, 1969); Bremner, *Children and Youth*, 3:1513–36; Tyor and Bell, *Caring for the Retarded*, pp. 122–51.

33. Patrick Murphy, *Our Kindly Parent—The State: The Juvenile Justice System and How It Works* (New York, 1974), pp. 32–44.

34. *Annual Report of the Illinois Department of Mental Health* [hereafter *AR IDMH*], 1960–61, pp. 24–25; *AR IDMH*, 1962–63, pp. 6, 43, 117; *AR IDMH*, 1964–65, p. 35; *AR IDMH*, 1963–64, p. 34.

35. *AR IDMH*, 1970, p. 10.

36. Wyatt v. Stickney, 344 F. Supp. 387 (1972) quoted in Bremner, *Children and Youth*, 3:1978–85.

37. Pennsylvania Association for Retarded Children et al. v. Commonwealth of Pennsylvania et al., 343 F. Supp. 279 (1972); Levine and Wexler, *P L 94–142*, pp. 38–39; Bremner, *Children and Youth*, 3:1972–78.

38. Levine and Wexler, *P L 94–142*, pp. 100–129, 153.

39. Office of Superintendent of Public Instruction, *The School Code of Illinois* (St. Paul, 1974), pp. 107–14; Julia Q. Dempsey and Gerry Kerr, "Comparison of Public Law 94–142 and the Illinois School Code" in Appendix to *Illinois School Problems*, #14, School Problems Commission, 1977, pp. 47–58; William P. McLure, Robert Burnham and Robert Henderson, *Special Education: Needs—Costs—Methods of Financing* (Urbana, 1975), p. 74.

40. Daniel Yohalem and Janet Dinsmore [Children's Defense Fund], *94–142 and 540: Numbers That Add Up to Educational Rights for Handicapped Children* (Washington, D.C., 1984), pp. 50–57.

41. Daniel P. Hallahan and James M. Kauffman, *Exceptional Children: Introduction to Special Education*, 3d ed. (Englewood Cliffs, N.J., 1986), pp. 25–32; The National Average Per Pupil Expenditure is a figure set yearly by the National Center for Education Statistics at the Department of Education. My figures for 1991 are from John George, Governmental Relations Liaison at the National Association of State Directors of Special Education. I spoke to Mr. George in a telephone interview on May 20, 1992. George asserts that the widely quoted 9 percent figure of federal expenditures for P. L. 94–142, adjusted for inflation, is in fact 6.7 percent of the National Average Per Pupil Expenditure.

42. Kenneth Katzen, "A Teacher's View," *Exceptional Children*, 12 (1980): 116–23; Interview with Susan O'Brien, Director of Curriculum Services, Palos Community Consolidated Schools, Palos Park, Ill., Feb. 28, 1988.

43. Coordinating Council for Handicapped Children, pamphlets and fliers, Feb.–Sept. 1981.

44. Jeanette Jennings, "Elderly Parents as Caregivers for their Adult Dependent Children," *Social Work* 32 (Sept.–Oct., 1987): 430–33.

45. Tom Joe and Cheryl Rogers, *By the Few, for the Few: The Reagan Welfare Legacy* (Lexington, Mass., 1980), pp. 19, 21.

46. *U.S. News*, June 20, 1983, p. 13; Jeff Lyon, *Playing God in the Nursery* (New York, 1985), pp. 259–65. For the particulars of the SSI controversy, see the *New York Times*, which covered the story extensively from February until June of 1981.

47. *AR IDMH*, 1966–67, pp. 7–8; *Report of the Governor's Task Force on the Future of Mental Health in Illinois* (n.p., 1987), p. 1.

48. *Chicago Tribune*, Sept. 5, 1986, p. 1; *Chicago Tribune*, Dec. 4, 1986, p. 2; *Chicago Tribune*, Aug. 7, 1986, sec. 2, p. 1; League of Women Voters, *Public Policy on Mental Illness in Illinois: A Report by the Mental Health Task Force* (n.p., 1986).

49. Mary Ellen Barry, League of Women Voters Press Conference, Feb. 21, 1988.

50. Lyon, *Playing God*, 264–67; Roy Petty and Donna Sassaman, "Dead Babies," *[Chicago] Reader*, Aug. 15, 1986, pp. 1, 26–33.

51. Lyon, *Playing God*, chaps. 10, 11.

52. *Youth Law News* (Jan./Feb. 1991): 1–5.

53. The Chicago Community Trust, "Equal Access to the American Dream: The Americans With Disabilities Act . . . What It Means To You," Supplement to *Chicago Tribune*, Nov. 12, 1991, pp. 1–11.

Bibliographic Essay

In writing a history that covers almost two centuries, I was fortunate that, with few exceptions, the documents I used were in a central location, the University of Chicago Libraries—specifically, the Regenstein Library, the John Crerar Library, the School of Social Service Administration Library, and the Law Library. Many of the materials that I found most valuable are by their nature ephemeral: reports that are often discarded without a thought, since all but historians regard them as outdated shortly after they are produced. The University of Chicago collections owe much to the strong historical sense of Edith Abbott and Sophonisba Breckinridge, founders and professors at the School of Social Service Administration from the 1920s through the 1940s, who preserved many of the materials I found so informative. This same appreciation of history is reflected in the master's theses written at the school under Abbott's and Breckinridge's direction. These examinations of various institutions' histories and policies were of immense help to me in piecing together the state's relationship with its children over such a long period of time.

Serials

Annual and biennial reports of institutions or conventions provided a wealth of information, including philosophical and theoretical discussions of the day. One of the most useful for all three sections of the book was the *Biennial Reports of the Illinois State Board of Commissioners of Public Charities*. From its creation in 1870 to its reorganization in the first decade of the twentieth century, the board was charged with visiting the institutions of the state and reporting on their condition. When the board was reorganized into the Illinois Charities Commission, in 1909–10, there were two annual reports issued, after which the *Institution Quarterly* took over the responsibility of reporting on the state's institutions. In 1926, this quarterly was renamed *Welfare Magazine.*

Other important annual or biennial reports were: *The Annual Reports of the Chicago Reform School* (located at the Chicago Historical Society); *The Annual and Biennial Reports of the Illinois Home for Female Juvenile Offenders* (later *The Illinois State Training School for Girls at Geneva*); *The Department of Visitation of Children Placed in Family Homes; The Annual Message of the Commissioners of Cook County; The Annual Reports of the Cook County Juvenile Court* (for the modern sections of the book); *The Annual and Biennial Reports of the Institution for the Blind; The Annual and Biennial Reports of the Institution for the Deaf; The Annual and Biennial Reports of the Institution for the Feeble-Minded* (originally called the Experimental School for Idiots and Feeble-Minded Children), the Illinois Commission for Handicapped Children's *Report of the Proceedings of the Annual Governor's Conference on Exceptional Children* (1940s and 1950s); and *The Annual Reports of the Illinois Department of Mental Health.*

Assessments of "The State of the Child"

A number of the works consulted surveyed the condition of children, either with an eye to improving the situation of a particular group of children or with the intention of assessing the general state of children in Illinois or the United States. One of the first of these assessments took place at the famous "Children of the State" Conference of 1898, which looked broadly at the question of children's needs in Illinois. The proceedings of this conference can be found in *The Sixteenth Biennial Report of the State Board of Commissioners of Public Charities* (Springfield, 1899).

Over the course of the twentieth century, various state committees convened to critique the "the state of the child." In 1920, the newly established Department of Public Welfare gathered a group of experts to review children's services. *The Report of the Children's Committee* (Springfield, 1921) is a comprehensive look at the problems in children's programs and the lack of programs in the state. (One of the few extant copies of this report is in the John Crerar Library at the University of Chicago.)

In 1931, a committee appointed by the Illinois legislature issued *A Report on Child Welfare Legislation.* Also useful for assessing the general condition of services to children in Illinois in the 1930s are: Elizabeth Milchrist, *State Administration of Child Welfare in Illinois* (Chicago, 1937), and John Kahlert, *Child Dependency in Illinois* (Springfield, 1941).

There were a number of reports to the legislature in the 1940s reviewing the state's child welfare functions and activities. The Committee on Child Welfare Functions issued reports in 1943, 1945, 1947, and 1949, all of which provide a wealth of information about the condition of children in Illinois and illustrate the fragmented and inadequate nature of public provisions for children in need.

In 1955, the Committee of Eighteen Health, Welfare, and Educational Agencies reported on *Public State-Wide Services for Children in Illinois.* The Illinois Commission on Children issued *A Report of a Committee for a Comprehensive Family and Child Welfare Program in Illinois* (Springfield, 1962) calling for a separate Department of Children and Family Services and demonstrating that conditions in Illinois children's services were no less fragmented and chaotic than they had been a generation earlier.

The White House Conference on Children called by President Theodore Roosevelt in 1909 proved to be an excellent source for a discussion of the developing vision of the Child Welfare Progressives in regard to children and families. The 1930 and 1940 White House conferences provided specific information as well as a general overview of the mentality of social welfare advocates. Specific to Illinois were the state committees convened every decade to assess the situation preparatory to attending the White House Conference on Children.

Some excellent collections of documents pertaining to the condition of children nationally are: Grace Abbott, *The Child and the State* (2 vols., Chicago, 1938), and Robert Bremner et al., *Children and Youth in America: A Documentary History* (3 vols., 4 pts., Cambridge, Mass., 1970–74). For modern issues regarding children and the law, Robert Mnookin's *Child, Family, State: Problems and Materials on Children and the Law* (Boston, 1978) is an excellent resource.

The Child in the City (Chicago, 1912), edited by Sophonisba Breckinridge, is a collection of papers given at the national Child Welfare Exhibit held in Chicago in 1911. It offers a wealth of information and opinions about the state of children and attitudes about them at the height of the Progressive Era. *Children in a Depression Decade* (Philadelphia, 1940), edited by James H. S. Bossard, serves the same function for the 1930s.

Dependency

The following material proved useful for the section of *The Children of the State* dealing with dependency:

The issue of children in poverty, from the poorhouse through Aid to Families with Dependent Children, afforded extensive materials:

Homer Folks, *The Care of Destitute, Neglected and Delinquent Children* (New York, 1900), is critical, because it provides a history as well as a comprehensive look at conditions for children in the United States at the end of the nineteenth century. Folks also articulates the philosophy and aims of child welfare advocates moving into the Progressive Era. Henry Thurston, *The Dependent Child: A Story of Changing Aims and Methods in the Care of Dependent Children* (New York, 1930), serves the same function for a somewhat later time period, both for Illinois and the nation.

"A Centennial History of Charitable Legislation in the State of Illinois" in the *4th Biennial Report of the Board of State Commissioners of Public Charities* (Springfield, 1876) is a useful essay for nineteenth-century policy. Naomi Harwood, "The History of the Care of Dependent Children in Cook County to 1899," Field Study, School of Social Service Administration [SSA], University of Chicago, 1941, is an invaluable work for information on nineteenth-century Illinois' care of dependent children. This excellent work is available only on microfilm in the SSA Library. Julia Lathrop, "The Cook County Charities" in *Hull-House Maps and Papers: A Presentation of Nationalities and Wages in a Congested District of Chicago* (1894; reprint, New York, 1970), discusses the children in the Cook County poorhouse at the end of the nineteenth century.

Arlien Johnson, *Public Policy and Private Charities: A Study of Legislation in the United States and of Administration in Illinois* (Chicago, 1941); James Brown, *The History of Public Assistance in Chicago* (Chicago, 1941); and Sophonisba Breckinridge, *The Illinois Poor Law and Its Administration* (Chicago, 1939), are all very helpful in discussing Illinois policy toward children and families dependent because of poverty.

Edna Bullock, ed., *Selected Articles on Mothers' Pensions* (New York, 1915) is an excellent cross section of early views on mothers' pensions. Graham W. Morland, "Mothers' Pensions and Their Failure in Illinois," *Institution Quarterly* 7 (Sept. 1916); Edith Abbott and Sophonisba Breckinridge, *The Administration of the Aid to Mothers' Law in Illinois* (Children's Bureau Publication #82: Washington, D.C., 1921); Helen Wright, *Children of Wage-Earning Mothers: a Study of a Select Group in Chicago* (Children's Bureau Publication #102: Washington, D.C., 1922); Annette Marie Garrett, "The Administration of the Aid to Mothers' Law in Illinois, 1917–1925" (Master's thesis, University of Chicago, 1925), all give an extensive analysis of the workings of mothers' pensions in Illinois.

Arthur Miles, *Federal Aid and Public Assistance in Illinois* (Chicago, 1941) and Wallace Clarke, *An Appraisal of ADC in Illinois* (n.p., 1943), discuss the difficulties of getting A.D.C. established in Illinois, while Kathryn Goodwin, *A.D.C.: Problems and Promise* (n.p., 1959), discusses the issue on a national level some years after its inception.

Robert Bremner, *From the Depths: The Discovery of Poverty in the United States* (New York, 1956), and Walter Trattner, *From Poor Law to Welfare State: A History of Social Welfare in America*, 3d ed. (New York, 1984) provide useful background on this issue. Michael Katz, *In the Shadow of the Poorhouse: A Social History of Welfare in America* (New York, 1986), is an excellent resource, especially for modern welfare issues.

For contemporary aspects of welfare, I am indebted to the Illinois Public Welfare Coalition for materials and analysis of both state and federal welfare policy.

For the issue of institutionalized children, foster children, and neglect and abuse, the following were especially useful: Harwood, "Dependent Children in Cook County"; Folks, *Destitute, Neglected, and Dependent Children*; Thurston, *The Dependent Child*, cited above; Alice Channing, "The Illinois Soldiers' Orphans' Home" (Master's thesis, University of Chicago, 1926); Oscar Dudley, "Saving the Children: Sixteen Years' Work Among the Dependent Youth of Chicago" in *History of Child Saving in the United States* in *Twentieth National Conference of Charities and Corrections in Chicago, 1893* (Boston, 1893); Charles Loring Brace, *The Dangerous Classes of New York and Twenty Years Work Among Them* (New York, 1872); Arthur Guild, *Baby Farms in Chicago: An Investigation for the Juvenile Protective Association*, (n.p., 1917); Charlotte Ashby, "Dependent Negro Children in Chicago in 1926" (Master's thesis, University of Chicago, 1927); Sandra Stehno, "Foster Care for Dependent Black Children in Chicago, 1899–1934" (Ph.D diss., University of Chicago, 1985). An excellent and comprehensive secondary source on dependent children in the Progressive Era is Susan Tiffin, *In Whose Best Interests? Child Welfare Reform in the Progressive Era* (Westport, Conn., 1982).

In discussing modern issues of foster care and neglect and abuse, the documents collection *Children and Youth in America,* cited above, was very useful, as was *Foster Care in Question: A National Reassessment by Twenty-one Experts* (New York, 1974). Douglas Besharov, "Right Versus Rights: the Dilemma of Child Protection," *Public Welfare* (Spring, 1985), afforded me many insights about contemporary problems of child protection. In *Recognizing Child Abuse: A Guide for the Concerned* (New York, 1989), Besharov develops some of the ideas in the *Public Welfare* article. Another critical source was Malcolm Bush, *Families in Distress: Public, Private, and Civic Responses* (Berkeley, Calif., 1988). Malcolm Bush and Harold Goldman, "Psychological Parenting and Permanency Principles in Child Welfare: A Reappraisal and Critique," *The American Journal of Orthopsychiatry* 52 (April 1982), raised important questions about the philosophy underlying permanency planning.

For the more recent aspects of each issue, I was fortunate in being able to draw on the knowledge and resources of experts in the social welfare community. For the issue of foster care and neglect and abuse I am especially grateful for the help of social policy and child welfare scholar Dr. Malcolm Bush; Marlene Stern, Director of the Citizens Committee for the Juvenile Court of Cook County, Illinois; and Marilyn Clarke, a social worker with more than twenty years experience with child welfare in Illinois. Many of the pamphlets and unpublished papers I used as sources were obtained through this child welfare network.

I wrote a first draft of the dependency and delinquency sections of this manuscript while at The Social Policy Research Center at the University of Chicago, another general resource that provided information and discussion about contemporary issues to which I might not otherwise have had access.

The Department of Children and Family Services provided assistance and clarification of laws and policies from time to time, and the Illinois chapter of the American Civil Liberties Union was especially helpful in explaining the "B.H." lawsuit and consent decree and its implications for child welfare in Illinois.

In addition to the information and resources obtained from these experts in the field, I was also able to observe dependency proceedings in the Cook County Juvenile Court for six months under the auspices of the Citizens Committee for the Juvenile Court and was thus able to become familiar with the practical workings and problems of the court in a concrete way that would not have been possible through strictly literary sources.

I also made extensive use of the *Chicago Tribune* coverage of issues relating to child welfare and especially DCFS in the late 1980s and early 1990s.

Delinquency

For the Delinquency section of *The Children of the State*, some of the materials I found most helpful for the nineteenth century were: E. C. Wines and Theodore Dwight, *Report on the Prisons and Reformatories of the United States and Canada* (New York, 1867); E. C. Wines, *The State of the Prisons and Child-Saving Institutions in the Civilized World* (Cambridge, Mass., 1880); Andrew Bruce, "One Hundred Years of Criminalized Development in Illinois," *Journal of the American Institute of Criminal Law and Criminology* 24 (May 1933–Apr. 1934): 21–22; Leslie Cranston, *Early Criminal Codes of Illinois and Their Relation to the Common Law of England* (DuQuoin, Ill., 1930).

The conflict between Bishop McMullen and the Chicago Reform School, as well as other Chicago Reform School documents and pamphlets, are housed in the Chicago Historical Society.

The materials on the establishment of the Juvenile Court are extensive: One of the best sources is *The Child, the Clinic and the Court*, a collection of talks in honor of the twenty-fifth anniversary of the court, edited by Sophonisba Breckinridge (New York, 1927). Timothy Hurley, *Origin of the Juvenile Court Law* (Chicago, 1907), is also useful, though utterly partisan in behalf of the court. Bernard Flexner, "A Decade of the Juvenile Court" in *Proceedings of the National Conference of Charities and Corrections* (Fort Wayne, Ind., 1910) and Henry Thurston, "Ten Years of the Juvenile Court of Chicago," *Survey* 23 (Oct. 1909–Mar. 1910) gives a good assessment of the problems faced by the Illinois Juvenile Court in its first decade. By 1911, the court was already experiencing an investigation, summarized in *The Report of the Committee Appointed Under Resolution of the Board of Commissioners of Cook County, August 8, 1911* (Chicago, 1912). (This committee was also known as the Hotchkiss Committee.) Echoes of the political turmoil surrounding the court can be heard in Sophonisba Breckinridge and Edith Abbott, *The Delinquent Child in the Home: A Study of the Delinquent Wards of the Juvenile Court of Chicago* (New York, 1912), especially in Julia Lathrop's introduction to the book. Helen Jeter, *The Chicago Juvenile Court* (Children's Bureau Publication #104: Washington, D.C., 1922), gives a thorough assessment of the court's limitations and problems, as do Grace Benjamin, "The Constitutionality and Jurisdiction of the Juvenile Court of Cook County" (Ph.D. diss. University of Chicago, 1932) and Elizabeth Parker, "Personnel and Organization of the Probation Department of the Juvenile Court of Cook County, 1899–1933" (Master's thesis, University of Chicago, 1934). Another useful thesis is Bertha Corman, "A Study of 446 Delinquent Girls with Institutional Experiences" (Master's thesis, University of Chicago, 1926).

Edith Abbot and Sophonisba Breckinridge, *Truancy and Non-Attendance in the Chicago Schools* (Chicago, 1917), and Mary Aydelott, "Children in the Street Trades in Chicago" (Master's thesis, University of Chicago, 1924), develop the connection between child labor and delinquency.

Louise de Koven Bowen's memoirs, *Growing Up with a City* (New York, 1926), and Jane Addams's biography *My Friend Julia Lathrop* (New York, 1935) both give some texture to the story of the establishment of the Juvenile Court and its difficult early years.

For the problems of the Illinois Juvenile Court in the 1930s and 1940s, see Bernard Alper, "Forty Years of the Juvenile Court," *American Sociological Review* 6 (1941); William Trumball, "Boys and Girls of Juvenile Court Age Held in Cook County Jail, 1936 and 1937" (Master's thesis, University of Chicago, 1936); Fred Gross, *Detention and Criminal Prosecution of Children of Juvenile Court Age in Cook County, 1938–1942* (Chicago, 1942); *A History, Report and Recommendations Submitted by the Committee Appointed by the Legislature to Study the Illinois St. Charles School for Boys and the Whole Subject of Juvenile Delinquency* (Springfield, 1939); Illinois Board of Public Welfare Commissioners, *Study and Reorganization of the Illinois State Training School for Boys, 1941* (n.p., 1942); *Joint Report and Recommendations of the Training School for Boys Commission and the Youthful Offenders Commission* (Springfield, 1943); Juvenile Court of Cook County, Illinois, *Fiftieth Anniversary Report* (Chicago, 1949).

For the study of the juvenile court and delinquency in the second half of the twentieth century, I found the following materials useful: National Council on Crime and Delinquency, *The Cook County Family (Juvenile) Court and Arthur J. Audy Home: An Appraisal and Recommendations* (n.p., 1963); William Trumball, "Proposed New Juvenile Court Act for Illinois," *Illinois Bar Journal* (Mar. 1965); League of Women Voters, *Analysis of the Juvenile Court Act* (Chicago, 1966); George Davidson, "The Juvenile's Gideon," *Illinois Bar Journal* (Feb. 1968); Margaret Rosenheim, ed.,

Justice for the Child: the Juvenile Court in Transition (New York, 1962); Margaret Rosenheim, ed., *Pursuing Justice for the Child* (Chicago, 1976); National Council on Crime and Delinquency, *Status Offenders and the Juvenile Justice System: An Anthology,* ed. by Richard Allinson (Hackensack, N.J., 1978); David Reed et al., *Promises, Promises. . . . Does the Juvenile Court Deliver for Status Offenders? The Record in Cook County, Illinois* (Chicago, 1981); National Advisory Committee for Juvenile Justice and Delinquency Prevention, *Serious Juvenile Crime: A Redirected Federal Effort* (Washington, D.C., 1984).

I found the following histories of juvenile justice especially useful: Sanford Fox, "Juvenile Justice Reform," *Stanford Law Review* 22 (June 1970): 1187–1239 and Anthony Platt, *The Child Savers: The Invention of Delinquency* (Chicago, 1969), are very critical of the motives of the juvenile court founders; Joseph Hawes, *Children in Urban Society: Juvenile Delinquency in Nineteenth Century America* (New York, 1971) and Robert Mennel, *Thorns and Thistles: Juvenile Delinquents in the United States, 1825–1940* provide a nineteenth-century context for the establishment of the juvenile court; Steven Schlossman, *Love and the American Delinquent* (Chicago, 1977), focuses on the juvenile court, as does Ellen Ryerson, *The Best Laid Plans: America's Juvenile Court Experiment* (New York, 1978). Both Barbara Meil Hobson, *Uneasy Virtue: The Politics of Prostitution and the American Reform Tradition* (New York, 1987), and Estelle Freedman, *Their Sisters' Keepers: Women's Prison Reform in America, 1830–1930* (Ann Arbor, Mich., 1981), discuss American attitudes toward the criminality of women. John R. Sutton, *Stubborn Children: Controlling Delinquency in the United States, 1640–1981* (Berkeley, Calif., 1988), gives a sociological interpretation of American delinquency over more than three hundred years.

In writing about modern issues of delinquency, I drew on the resources of the Citizens Committee for the Juvenile Court, as I did with the dependency section. I was also able to observe the delinquency calendar of the Cook County Juvenile Court through the auspices of the Citizens Committee.

Handicapped Children

Annual and biennial reports were especially important in writing the history of the state's relationship with handicapped children in the nineteenth century and the Progressive Era. The reports of the institutions for the deaf, blind, and feeble-minded, along with the reports of the State Board of Commissioners of Public Charities and later the *Institution Quarterly* provided much of the substance of the study. In addition, the following materials were useful:

Phillip Gillette, "History of the Illinois Institution for the Education of the Deaf and Dumb" in *26th Biennial Report of the Illinois Institution for the Deaf and Dumb* (Springfield, 1892); Elizabeth Davis, "State Care of the Feeble-Minded in Illinois" (Master's thesis, University of Chicago, 1928); Julia Scott Reichman, "A Study of the State Care of the Blind in Illinois" (Master's thesis, University of Chicago, 1928).

In studying the 1907 scandal and investigation at the Lincoln Institution for the Feebleminded, I found the most useful source to be the State of Illinois, 45th General Assembly, House of Representatives, *Report of the Special Committee to Investigate State Institutions* (Chicago, 1908). (This document was one of the few not available in the University of Chicago libraries. I located it at the University of Illinois at Chicago central library.) "Governor Charles Deneen's Message to the 45th General Assembly, May 23, 1908" in *21st Biennial Report of The State Board of Commissioners of Public Charities* (Springfield, 1909), was also important for the discussion.

John Ransom, *A Study of Mentally Defective Children in Chicago* (Chicago, 1915), was an excellent source for assessing the mentality of reformers just before the involuntary commitment law for the mentally retarded was passed in Illinois. The publication that replaced the State Board of Charities *Biennial Reports, The Institution Quarterly*, was a rich source for particulars of institutional care in the Progressive Era and a forum for attitudes and theories about the disabled in the first twenty-five years of the twentieth century. The Progressive Era panic concerning eugenics comes through in virtually every issue of the journal. The most comprehensive secondary source for this topic is Carl Degler, *In Search of Human Nature: The Decline and Revival of Darwinism in American Social Thought* (New York, 1991). Bertha Schlotter and Margaret Svendson, *An Experiment in Recreation with the Retarded* (Chicago, 1932), discusses the bleak institutional conditions for retarded people in Illinois, as well as noting the improvements that their program effected at the Lincoln institution.

By the 1940s, the Illinois Commission on Handicapped Children was issuing the yearly proceedings of the Governor's Conference on Exceptional Children, as well as other reports, such as:

The Commission [on Handicapped Children] Reports to the People of Illinois, June, 1941–June, 1946 (Springfield?, 1946); Lawrence Linck, *Some Unmet Needs of Physically Handicapped Children in Illinois* (n.p., 1940); and *Facilities for the Education and Institutional Care of Mentally Handicapped Children in Illinois* (Chicago, 1942).

One of the clearest statements of the "professional" perspective, a highly sanitized view of the care provided for disabled children at midcentury is Edith Stern, *The Handicapped Child: A Guide for Parents* (New York, 1950). On the other hand, Elizabeth Kramm, "Families of Mongoloid Children" (Children's Bureau Publication #401: Washington, D.C., 1963), is a study describing the failure of medical support for the parents of mentally disabled children.

On the critique of institutions that began in the 1960s, Erving Goffman's classic, *Asylums: Essays on the Social Situation of Mental Patients and Other Inmates* (New York, 1961), provided a useful background; Pauline Morris, *Put Away: A Sociological Study of Institutions for the Mentally Retarded* (London, 1969), and Wolf Wolfensberger, *Normalization: The Principle of Normalization in Human Services* (Toronto, 1972), make the case for deinstitutionalization.

Erwine Levine and Elizabeth Wexler, *P L 94-142: An Act of Congress* (New York, 1981), discuss the history and impact of the critical 1975 civil rights/education law for children, while Daniel Yohalem and Janet Dinsmore, *94-142 and 504: Numbers that Add Up to Educational Rights for Handicapped Children* (Washington, D.C., 1984), a Children's Defense Fund pamphlet for parents, give a clear statement of the laws supporting handicapped children passed in the 1970s. William P. McLure, Robert Burnham, and Robert Henderson, *Special Education: Needs, Costs, Methods of Financing* (Urbana, Ill., 1975), discuss Illinois education laws for handicapped children just before the passage of P.L. 94-142. Daniel Hallahan and James Kauffman, *Exceptional Children: Introduction to Special Education*, 3d ed. (Englewood Cliffs, N.J., 1986), discuss the educational needs and rights of disabled children. Kenneth Katzen, "A Teacher's View" in *Exceptional Children* 12 (1980): 116–23 is a poignant discussion of some of the frustrations connected with the implementation of P.L. 94-142. Jeanette Jennings, "Elderly Parents as Caregivers for Their Adult Disabled Children" in *Social Work* 32 (Sept.–Oct. 1987): 430–33, discusses the limits of assistance for families with adult disabled children.

For the modern section on handicapped children, I consulted the

Chicago-based educational reform and advocacy organization Designs for Change; the Coordinating Council for Handicapped Children; and the National Association of State Directors of Special Education for particular questions regarding laws and policies. In addition, I was able to draw on the expertise of Mary Lopata, a speech pathologist who has worked with special education issues in Illinois for over twenty years, and Debbie Greenebaum, a long time advocate for the mentally handicapped/developmentally disabled in Chicago. As was true with the dependency and delinquency sections, these professionals in the field saw me through the intricacies of the system and gave me a sense of context that I could not have achieved without them.

For a discussion of the impact of "The Reagan Revolution" on the treatment of handicapped children, see Tom Joe and Cheryl Rogers, *By the Few, for the Few: The Reagan Welfare Legacy* (Lexington, Mass., 1980) and Jeff Lyon, *Playing God in the Nursery* (New York, 1985). Lyon's book is also an excellent general study of the dilemmas that technology poses in the care of handicapped infants.

Peter L. Tyor and Leland Bell's *Caring for the Retarded in America: A History* (Westport, Conn., 1984) was an invaluable source for the entire section on handicapped children. Frances Koestler, *The Unseen Minority: A Social History of Blindness in America* (New York, 1976), was also helpful, as was John Gliedman and William Roth, *The Unexpected Minority: Handicapped Children in America* (New York, 1980).

General Materials

There is a vast literature on the Progressive Era, much of it directed to the question of the Progressive reformers' motives in relation to the poor and immigrant population with which they were concerned. I made a deliberate decision to address this question of motivation in the introduction and as a theme throughout the manuscript as part of the late twentieth century's rejection of Progressive "modernism." But I did not want to interrupt the flow of the narrative to consider this as a historiographical question. Certainly in regard to the child welfare reformers coming out of Hull-House, I would contend that the accusations that they were motivated largely by fear and a desire to re-establish an older social order show a misreading of their intentions, as their own writings demonstrate to my satisfaction. The secondary sources that I found most useful in regard to the child welfare Progressives were Clarke

Chambers, *Seedtime of Reform: American Social Service and Social Action, 1918–1933* (Minneapolis, 1963); Lela Costin, *Two Sisters for Social Justice: A Biography of Grace and Edith Abbott* (Urbana, 1983); and Robyn Muncy, *Creating a Female Dominion in American Reform, 1890–1935* (New York, 1991).

David Rothman, *Conscience and Convenience: The Asylum and Its Alternatives in Progressive America* (Boston, 1980), I found to be the most insightful explanation of Progressive good intentions turned to ill account by already established bureaucracies. Rothman's *The Discovery of the Asylum: Social Order and Disorder in the New Republic* (Boston, 1971), gave a helpful background for reform in the antebellum period.

For the history of social work, Roy Lubove, *The Professional Altruist: The Emergence of Social Work as a Career, 1880–1930* (New York, 1965); John Ehrenreich, *The Altruistic Imagination: A History of Social Work and Social Policy in the United States* (Ithaca, N.Y., 1985); and *Compassion and Responsibility: Readings in the History of Social Welfare Policy in the United States*, ed. Frank Breul and Steven Diner (Chicago, 1980) all proved very helpful.

One of the best expressions of late twentieth-century disillusionment with Progressive interventions and the hazards of altruism is Willard Gaylin, Ira Glasser, Steven Marcus, and David Rothman, *Doing Good: The Limits of Benevolence* (New York, 1981). On the other hand, Lisbeth Schorr, *Within Our Reach: Breaking the Cycle of Disadvantage and Despair* (New York, 1988), is a discussion of late twentieth-century children's programs that have worked and a consideration of what factors are necessary to make intervention effective.

An excellent resource that covers the history of childhood in America, including public policy issues through a collection of essays and an extensive bibliography is *American Childhood: A Research Guide and Historical Handbook*, ed. Joseph Hawes and N. Ray Hiner (Westport, Conn., 1985). Joseph Hawes, *The Children's Rights Movement: a History of Advocacy and Protection* (Boston, 1991) provides a broad historical perspective on a national level of many issues considered in this manuscript.

For the modern portion of all three sections of the book, I used materials from the Children's Defense Fund, both the *Newsletter* and various pamphlets. The *Youth Law News*, published out of The National Center for Youth Law in San Francisco provided a national view of contemporary legal issues regarding children.

Index

JOAN GITTENS lived in Illinois for ten years, studying the intricacies of the state's child welfare system, past and present. She is currently an associate professor of American history at Southwest State University in Marshall, Minnesota, where she teaches a history of American childhood and is working on a history of foster care and adoption in the United States.